T·H·E
FATHER
BOOK

Other Books in the Minirth-Meier Clinic Series

For general information about Minirth Clinic offices, counseling services, educational resources and hospital programs, call (214) 669-1733.

THE
FATHER
BOOK

Dr. Frank Minirth
Dr. Brian Newman
Dr. Paul Warren

A
JANET
THOMA
BOOK

Thomas Nelson Publishers
Nashville • Atlanta • London • Vancouver

Copyright © 1992 by Dr. Frank Minirth, Dr. Brian Newman, and Dr. Paul Warren

Published in Nashville, Tennessee, by Thomas Nelson, Inc.

Scripture quotations are from the NEW KING JAMES VERSION of the Bible. Copyright © 1979, 1980, 1982, Thomas Nelson, Inc., Publishers.

Library of Congress Cataloging-in-Publication Data

Warren, Paul, 1949–
    The father book / by Paul Warren, Frank Minirth, Brian Newman.
        p.   m.
    "A Janet Thoma Book"
    ISBN 0-7852-7361-1 MP
    ISBN 0-7852-8188-6 PB
    ISBN 0-8407-7775-2 CB
    1. Fatherhood—United States.   2. Fathers—United States.   3. Father and child—United States.   I. Minirth, Frank B.   II. Newman, Brian.   III. Title.
HQ756.W37   1992
306.874'2—dc20   92–28633
                                                    CIP

Printed in the United States of America
1 2 3 4 5 6 — 01 00 99 98 97 96

To our fathers

Ike Minirth, Danny Newman, Robert Warren

whose wisdom and guidance provides strength and
encouragement as we continue to run the race set
before us. Thank you for your godly example
of dependence on the only perfect father—
the Heavenly Father.

Contents

Acknowledgments

The authors wish to express appreciation to the many people who have made *The Father Book* a reality.

Heartfelt thanks and praise go to Sandy Dengler whose creativity and writing talent brought our deepest concerns and desires for all fathers to life on these pages; and to Janet Thoma whose continued vision and encouragement combined with her editorial expertise, drive and genius are the lifeblood of this project. Many thanks to Susan Salmon for her diligence in keeping us on schedule and her attention to details that would have eluded us! And to Bob Zaloba for his unwavering support and excitement about this project.

We thank our wives, Mary Alice Minirth, Deborah Newman, and Vicky Warren for their love, patience, and encouragement. And finally, we thank our children, Rachel, Renee, Carrie, and Alicia Minirth; Rachel and Benjamin Newman; and Matthew Warren for teaching us what we know about fatherhood . . . and what we still have to learn! You provided the inspiration for this book and are truly gifts from God!

ONE

The Birth
of a Father

There were a lot of places Charles Mayer would rather be: Outside. Idaho. Teheran, maybe. But not here in a hospital delivery room, surrounded by women. Not here. Even the obstetrician was a woman, Dr. Maria Alvarez. She presided over this "torture chamber" with a casual arrogance. Well, maybe not arrogance, but she obviously knew exactly what was going on, and she was comfortable doing her job.

Charles Mayer had taken all the childbirth lessons, and he still didn't know what in the world was happening.

Meghan sure knew. She tightened and made that funny little squeaking sound again as a fresh labor contraction hit her. She seemed so frail, so tiny to be going through this ordeal. At five feet four and not much more than a hundred pounds, she was much too small to be a mother. To Charles, "Mother" meant a jolly, bulky, billowing woman, like his own mom.

Jean Mayer, Charles's ample mom, hovered near Meghan's head, an endless font of good cheer. In some ways, Meghan got along better with his mother than did Charles. Today, especially, the two women shared a common bond. Childbirth.

Charles glanced toward the big swinging steel doors. A smallish man in rubber gloves, gown, and mask stood huddled in the corner, like a shy ninth grader at a high school prom.

"Pop! What are you doing here?" Charles hurried over to

him. Do you shake hands in surgical gloves? Charles glanced at his own rubber-coated paw and decided against it.

"Wish I knew." Charles's dad looked a lot older now than he did, say, an hour ago. "Can you imagine this? According to natural law, the father's supposed to sit in a waiting room and chain-smoke and read out-of-date hunting magazines. And the grandfather-to-be? Ridiculous. We don't belong in here." He jabbed Charles with an elbow. "Let's disappear."

"After I spent all that time and money on childbirth lessons? I don't dare." Charles did, when you came right down to it, feel a lot like bolting. "How did you get snookered into being here?"

"Not sure." The older man watched the goings-on at the delivery table from afar. "I was talking to that little receptionist, and she said they encourage the whole family to take part. Says it's great for the baby. A bonding something or other. All of a sudden she's slipping me into this stuff and shoving me through the doors."

Charles snickered. He could just picture Dad getting manipulated by the young woman on the reception desk.

Dad's watery gray eyes flicked toward Charles and quickly looked away. "Guess I was curious, mostly. This is so different from when you were born. Then, the only outsider in the delivery room was the mother. Bet the doctor hated to let even her in, but he couldn't do it without her. You were three days old before I touched you for the first time."

"Male doctor."

"Darned right. Hundred and fifty years old if he was a day. He delivered me, and he delivered you."

"Charles," Dr. Alvarez called, "got some action here."

Charles found himself back at Meghan's bedside and couldn't remember walking there.

A bulge, a wet, dark bulge, was pushing toward the light. Meghan squeaked, Mom purred something, and the tiny head suddenly dropped.

Charles's heart jumped up into his throat. "Is its neck broke?"

"Not 'it,' Charles. Your son." Dr. Alvarez corrected him, her dark eyes flashing. "He is the next generation of Mayers. I understand this is the first grandchild on either side of the family."

Charles nodded numbly. He watched, still numb, as the rest of the birth went smoothly. So smoothly. The first grandchild on either side of the family was a weird color, covered with a weird gunk, shaped in rather weird proportions, and still attached to the ugliest, slimiest piece of garden hose Charles had ever seen. He was supposed to be reveling in this moment. He felt drugged.

Dr. Alvarez's dark eyes twinkled. "You look a little pale, but compared to most fathers who come through this room, you're doing great. I'm not sure you're in shape to be allowed near sharp instruments, but here. You can cut the cord now." She handed him a pair of surgical scissors.

He stared at them. He stared at the baby. At the cord. At the scissors.

"Between the clamps," Dr. Alvarez prompted.

The flaccid, rubbery flesh of the umbilical cord resisted his scissors. The blades slipped a little, then bit in. He squeezed, squeezed again, and thought of the profound symbolism of this moment. Exhilaration displaced the drugged feeling. His child had been attached to Meghan for nine months. Now he, the father, was severing that attachment, releasing this child from its mother, initiating his child—*his* child—into the world.

Claiming his child.

Charles Mayer began to weep.

Suddenly he felt intensely, hotly embarrassed. His father still stood in the corner. Dad would see his tears.

With a loud honk, the man in the corner blew his nose.

—Fathering Today—

When the family's first child is born, a father is born. Mom has been carrying the child nine months. She has been feeling it kick and squirm; she's been getting punched in the diaphragm—from the inside. For months she has been unable to fold in the middle, touch her toes, or even greet them warmly. She's relieved the pregnancy is over. Dad, though, has not experienced this child firsthand before birth. Watching his wife's belly move is in no way the same thing as holding a seven- or eight-pound infant.

Charles Mayer was absolutely starting from ground zero on this father business, despite all his preparations. He had gone to the hospital's childbirth class with Meghan and did all the things expected of daddies these days. But it was not always so.

In the past, birthing and new-parent classes were only for mothers. Mother alone was expected to feed, bathe, rock, burp, diaper, and clothe the baby. She would then hand the completed infant to the father for a good-night kiss. He would dutifully kiss the cute little tyke and hand it back for mother to put to bed. Dad's job was not to actually touch the child. His was to go out and make the living. He bought the baby food. Mom spooned it into the baby.

That is yesterday's stereotype. People who work with children are rapidly discovering that the old stereotype father falls seriously short when it comes to nurturing today's next generation. Kids face a host of fears and challenges adults did not know in their own youth. And they face them earlier. Kids need every bit of help they can get, and they no longer have time to mature slowly, as in the old days when fathers and children together sort of groped their way into the future. Today, Dad has to know what he's doing and hit the ground running, from the very beginning of a child's growth and development.

"Whether or not you choose to acknowledge the fact, the father's impact on the child is tremendous. Just tremendous!" says Dr. Frank Minirth. "By far the most issues adults bring into counseling are related directly with the father. If the father backs off—steps out of the picture—he exerts a tremendous negative impact. You can't take the responsibility lightly."

Dr. Brian Newman agrees. "Don't minimize, even with single fathers, the impact on a kid's life. I have divorcing fathers sit in my office and tell me, 'Oh well, better off if I slip out of the picture.' Wrong, wrong, wrong!"

But it is not only the child who benefits from a father's increased involvement. The father who steps beyond the stereotype of yesterday invests more of himself in the family. Because his family is so much a part of him, he is actually investing in his own life both directly and indirectly. Certainly, he invests materially with his paycheck. But when he makes a heavy relationship investment in addition, the chances of his marriage succeeding will go way up. The chances of his children succeeding will skyrocket. And as he leads his children spiritually, he grows spiritually himself. The father himself benefits, in every dimension.

—The Maximum Return on Your Investment—

Enormous National Bank has made some interest rate changes, explained in your latest monthly certificate of deposit interest statement:

A. Accounts averaging $200,000 and up earn 3.7 percent
B. Accounts averaging $100,000 to $200,000 earn 1.9 percent
C. Accounts averaging less than $100,000 earn −0.9 percent

Dear Depositor,

Because your account falls into Category C, popularly known as our "poor sucker" rate level, please note that you owe us $12.80 this month.

It's hard to make a buck these days and even harder to hang on to it. . . . And nearly impossible to make it multiply. When a good deal does come along, there are always strings attached. So you find yourself looking not just at deals but at the complexity of their attached strings. That's especially true when you're seeking long-term investments.

Fathering is one of the longest term investments, and by any measure your most important one. You want a deal with the best return and the least strings. An investment with fewer hoops to jump through is more efficient in terms of time and energy than one that's constantly causing you grief one way or another.

This book can help you realize a maximum return on your most important long-term investment, your kids. We can show you where to invest your time and energy to receive the brightest payoff. We will show you how the fathering process operates, and help you understand how fathers influence the way kids grow—the deep-down basics, the nuts and bolts of your investment. We'll explain how the kids change as they mature and how best to respond to those changes. For as you know, the better you understand how your investment works, the more wisely you can shape your strategy.

Much of our knowledge comes from extensive clinical experience as we probe the depths of how thousands of dads and kids interact, and what they need of each other. But this is not just head knowledge. All three of us are working dads ourselves, involved in the day-to-day application of the principles we explain here.

Psychiatrist Frank Minirth, president of the Minirth Clinic, takes particular interest in family dynamics, having four girls. Dr. Paul Warren, behavioral pediatrician, understands children as few do, for he has treated hundreds. He has one son, Matthew. When Dr. Brian Newman, psychotherapist at the clinic, talks about his children, Rachel and Benjamin, his grin is too wide to fit through a door. We take great pleasure in our fathering, and happiness is a part of the return a really good investment provides.

Together, we three can provide the information you need for successful everyday fathering and for troubleshooting the problems that are bound to crop up.

We will pay particular attention to ways you can help your children grow spiritually. Discipline? Tough subject, but understandable. Fathering a dating kid (my baby?!)? How about that music, and the hairstyles. . . . If kids are shaving half their hair and spiking the rest now, what will kids look like ten years from now? It staggers the imagination. We will touch upon the special considerations of stepfathering and grandfathering. Single and absent fathers have unique challenges. We'll discuss them.

"Whoa," you respond. "My dad did okay. Look how I turned out. Who needs a how-to for something that comes naturally?"

Good point, except that fathering is not something that comes naturally. You learn fathering not by instinct but by the way you were fathered. However, that was years ago. All aspects of society are changing. Labor and industry are shifting exponentially; jobs aren't what they used to be. Risks are different these days, as are attitudes (boy, are they!) and technology.

"Think of the changes in just the last few years: my Rachel, at four, is growing up with a phone in the car," says Brian Newman. "She can page my beeper and knows three or four phone numbers by heart. Doesn't think a thing of it."

"I remember, growing up in Arkansas, when it wasn't a common thing to have a telephone in the house," Frank Minirth muses.

What used to work doesn't always work anymore. Your children face a very different world from the one you grew up in, and if you're going to see your investment in them reap its richest rewards, you're going to have to move beyond the old ways.

But if today's father must step beyond the stereotype of yesterday, how does he know where to go? He's being called upon to explore new territory. If he learned about fathering by being fathered, and that being-fathered experience is no longer adequate, where does he learn new ways? He needs an owner's guide. A manual.

The Operator's Manual

"I was teasing the nurses when Rachel was born," Brian Newman says with a grin. "I tipped the baby this way and that, and looked underneath her. 'Where's the instruction book?' I asked. 'Every new model comes with an instruction book, at least so you can identify the parts. You can't tell how to program your VCR without instructions. Same with this.'"

Drivers, truckers, hunters, food handlers, people who curl and dye your hair—all receive more preparation, training, and testing than do men who get married and sire children. To earn a driver's license you must study the manual, take a written test, and show your stuff out on the road. The man who finds himself a father receives no manual and takes no test. But if he messes up out on the road, the blame reflects back on him.

For all you fathers who wish you could find the manual that would tell you what in tarnation you're doing, that's what this book is. As for a written test, however, you're on your own.

Charles Mayer was starting off along a path his own father was never given the opportunity to travel. Charles was taking part in his child's life from the moment of birth. In fact, Charles's father, kicking and screaming, was also being dragged along on the adventure. And an exhilarating adventure it would be, for Baby, Dad, and Grampa, all three.

Did the brand new infant, Sean Michael Mayer, know Daddy was there? Can a newborn identify the father? For that matter, does a newborn care? What is Dad's role in the first minutes and the first year? It's an extremely important one, as we shall see.

To Think About

. . . When you're waiting in the lunch line, stuck in traffic, riding on the bus, at other odd times. . . .

When I was born:

As far as I've been able to learn, my own father took part in my birth in these ways (driving Mom to the hospital, waiting for hours, visiting, looking through a glass window into the nursery [It may be worth a call to Dad, if possible, to find out the details firsthand.]):

_____

_____

_____

_____

_____

This would have been considered (usual) (unusual) involvement for his day because:

_____

_____

_____

If that was the stereotype when I was born, the "new stereotype" these days calls for the father to (go to childbirth classes, help Mom with exercises, be present at delivery . . .):

_____

_____

_____

_____

_____

Just off the top of my head, I can think of these reasons why I like the old stereotypical way better:

1. _____
2. _____
3. _____

This is why I think the new way might be better for my child(ren):

1. _____
2. _____
3. _____

As your child grows, obviously, your strategies change. In subsequent chapters we'll discuss strategies in detail. No matter what ages your kids are and what stages of fathering you're going through right now, you can profit from insider information. And you know other men who need this book too. We will provide the resources you need to see your children reach their maximum potential in today's strange world, but we won't lose sight of what worked in the past. We will bring past and future together in your fathering today.

TWO

Gearing Up
for Fatherhood

By no stretch of the imagination could you call Elgin Mayer a wimp. Sure, he only stood about five seven, and sure, he didn't exactly weigh in like a sumo wrestler, but he was as strong as any two men, even now at age fifty-seven. He drove a truck, a big cross-continental rig, for a major moving company, and that meant loading and unloading those puppies a couple times a week. Sometimes he picked up a tandem, which doubled the pay and the work. Elgin Mayer made a very good living in a macho job, and he was understandably proud of himself.

He pulled out of the North Side Truck Stop in Springfield. His rig waddled onto the feeder road; the manager ought to fill in where his blacktop was crumbling there. Elgin ran up through his gears as he took the on-ramp to the interstate, headed for Columbus.

A grandson. Sean Michael Mayer. How about that?!

But why did his eyes and nose start running there in the delivery room when his son Charles cut Sean Michael's umbilical cord? Jean, his wife, didn't seem to feel the least bit weepy. She laughed before the baby came, and she was still laughing afterward.

Elgin thought about the women in that delivery room. Meghan, his daughter-in-law, had never had a baby before, but she took it in her arms instantly, like she knew what she was doing. Jean handled the baby like a pro and dived right in to help the staff clean things up afterward. They acted as if they felt totally comfortable with the situation.

That woman doctor (a young woman doctor at that—what were things coming to?) synchromeshed with mother and grandmother like the gears in his transmission.

Meanwhile, he and Charles hung around the edges watching and trying to figure out how to feel. The women didn't have the confusion the men were going through. Oh well. Let's see those women load a twenty-thousand-pound house and deliver it in five days.

Come to think of it, Jean had done that ten days ago when she went with him to Indianapolis on a run. And the woman doctor. Women were doing all these things men were traditionally supposed to be doing, and men couldn't get the hang of woman-stuff to save their lives. Elgin Mayer felt more than a little inadequate in some respects.

Elgin Mayer didn't know it, but he was experiencing pretty much the same feelings his son Charles was. Just about every father feels them, and yes, so do grandfathers who for years knew only the stereotype. If you don't realize they're there, doubts and other feelings can short-circuit your attempts to be a good father. They shape the way you think, and they do it behind your back; you don't know it's happening. They'll cripple your effectiveness as a father and husband, and you'll have no idea what's going on. No matter where you are as a father or grandfather—brand new, an old hand, or simply contemplating fatherhood as an option for the future—it will pay dividends to bring those feelings out where you can see them. Once you know they're there, they can't do their sneaky mischief.

—Combatting the Nagging Questions—

Two kinds of feelings plague fathers, grief and fear, and those feelings raise nagging questions that distract men from the real problems of fathering. Unfortunately, in our culture it's not manly to admit fear and grief, so "real men" often just put those thoughts aside. When they're buried without being resolved, the feelings are free to work below the conscious level.

Doubt breeds worry, and worry is always counterproductive. Men find themselves investing enormous resources—emotional energy, time, stress—on questions that could be resolved by chopping out their roots, the common feelings of fathers. The most common feeling men face in fatherhood is grief. Sounds unbelievable, but think about it for a minute.

Grief

Some years ago, a television documentary crew interviewed a young inner-city man who had fathered a number of kids so far, that he knew of. Why didn't he marry and start a family? "Ain't no woman gonna mess up my life," he responded.

Freedom.

No responsibilities.

In a way, he was articulating a deep-down dream of the heart—to range wide and play the field without consequences. Traditionally, becoming a family man shoots that hidden desire down in flames. When the kids start coming along, responsibility multiplies exponentially.

Never mind that statistically, family men live longer, healthier lives than do bachelors. Never mind all those men who claim that the most rewarding thing in this world that you can be is a father. Never mind that not only is playing the field immoral, and odious in God's eyes, but the field rarely lets you play. The siren call of freedom without responsibility persists. Responsibility is a scary thing. Who wants it? And who wants to grieve?

"I experienced a definite grieving period when Debi was pregnant with Rachel," Brian Newman reports. "Our marriage was about to change forever. We were comfortable just by ourselves. Our lives were busy but settled. Productive. Now a little someone was going to disrupt all that—going to rock our boat. We were losing our freedom to just come and go and do whatever we wanted."

This loss of convenience and freedom is very real and must be grieved like any other loss.

The five familiar steps in the grieving process operate here as they operate with other sorts of losses.

1. Shock and disbelief.
"This can't be happening to me!"
Ah, but it is.

2. Anger turned outward.
A man may well add guilt feelings to his emotional load about now. What father-to-be in his right mind gets angry about the situation? This is supposed to be a happy time. For shame!

Bear in mind that anger is a perfectly normal part of the process. The anger is all part of those feelings you want to dig out, and it won't last. No need to feel guilty.

3. Anger turned inward.
That's a three-word phrase that means, simply, depression. You feel lousy, in the dumps. It can last ten minutes or it can last for months. This, too, shall pass. All by itself, depression can invite doubts and worries about inadequacy. Be aware what it's doing.

4. Bargaining.
"If this thing will only turn out right (or go away), I promise I'll [make more money] [be a better Christian] [pay better attention to God] [eat my vegetables] [_____]." Bargaining is trying to weasel a good ending for a frightening new venture. Everybody does it to some extent.

5. Resolution.
"Guess I'll just have to deal with it."
You might call this final stage "Coming to Grips with It." Sometimes this stage does not really take over until the child is born. Even then, the grief process is not done. It must be repeated as the circumstances of fatherhood change.

Brian Newman describes it from personal experience. "Our firstborn Rachel arrived, and everything was great.

We had Rachel three or four years and got comfortable with our family as a threesome. Then Debi was pregnant with Benjamin. Again, Benjamin was going to disrupt our family. Rock the boat again. Now, in five months, it's like Benjamin has always been here; he's so much a part of our family—he's always been there. The fear and grief came and went quickly." Dr. Newman muses, "I believe all men probably feel that way, but they don't always realize it."

Along with grief comes a whole set of fears. They aren't any more fun than grief is.

Fear

Brian Newman continues. "When Rachel was born it was a fearful time too. Persistent feelings of inadequacy. Can I relate to this child? Can I father well? Can I provide financially? I was afraid I wouldn't make the grade as a provider."

Fear comes in various guises. Three of the most prominent in the pending father's life are plain and simple fear of the unknown, fear of making some horrible and irreversible error, and the nagging fear that his own children will fail to honor and appreciate him.

Fear of the Unknown

Paul Warren comments, "There are very few rites of passage in our culture. We'll talk about the few there are later. Fatherhood is a rite of passage of sorts. No matter how thoroughly you prepare for it, you're not prepared. You can't know what it's going to be like until you go through it. . . . Which is pretty much true of all rites of passage.

"And it's only that one time, when you have the first child. The second child is more routine. There's less anxiety. You think, 'I'm a father already; I've passed through this before; it's no big deal.'"

Fortunately, there's nothing like a little practical experience to ease the first-time father's terror. The fear of what is coming, and what may already be here, abates naturally with time and experience.

How do you master the fear, or at least cope with it?

Paul Warren says, "Talking to other men can be a big help. Seek out other men in the same position. Childbirth class is good for that. Listening to other men does two things. It clues you in to what to expect a little bit. And in this class, for instance, you see that first-time fathers are all pretty clumsy at the process—clumsy at the process of helping their wives. You don't feel quite like the only person in the world who's inept."

. . . Or alone. What was going through your own father's mind when you were born? "I got to thinking about what my father must have been feeling when I was born," Paul Warren recalls. "But we had never talked about that. It never occurred to us to ever talk about that. When Vicky was in labor, I found myself wishing I could ask my father what it was like."

If you are about to become a father, perhaps you may find that talking to your father or another close adult male would be of help. In fact, no matter what stage of fathering you're in, no matter how old your kids are now, discussing the feelings, problems, and experiences of fathering can blunt the sharp edge of the future and make it less foreboding.

This fear of the unknown produces a real urge to just back away and run. If fathers-to-be are being brutally honest, they find themselves thinking, "It's the woman's job to bear this child. Don't bother me with this." Flight can look pretty attractive.

Paramedics with a good working knowledge of the birthing process may have delivered babies under stressful circumstances, from accidents through storms. That knowledge doesn't help a bit when it comes to them becoming dads.

"You don't learn to be a father in medical school," says Paul Warren. "Just the opposite. You learn how to be God. I was resentful when everyone was sending me off to childbirthing classes with Vicky. I knew all about this. I could teach this class. You know—actually I knew none of it. The perspective of the father-to-be is nothing like that of a trained professional. It's different. It's not physical; it's emotional. I can't explain it, but no amount of training prepares you for it."

Fear of Making Some Irreversible Error

As we will discuss later, men by nature tend to be success-oriented. Goal-completion-oriented. Because the completion rather than the process is primary with men, they quite naturally fear they might make some inadvertent error that would deny them success as fathers.

For example, new fathers are usually afraid, to a greater or lesser extent, of handling fragile little tots. Men tend to be rather uncomfortable with small kids, and for good reason—they simply aren't very used to it. Here is this huge, strong, hulking, ham-handed galoot trying to manage a miniature person that he can fit in his ten-gallon hat and still have room for eight or nine gallons of something else. "Will I break the kid? What if I drop it? Or it squirms. Babies have a reputation for squirming, you know."

In the past, baby-sitting was usually a girl's first paying job. She handled everything from sleepy newborns to rocket-propelled two-year-olds. Her brother almost never baby-sat. Girls ended up taking care of younger siblings. Boys were "too busy" to.

Cultural change is taking place, though, even as we speak. Boys are learning that a first-class, dependable baby-sitter brings top dollar. That baby-sitting experience, profitable as it is in the short term, is even more profitable in the long term. It provides splendid training and acclimatization for the someday-father. Think how comfortable a new father will be with his infant if he's already had some years' experience handling kids.

Charles Mayer's next-door neighbor, Bill, became a father for the third time a month before Charles did.

Bill poured himself another cup of coffee and draped himself across Charles's kitchen counter. "Initially, I wasn't really interested in going into the delivery room. With Betsy, our first kid, I wanted to sit out in the waiting room and smoke cigars."

"You don't smoke," Charles interrupted.

"So I'd substitute tortilla chips. Whatever." Bill shrugged. "Rhoda gave me the choice of going in or getting a divorce."

"So how did you like the delivery room?"

"You know, I didn't think I'd survive, but I actually warmed up and came around to it. Anyway, here's Rhoda over in the maternity ward, and here am I, without a clue to what I'm supposed to do. So I walked over to the nursery."

"Wait a minute. You told me once that your baby wasn't in the nursery. She stayed in Rhoda's room." Charles's baby son was with Meghan in her room this very moment.

"Yeah, I know. It's about two in the morning. The nurse taking care of the nursery wasn't too busy because most of the babies were asleep. I asked her to show me what to do."

"Diapers, that kind of thing?"

"That I could learn from Rhoda. But I was scared to look like a clumsy idiot in front of her. No, I wanted to learn how to handle the baby so I didn't snap it in two or spike it at the goal line. The nurse showed me some stuff . . . ."

"Yeah, I've watched nurses with babies." Charles admired anyone who could handle a baby like they did. "They sling 'em around like they're handling flour sacks."

"Never drop one."

"No, they never drop one. But if I tried that . . . ."

Bill grinned. "You'd do fine. She showed me how. And if the Klutz King here can handle a baby, anyone can. Then she sat me down in a rocker. Did you know babies don't grow well if they're not handled and cuddled?"

"No, I didn't know that."

"So they handle babies and rock them, even the little preemies with the tubes and oxygen stuff." Bill's eyes misted. "I never knew you could get a real, zinging charge out of rocking a kid who can't even talk yet. Hey. I'm not worried anymore about tripping up."

The changing roles of just about everyone in today's society don't help this fear of tripping up. Brian Newman articulates what many men never openly admit: "I was really scared to death of having a son, more than a daughter. You might say it was a threat to my own adequacy. Because of changing male roles, I don't know if I'm raising my male child in a wholesome way. I don't have a solid role model because my own father was raised under different role patterns, a different kind of attitude in society."

He pauses and considers. "At the very deepest level, this fear lurks in another form. For most men, I believe, this bottom line keeps showing up: How can I help my son grow up to be a man?"

Acknowledging these fears is usually enough to allay them. At the very least, acknowledging them robs them of their power to influence you adversely without your knowledge.

Fear of Failing to Earn the Child's Respect

"What if my kid thinks I'm a dud?"

"What if all the other fathers outshine me as my kid is growing up?"

"What if some other man steals my kid's affection and respect?"

These are legitimate fears that gnaw deep inside. It doesn't help much to glibly tell a father-to-be, "These fears will go away as your child grows, and you realize that your child loves and respects you simply because you are Dad." You'll do much better if you can dig them out and examine them in the beginning.

Charles Mayer snorted derisively. "When you're a football player, it's easy to earn your kid's respect. Just hover over him a little. But I'm not a big man. And it doesn't help when I'm around Bill's kids next door and Meghan calls me 'the Marshmallow.'"

Size? Brute force? Macho job? These impress adults. But to a child, every adult represents brute force. An adult is a BIG person, and careers don't mean much. A stable hand and the head horse trainer weigh equally in a child's mind.

The terms *hulking brute* and *sensitive father* are not mutually exclusive. Neither is *wimp*. The ninety-seven-pound weakling who flies into a howling rage at his kid does just as much lasting damage as if he used physical power. Physical appearance and particular characteristics or job-related specifics do not define a father. Kids know that. Adults tend to overlook it.

The stereotypical father is stern and judgmental. The real father is also tender and merciful. The stereotype is strong. The real father tempers that strength with control. Stereotypes happen when we focus only on a narrow band of expectations, a limited part of what it means to be a real man. The man who focuses on his child's best interests will move beyond the stereotype. He need not harbor any fears or worries that his children will not love and respect him.

Don't, therefore, view yourself and your supposed influence on a child from an adult's perspective. Look at yourself from the perspective of the child, who considers every grown-up awesome.

Some Things to Think About

What fears push your button? It pays to know. These questions may lead you to insight, helping you to identify your own fears.

Being around these things makes me uneasy (or they used to):

_____ Snakes

_____ Computers

_____ People who made A's in school

_____ Girls

_____ Large animals

_____ Babies

Being around people in these walks of life makes me uneasy:

_____

_____

_____

And also, I specifically feel uneasy about:

_____

_____

_____

_____

As I look at the things that make me uneasy, I can see these underlying adequacy issues lurking:

_____ Fear of being outshone

_____ Fear of messing up

_____ Fear of the unknown

_____ Fear of being denied respect or losing respect

These underlying fears could translate over into my fathering experience in these ways (avoiding emotional or physical contact with my kids, being too harsh, being too lenient . . .):

1. _____

2. _____

3. _____

"A few words and a pat on the head—there, there, it's all right—won't help a man allay his fears. We know that," says Brian Newman. "It's not easy to slip into a role you don't know anything about. Fathers today never saw this new fathering modeled for us."

He studies the tops of his shoes a moment, trying to pluck solid words to describe a nebulous concept. "I guess you'd call the old role (the stereotypical father) the caterpillar and the new role the butterfly." He brightens. "You know, as the butterfly is emerging from its cocoon it's the same individual you started with. The new role contains everything that was in the cocoon the caterpillar spun around itself, including the caterpillar. In other words, the old father role is part of it. But the new role looks altogether different because it includes what used to be called female traits—affection, nurturing, understanding—plus an increased use of the traditional male strong points. The butterfly can accomplish more than the caterpillar ever could; it can fly farther; it's more beautiful; it will foster the next generation of butterflies."

That boyish grin spreads out across his face. "That was kind of poetic.

"We fathers who have children right now, we're caught on the change. We're the first generation trying to bumble it through. Our kids will have a better shot at it; an easier time. They will have seen and experienced the new, more inclusive role of fatherhood. The times demand it; you've got to keep up. So we do."

—Step Beyond the Traditional from the Start—

Women are "authorities" on kids. When a woman does something with a child, it's immediately assumed she's doing it correctly. She can do some truly strange things, and no one calls her on it. Sometimes men feel no matter what a man does with a child, some woman is bound to peer over his shoulder questioning why he's doing it that way.

Men, even when they are competent, are not assumed to be competent as nurturers.

That doesn't sit well with a man who already has adequacy fears.

It pays, though, to persevere. An investment representing the easy way out is probably not the best investment you can make. It takes thought and wisdom to find the better way. Anyone can take the easy way.

From both clinical practice and personal experience, Brian Newman confidently advises the new father, "Don't hesitate! Risk failure because the risk is worth it. Dive in and challenge your fear of inadequacy. You're going to have to face it throughout the fathering process, so it's in your own best interests to become accustomed to challenging it."

Paul Warren says the same thing in other words. "I know what it's like to find yourself alone with this little baby. You feel uncertain. 'What if so and so happens? I don't know what to do.' That's the stereotypical man speaking. The task-centered attitude. So what if you don't know what to do? Women know they can't afford to entertain that fear; they just go with the moment."

He speaks of the first few days of his Matthew's life. "I didn't do very well back then. I knew all the latest thinking. I counseled new fathers frequently." He snorts. "A lot of good that did. I was scared, not of the baby, but of myself. I was still unsure that I was ready to be a father.

"Looking back, I wish I had taken time to talk to other fathers about fears of failure. But I didn't recognize them then. I was a pediatrician; I knew what babies needed. But I wasn't aware of what I needed. My own fears of being a father failure were there; I simply wasn't aware of them."

His wife, Vicky, wishes she had been more firm about saying, "I need help in this process." Instead, Vicky took the typical position a lot of moms take. She told herself, "He works hard. He's busy. So I'll take care of the dirty work. I'll wash the baby, feed him, and get up with him at night." She should have said, "Next time Matthew wakes up, you take him."

Drs. Minirth, Newman, and Warren all emphasize that Mom has to get away on occasion. She needs an escape from the twenty-four-hour job of mothering. Indeed, Mom and Dad together must get away, too, for a variety of reasons. However, Mom is normally reluctant to take the initiative about going out.

Here, Dad in his traditional role of leadership must take the initiative. It is up to the father to step forward and assume some of the nurturing duties.

That's not easy to do. It means stepping out of the stereotype, which is always difficult. Stepping beyond pays off, though. It's also not easy because mothers may actually resist receiving help. To surrender some of the tedium and "baby-sitting" to the father means surrendering control. Yielding control is no easier for a woman than it is for a man. Both father and mother must be aware of the control issue and work around it.

"I was supportive of Vicky," Paul Warren concludes. "I was making the money, working hard, doing the stereotypical role. I even made sure she had a morning off or an evening off to be with friends. I didn't think about it and neither did she, really. But in the process of being the traditional father, I lost the pure pleasure of nurturing Matt. I missed a very satisfying time, a rewarding part of being Dad."

"And don't forget about fathers who are middle-aged and have newborns," adds Frank Minirth. "We're probably more able to change from the way we were fathered because we've been through the process with our older kids. Practice, is what it is. Also, my career is established. I have more time now. I can make up what I missed with my other kids."

What I missed. Pleasure. Satisfaction. The kick a man gets out of challenging his adequacy fears and winning. That's part of the father's payback for stepping beyond the stereotype. A lot of men who are now entering their later years look back at their yesterdays and see no such pleasure and satisfaction. Not only did they miss out, they're just now realizing that fact as they assume their role of grandfather.

The trick is to avoid letting their lives unduly influence yours.

Evaluating How I Myself Was Fathered

Our fathers harbored exactly the same grief and fears we do. Those feelings, whether expressed or not, shaped the way they fathered us. Their methods of fathering shaped ours; we either father the way we were fathered or we rebel against Dad's ways by doing opposite things. For example, if my father was abusive and ugly, either I will be abusive and ugly or overly sticky and smothering. It pays, therefore, to give your past some thought. It shaped your present and will shape your future as well as your kids'.

1. What are your memories of how your father felt toward you? Good? Angry? Indifferent? Mention a specific memory that led you to feel this way.

_____

_____

_____

2. In what ways did your dad punish (that is, discipline) you?

_____ Physical contact: spanking, slapping, swatting, shaking

_____ Verbal: yelling, belittling, mocking, name-calling, "chewing out"

_____ Tactical: removing privileges, grounding, forcing behaviors such as sitting in a certain chair or standing in a corner

_____ Other _____

3. Of these methods, from the viewpoint of adulthood, which do you think were most effective in keeping you on the straight and narrow?

_____

Which ones didn't really work at all on you?

_____

4. How did you feel when you walked into a room where he was, or when he walked into a room where you were?

_____ Glad he came in?

_____ Indifferent?

_____ A little uneasy, perhaps?

_____ You could feel anger or resentment stirring.

_____ Other _____

5. And how do you feel now as an adult when that happens?

_____ Glad to see him?
_____ Indifferent?
_____ A little uneasy, perhaps?
_____ You can feel anger or resentment stirring.
_____ Other _____

6. What are some positive events you remember with your dad (attendance at sporting events, activities such as working on the car, work you performed together, goof-off things such as playing catch or one-on-one, family outings . . .)?

a. _____
b. _____
c. _____

7. Some negative events (an activity or event he promised you and had to renege on; things you intensely wished he'd do and he did not; trips or activities that went sour; times you screwed up or he did; times he caught you when you were up to no good, or others ratted on you; an occasion in which you discovered him in something he shouldn't be doing):

a. _____
b. _____
c. _____

8. As you look at the specific events above from an adult perspective, how might common fears have been influencing your father's actions and attitudes?

Fear of being outshone _____
Fear of messing up _____
Fear of the unknown _____
Fear of being denied respect or losing respect _____

_____

The memories and insights you explored in this exercise are shaping the kind of father you are, or will become. Some are very positive, some negative. This is not a witch hunt (okay, a warlock hunt), trying to find fault with Dad. By no means. Dad isn't bad. He was doing his best, and most probably, quite well. However, only by becoming aware of how the past is working on you can you accentuate the positive and minimize the negative.

We ask you therefore to think long and hard about the kind of fathering you experienced (or, for that matter, lacked), and how the experience has influenced you, for better or worse. Out of that thinking will come a picture of the kind of father you yourself want to become.

Building a Life

Not your life—your children's. Yours is pretty much built. Let us begin with the expanded role fathers can play in the lives of their infants and follow through with preschoolers, grade schoolers, early adolescents, and boisterous teens. Along the way, we'll discuss discipline, the differences between raising boys and raising girls, and other aspects of fathering that span all ages.

Whether your children are teens, babies, or still just a twinkle in your eye, we suggest you read everything, including the parts that don't seem to pertain to your immediate situation. It will benefit you immensely to understand not just how your kids operate now but how they used to function and will in the future.

THREE

Dad and His Newborn

On the day Debi Newman gave birth to Benjamin, Brian gleefully busied himself building history. He taped a morning news-and-entertainment show so that Benjamin someday could see what was happening in the world when he arrived. Brian borrowed Dr. Minirth's portable phone with which he could call from anywhere, anywhere at all, to give and receive the latest news. And he juiced up his video camcorder.

Off they went to the hospital, Brian and Deborah Newman, both eagerly commencing the first step in the birth of their son. And therein lies a tale—a couple different tales, in fact. For Brian, with Debi, illustrated several important basic principles of fathering that day.

—Getting It Right, from the First—

His name was Miles, and at thirteen he had a school problem, an attitude problem, and an arrest record. It was the arrest that tipped his parents into doing something. His father claimed the ungrateful kid needed a good, old-fashioned reform school. His mother demurred and brought him to our clinic.

So there he sat beside the third floor elevator, his arms crossed, his lower lip out, scowling. When Dr. Paul Warren appeared to escort him back to the office, Miles jerked his arm out, a much exaggerated gesture, and glared at his watch. "You're late. You owe me twenty-six dollars."

He then became silent, seething, on that endless walk back to the office. He plopped into a chair.

Dr. Warren, already somewhat nonplussed, launched into his standard introductory comments—rather ineptly, he felt, considering that he explained it to every new and potential client.

Midway through it, Miles interrupted him. "I'm here because I'm daddyless." There were tears in his eyes.

And tears in Dr. Warren's.

Miles had grown up in a two-parent household and still considered himself without a father. In too many ways, he was right. His father, Arnold, was a busy man. Miles's mother hung in with the loneliness and neglect because her husband was, after all, an excellent provider. More important, she served God faithfully and for that reason refused to consider divorce. It was a continual decision on her part to hold her marriage together.

A child does not have that decision. A child cannot contemplate some other living situation; this family is all the child knows. Even if the child senses that needs are not being met, rarely can he or she articulate the intuition. Miles knew, but it took him thirteen years to figure it out.

Arnold considered it sufficient that he provided the best of everything for his wife and son. Frequently, particularly during Miles's first years, his wife begged him to spend more time with her and the boy. His standard reply was, "I'd like to, but I have to get my business off the ground." He considered this his most demanding career juncture. He couldn't afford to waste time now if they were going to be well set in the future. Besides, that's a woman for you: emotional. No practical understanding of how life is.

Arnold had invested his time and money—in fact, his whole life—into building a career that would keep everyone in clover for the next century. In so doing he denied his wife and child happiness, but that was only the half of his investment return.

Now he was having to spend some major bucks getting Miles straightened out, if it could be done at all. Can you imagine? After a lifetime of luxury, his son had turned on him. Arnold could point to his financial success with pride, but how many business associates and their wives were tittering behind his back, gossiping that he had failed as a father and family man? He fought having to admit it, but Miles and his whining mother were making Arnold a laughingstock. And that hurt. It really hurt.

And yet, let us emphasize that Arnold was not the bad guy here. Establishing financial security for his family right down through the great-grandkids-to-be was an immense undertaking and stunning accomplishment. The negative results of his work ethic tended to take center stage over the positive accomplishments, and unfairly so. Human nature too often focuses on the bad and selectively ignores the good.

Most important of all, Arnold was doing his best to father *exactly as he had been fathered*. His own dad also worked hard and long. In the fifties, Mom usually stayed home and tried to be more like Donna Reed, while Dad went out and earned scads of money at a respectable career and wore a suit. Arnold's mom didn't look the least bit like Donna Reed, but Dad was a Father Knows Best look-alike. He dressed in gray suits (TV was black-and-white in those days) and worked for a major accounting firm. Arnold's dad made a nice living, but in the end, in his old age, he had only some modest stocks and bonds and his retirement pay. Arnold determined that his own family's future would fare better.

Still, had Arnold played his cards differently, redirecting his initial investment as best he could, he could have avoided the costs and pain of an alienated son and a sad wife. Let's explore some other options he could have taken.

• **Prepare Physically, Physiologically**

Arnold's wife needed his wholehearted support even before the birth of Miles. Every wife does. Not every wife receives it, but that makes it no less a need. Had Arnold committed himself to this ultimate investment in the generations right at the outset, he would have felt more comfortable about leaving the traditional, comfortable father role he grew up with. He would thereby have appreciated the importance of protecting his generational investment better because it was already an integral part of him.

Frank Minirth and Mary Alice suffered several miscarriages. During those painful, trying years, Frank developed a plan. After receiving her assurance that she indeed wanted to go any distance to bear a child, he told Mary Alice, "Okay. Then we're going to try again. You may have to spend nine months in bed, but whatever it takes, we'll commit to this, together."

As part of the preparation to become parents, Frank Minirth made whatever sacrifices were necessary to stand by Mary Alice and help her. That meant, to an extent, putting his career plans on hold, on a slower track. She, too, pulled out all the stops. She monitored food and exercise and spent weeks flat on her back. She fought boredom. They both fought fear and the gnawing doubt that all this was worth it.

Finally after seven years of disappointment, Rachel was born. She was greeted into this world with jubilation. She happened because her father joined with her mother to prepare, to do whatever it took, to bring her to term. Together.

The pattern did not change much with subsequent pregnancies. Mary Alice soon learned that she had to help her body rest and heal for at least a year following a miscarriage before she tried again. During the last pregnancy, Frank canceled all his out-of-town travel plans and reduced his workload so that he might remain close by regardless what happened. Their diligence and efforts, together, bore good fruit when Alicia arrived, healthy and bright.

Most childbirths are not so fraught with danger as were the Minirths', but all require physical preparation. Mom must monitor her health, her eating habits, her exercise, her environment. It's not a one-man (rather, one-woman) show. Dad can help, and not in the role of pregnancy police, either. His enthusiastic support, giving whatever gifts of time and affection his wife requires, renders the long, taxing vigil less taxing. His wife no longer feels alone as she makes whatever sacrifices and adjustments she must. Check some of the situations in this table. We've left some blank lines, trusting you will think of ways you, specifically, can help out. Your wife may want to fill in the blanks for you! Ask her.

What Mom should do:	What Dad can do to support:
Avoid smoking and second-hand smoke.	Refrain from smoking.
Monitor nutrition.	Bone up on nutrition and alter meal habits to reflect her needs. Be not a tempter (No "Let's go out for ice cream").
Monitor exercise.	Share housework. Understand her exercise needs and help her meet them (walk, avoid heavy lifting . . .).
Monitor environment.	Avoid any activity that endangers the pregnancy. (Some paint fumes can cause miscarriage.) Empty the cat box often. Cat feces and urine, especially males', can cause trouble.

Physical preparation links with emotional preparation. Buying baby furniture. Choosing names. Those decisions, made together, provide a very positive influence, for they improve mutual understanding and intimacy, and that further solidifies the marriage.

Paul Warren tacks on, "Deciding on a name improves your relationship eventually. At first, Vicky and I had to really struggle through selecting a name. I picked rousing Scandinavian names. Not quite Thor or Harald Bluetooth, but close. Vicky had others. Coming to an agreement was very good for our intimacy; we learned each other better, and therefore it was ultimately good for Matthew."

Investments in intimacy always pay rich dividends—for everybody.

• **Prepare Mentally and Emotionally**

Had Arnold invested in his wife's emotional state prior to the birth, he would have found he benefitted even more than she did. Women are generally better prepared emotionally and mentally for childbearing; it's pretty much natural to them. It is also a necessity to them, for they are tossed into the pool, so to speak, whether they have ever gone swimming before or not. By talking about it with his wife, by sharing thoughts and plans, Arnold would have found that he was preparing himself emotionally even more so than she. It's a big, big jolt, becoming a father. It helps to mentally brace oneself.

Childbirth classes for that reason may be very interesting, but very uncomfortable. They force the father-to-be to come to grips with his approaching fatherhood. They can trigger the grieving process, and that is ultimately a healthy step forward, as we have seen.

"Come to grips with approaching fatherhood?" you ask. "You know you're going to be a father the moment your wife tells you the baby's coming. What's to come to grips with?" True, the man's head understands almost from the beginning that he is going to be a father. But the heart is generally pretty slow to catch on.

"The day Vicky's water broke," Paul Warren recalls. "That was the first time I actually realized I would be a father. Certainly, I knew it in my head. I thought I had it cold. Hah!

"I remember it all very clearly. We were trimming a tree out back. I was climbing the ladder, lopping the branches, and Vicky was picking them up in the alleyway. All of a sudden her water broke. I froze. What do we do now? I'm a medical doctor, remember.

"I asked her, of all the silly questions, 'Are you sure?' Water was running down her legs, down the alley. It was Sunday, at four P.M. I remember it vividly."

Paul Warren somewhat ruefully reflects that childbirth is usually not a time in which you use what you learned in childbirth classes. At seven the next morning, when he and Vicky were both numb, the attending physician recommended a Caesarean section.

"That's it," Dr. Warren finally told himself. "We're parents now."

If childbirth classes do not sufficiently force the painful reality, and are so often ignored in the delivery room, are they worth the effort? In fact, surely they'd do no good at all for some fathers, even first-timers, who like Dr. Warren may know more about the process than the instructor.

For example, Joe, a paramedic for a suburban ambulance service, had already delivered half a dozen babies when his wife became pregnant with their first child. Two of the infants he delivered he called "miracle babies" because their mothers gave birth under the perilous, filthy conditions of major traffic accidents. Both mothers and both babies were doing fine. Nobody was going to tell him about childbirth.

Joe learned to his amazement that he needed to talk to other fathers just as much as anyone else did. Those conversations alleviated the fears he was slow to recognize and reassured him. In his years as a paramedic, Joe had talked to dozens of distraught men whose pregnant wives were being rushed to the emergency room for some problem or other. He had acted as reassurer and counselor to five of those six new fathers whose babies he had helped into the world. He found that none of that was like talking about his pending fatherhood to other pending fathers in the relaxed, casual atmosphere of the childbirth classes. In his job, fatherhood was clinical. In his private life, it was very, very personal.

No matter how much a man understands the physical events of birth, he needs help figuring out the emotional and psychological ramifications. Only contact with other people in the same boat could advance Joe's confidence in those areas.

Too, fathers-to-be need time and repetition to thoroughly process the full realization of fatherhood. Fathers-to-be need to know they're not alone. And childbirth classes serve that purpose well. They are, for that reason, more helpful to the father than to the mother. Even if she can't make it, he should go anyway.

• Prepare Any Way You Like

Finally, the wise father prepares in ways that are uniquely his own. Men's interests differ widely. Those diverse interests, being a part of the man, ought to be honored. Brian Newman provides the example.

Besides his cordless phone and camcorder, Brian carried a twenty- or thirty-person phone list for weeks before the birth, ready to call around on a moment's notice. And call he did. He joyously told family members about the birth even from the delivery room while minutes-old Benjamin howled.

When Rachel was born three and a half years earlier, Brian used a pay phone, in the traditional manner. He had to go through the operator for an outside line. "After the eighth or tenth call," he says, "the operator said, 'You sound familiar. Did you just have a baby?' She really got into the program; she asked weight and all the details." Brian shrugs, grinning. "I like gadgets, and in that way I'm typically male. The new dad will pick up the phone and call. 'Hey, old college buddy; guess what. . . .' The mom will probably write a note. It's more personal. Intimate. And send pictures."

Brian is indeed typical, for as a rule, men are gadget-oriented. A man is concerned more with the material than with relationships as such. We will see this phenomenon over and over throughout fatherhood. It happened to Arnold, as he prepared for a material future at the expense of his family's nonmaterial needs.

The differences can be summarized in this comparison table.

Men's Basic Makeup Compared with Women's

Father	Mother
Concerned with tangibles.	Comfortable with intangibles.
"Thing" (gadget) directed.	Relationship directed.
Task- or goal-oriented.	Process-oriented.
Strives for completion; the doing is secondary.	Enjoys the moment, the doing; completion is secondary.

We will refer to these differences often, because they profoundly affect how a father fathers.

That penchant for gadgets tends to surface particularly in times of stress. For men, gadgets—the material—are comforting. You can see, feel, and touch a solid object. You know it's there. You cannot see or touch, perhaps not even understand, nonmaterial things such as love, distrust, fear, the future. Shifting, formless, sometimes undetectable intangibles offer cold comfort.

Brian Newman prepared materially. He had the camcorder ready, the phone, the baby's layette. He had the route to the hospital picked. But there were deeper reasons for the videos of his baby's birth and the calls than merely an enthusiasm for things electronic. Brian searched himself in vain for a feeling of his own history. He knew very little about his heritage and even less about his parents'. He felt the lack keenly and determined to provide his children with the sense of history and continuity he himself did not know.

Praise God, Debi understood his needs and motivations; for no lesser reason would a mother-to-be allow a camcorder in the delivery room.

Be There at the Start

"When Rachel was born, I saw her head come out. It looked misshapen. I was scared to death! I was afraid she

was deformed." Brian Newman's fear evaporated instantly
as he took the infant in his arms. She was not deformed;
indeed, Rachel is an absolutely beautiful child; but had she
been, he still would have been full of joy. "I can't tell you
the excitement of what it felt like to be there at delivery,"
he says. "Both times, I just cried. It's exhilarating. Breath-
taking."

Brian Newman, a psychotherapist well in touch with his
own feelings, articulates with great enthusiasm what many
fathers know inside, even if they can't describe it. There is
no substitute for being there from the beginning, or as near
the beginning as you can.

The arrival of babies has a very strong bonding influence
for the whole family, not just the mother and father. Some
people go so far as to say the siblings should be there
through the birth process also.

If commencing fathering right at the beginning is such a
win-win situation, why doesn't every father dive right in?
Arnold happened to be in St. Paul when Miles was born.
Deliberately. What held Arnold back?

One of the reasons many fathers stay out of the fathering
process is simple logistics. They can't make it. Their work
or other obligations prevent their presence. Men in the
career military know the situation all too well. As a naval
officer phrased it, "The navy feels that you have to be there
for the laying of the keel, but not for the launching."

Some fathers-to-be simply put expedience or even necessity aside. A splendid, and pertinent, true-life story comes
from the 1924 Olympiad in Paris, France. Bill Havens was
selected to represent the United States in the singles event
of Canadian-style canoeing, then a demonstration sport.
But he and his wife expected a child sometime during the
games. He gave up his place on the U.S. team to remain
home at his wife's side. His son Frank arrived four days
after the games ended.

In the summer of 1952, Bill Havens received a telegram
from Helsinki, where the Olympics were again in full swing.

"Dear Dad . . . Thanks for waiting around for me to get born in 1924. I'm coming home with the gold medal you should have won." Frank, a world-class canoeist himself, had just taken the gold in the Canadian-style singles.

Expedience aside, another reason many fathers stay out of the fathering process is the issue of adequacy we touched upon before. The fear is, I don't know how to relate to a child. What if I make a fool of myself in that forbidding, unfamiliar delivery room, and that nursery? I don't know how to change a diaper. Afraid to do it wrong, afraid he will be revealed as the bumbler he feels as though he is, Dad sees the easy way out. Dump the nurturing on Mom. This is an age of specialization, and it's her job anyway.

Every father yearns for adequacy—that is, the ability to do a thing, perhaps even to do it well. No man can have an impact on the world without it. So many issues in the fathering process hinge upon this matter of adequacy because it reaches so deep inside a man. It's a core issue in men's lives, nowhere more evident than in fathering.

Generally speaking, a man feels more adequate in his work setting, and no wonder. He's better trained for his job than he is for fathering. Remember, too, that as women tend more to be relationship-oriented, men tend more to be gadget-oriented—materialistic. A man feels most confident in a work place where issues, jobs, and tasks are not relational. The best jobs involve concrete objects without emotional needs. That feeling of inadequacy, then, really surfaces when he goes home at night and has to face the complex relationship issues of home, marriage, and a growing family.

Arnold, for example, habitually backed away from those relational issues that threatened his feeling of adequacy. Essentially, he feared messing up. By definition, *home* equals *relationship*. But Arnold grew up with the unspoken message that dads don't have to shine in the relationship department. His own father didn't, and the family seemed to get along just fine. He simply followed a pattern ingrained in him from his first moment in the world and trusted it to be the right pattern.

But there is a better pattern. Step beyond the traditional from the start.

Beyond the Traditional Role of the Father

No matter how egalitarian the society, different expectations are required of fathers than are required of mothers. Feminists complain that this is all culturally ingrained in kids. Naturists say it's genetically programmed in along with eye color and raging chocoholism. The argument is moot. How such expectations and roles appear is not at issue; what we do with them is.

Consider these side-by-side lists of traditional role expectations. Most male readers would nod and say, "Sure. Everyone knows that." Many female readers, arguing against old stereotypes that limit women's choices, would fume, "Bunk!"

Bunk or truth, let's use these role expectations as a starting point from which to explore men's roles as fathers.

The Traditional Roles Compared

Father	Mother
Love the mother	Love the father
Introduce kids to the world	Introduce kids to the home
Skills-enabler	Nurturer
Protect from dangers	Protect from inner hurts
Promote socialization	Promote relationships
Provide the food	Cook and serve the food
Do the outside chores	Do the inside chores
Handle automotive needs	Sew, enjoy related crafts
Discipline major cases	Discipline minor cases
Be assertive	Be submissive

A word of explanation about the very important role of skills-enabler is in order. The term *enabler* has a specific and unhealthy meaning in the terminology of codependence, and we do not in any way mean that here. Rather, we talk about the father enabling his children to cope with the world. He introduces the big, wide world to his child. He helps his child to be able to do many things. So we call that role a *skills-enabler* for want of a better term.

Experienced parents know that in day-to-day practice, the roles in the chart shift constantly from one parent to the other. Jack and Arlene Brubaker, friends of ours, constantly swapped roles for reasons of necessity, convenience, preference, or for no reason at all. They had to. Dragging a flock of four headstrong kids through life without losing them to weirdness, drugs, the wrong mates, the wrong careers, or the wrong choices took two people full time.

Daughter Marla, at seventeen, was chafing for a car of her own. Son John, fourteen, had discovered that he could always find a barber who would cut his hair his way. It was never his father's barber. Lynna, ten, was the star of her soccer team. All her teammates were boys. Peter, seven, was the only sensible one. For Peter, when Mom or Dad said something, it was so.

Arlene never hesitated to discipline major infractions when Jack wasn't available. Working alone, Jack could get the kids through breakfast and out the door to school without suffering undo stress. They complemented each other well and met the kids' needs whenever the needs appeared, not when the "right" parent was handy for a particular role.

The male is traditionally the skills-enabler; that is, the parent who enables the child to master the skills needed to cope with our world. But Arlene taught Marla how to drive and helped Lynna learn to ride her bike without training wheels. The mother is traditionally the nurturer, but Jack took Lynna to her ballet lessons (inflicted lessons, incidentally; Lynna had scant interest in ballet, but her parents knew she needed training in poise and balance). He stayed home from work with Peter when the little guy got the measles.

Despite these daily role reversals, Jack and Arlene both harbored the traditional picture—the stereotype—down inside. They didn't notice how much they themselves ignored tradition every day. Most couples don't.

Most couples have their own definitions for the items in the chart too.

—Dad, the Teacher About the World—

Like the caterpillar within the butterfly, these traditional roles are an integral part of the new father. They serve the emotional happiness and well-being of both father and child. And once you, the father, understand what they are and can see them clearly, you can expand upon them more easily.

Dad, Usher into the World of People

Relationship. That in a word explains the roles of the truly effective father.

"In counsel, we are very careful when we talk about traditional roles," says Paul Warren. "It's a highly charged emotional issue, and people so often mis-hear what we're really saying. We're not asking anyone to abandon a traditional role. No. We ask the man or woman to start there and step beyond it. Stepping beyond tradition is crucial for today's father."

When Dad comes between Mom and baby (cutting the umbilical cord notwithstanding), he is providing his child's first socialization experience. That is, he is the first outside human being, so to speak, to enter the child's world. Socialization is one aspect of dealing with the outside world. So is learning to use tools, to drive, to buy an airline ticket. That's the sort of skills-enabling we see Dad as doing well.

Let us emphasize: this is not to say that Mom does not serve that function as well. She certainly does, in very practical ways. Too often, though, she ends up serving in all ways as Dad abrogates his role as skills-enabler in favor of some other role, such as provider.

Dad, Primary Protector

Again we emphasize: Mom can protect with the best of them. Dad's unique and special role is this:

Dads protect their kids from the dangers of the inside world, from the angry, destructive impulses that originate within. He can usually understand those impulses better because of his very manhood; a characteristic of the testosterone-rich male is aggressiveness and ready anger. This places him in the best position to teach his sons and daughters how to control anger and impulse. He teaches by edict, by instruction, by modeling. He can say from the heart, "No. I understand, but I won't allow you to give vent to that. That's destructive."

Dads protect their kids from the dangers of the outside world. That precept is biblical. Dad knows the outside world; the child does not, to start with. Dad, the child's intercessor for the big, wide world, also knows its dangers.

Frank Minirth explains one aspect of protecting children. "Watch how you program the computer. The human mind stores so much more than we might think it does. Millions of messages working in there. On the positive side, you protect them by the use of memorized Scripture. Oh, I'm very big on memorizing Scripture. When it's stored inside, it's there, working.

"Not only Scriptures program children, either. A lot of the old songs we repeat, that's programming. 'You're the only one of your kind'; wonderful builder-upper.

"On the negative side, you protect them from bad programming by not letting them watch bad TV, bad news. Six to eight hours of TV a day makes a profound difference; profound difference! You see, we're programmed by repetition."

Dr. Minirth contends that if the father builds a relationship of protection when his children are young, he will find turning them loose later much easier.

"I came home on one occasion last year; a baby-sitter was minding Allie—Alicia. Alicia was a year old, that's all. The sitter was watching an objectionable TV program. I asked her to turn it off. I didn't want it programmed in. A year old? Yes, I believe the mind is picking up messages then. Very much so.

"The children know that I take care to protect them because I love them."

Frank Minirth nods and smiles. "I really love them."

There is also, of course, the aspect of actual physical protection. That, too, says in no uncertain terms, "I care."

Artist Bill Holm, both a splendid artist and a recognized authority on Indian tribes of northwest North America, created a painting of a clan of Plains Indians on the move. In a distant column of horses, dogs, bundles, and people, the women, children, and some of the men are traveling to a new village site. Here in the foreground, and on the far distant rolling prairie, members of the group's elite warrior societies ride guard. Well-mounted, they range wide in a protective stance ahead of and beside the column, on the watch, ready to detect and repel attackers. The children travel within a net of security, their safety assured by crack horse soldiers. It is a stunning and symbolic picture.

As Mom can perform traditional fathering functions when necessary, so Dad is able to perform many of Mom's. Frequently he may not realize he's doing so. Too, he may think he's unable to do a good job as a "mother." Sure he can; it's the mental slowdown rather than any actual inability that he has to get past.

Dad, the Nurturer

Expanding beyond his traditional roles, Dad is also called to be a nurturer. Breast-feeding may be out, but many other facets of nurturing bring him genuine pleasure. Kissing the boo-boo to make it better (always best accompanied with a hug); snuggling the baby or small child as sleep time approaches; rocking, bathing, bottle-feeding, spoon-feeding, diapering, walking the floor to soothe the baby whose life has gone awry; doing a load of diapers or baby clothes; folding laundry; Dad can be just as adequate in the role as Mom.

Neither does the nurturing role end with potty training. As the child grows, the father's nurturing role shifts but does not diminish.

"To summarize the expanded role of today's father," concludes Paul Warren, "it's being involved with the kids. When you do that, you're gripping the future as well as the past. It used to be Dad whipped some school pictures out of his wallet when people asked and checked the kids off as dependents on his income tax. Kids were show and tell.

"Now Dad is directly involved with their nurturing and upbringing, that expanded role. And for today's man, that is a great source of pride."

And his involvement will make a big different even for his infant.

—Baby's First Lessons—

Baby specialists long assumed that a newborn simply lies there blotting up nourishment, shooting it out the bottom into a diaper, and growing. Period. They figured the baby didn't even try to focus and see until it was a couple months old. "Cry when you need something, vegetate when you don't" was traditionally thought to be Baby Philosophy. That is poles apart from reality.

In recent years, as we learn by sometimes ingenious means what a newborn is actually doing and feeling, a lot of change has come in our understanding of the importance of Dad at this age. He imparts important lessons to the newborn. Yes, the newborn.

Babies learn through three sources: touching, hearing, and seeing.

We don't believe that tiny babies learn cognitively. That is, they don't think in the same linear ways we do. For one thing, they don't have verbalization (try thinking without using words sometime). Also, they probably don't analyze what's coming in. They have no life experience yet with which to sort and compare events. But that doesn't mean they aren't learning.

Some of the lessons a newborn must master are:

- This is Mother. She differs from:
- This other person, Father. He differs from:
- All other persons.
- And I am safe.

The baby learns these primary lessons through the three avenues of hearing, seeing, and touching. In years past, fathers let Mom do it all. So that's all baby learned at first. Except for an occasional good-night kiss or a bit of dandling on the knee while Mom finished dinner, Dad was an entity in the periphery, out there among "the others."

As a weird sort of experiment, place yourself for the moment in a baby's shoes—rather, booties. You know quite a few things instinctively, and you know Mommy. You heard her voice even in utero. You know her rhythms and her face. You know her gentle touch and nurse at her breast. She provides. Now imagine how, using the three avenues of learning (hearing, seeing, and touching), you learn about Daddy.

Will you learn about him best if he's floating out there somewhere, or if he's snuggling you in his arms? His eyes make contact with yours. His hands change you and pick you up; they may offer you a bottle. His mouth smiles at you. His voice, different in both timbre and inflection from Mommy's, speaks to you.

See the difference?

"I highly recommend skin-to-skin contact," says Dr. Warren, and Dr. Newman agrees. "That's the baby's first line of learning. It's important for babies to feel what the father feels like because he feels different from Mommy. It's better for the father too. It enhances the process of becoming a father. Enriches it."

Isn't this unnatural for fathers? Not at all. Brian Newman relates, "I stopped at the car dealership, where we were getting Debi's car worked on. I had Benjamin along; he was maybe two months old. I set him down in his carrier and whoosh! six male salesmen were hovering over him laughing. Those macho Texans were making baby talk at him. One of them offered me a trade: Benjamin for anything on the lot. He was kidding, of course, but there was some sadness there. He wanted a baby but his wife didn't."

Just talking to the baby is important; it's part of bonding with Dad. Therefore, taking those first important steps in socializing—that is, building a life with people other than Mommy—is hearing Dad talk.

"Dads," says Frank Minirth, "should sing to their babies. Sing what? Well, what kind of messages do you want to give your children? Start delivering those messages right from the beginning."

—The Fun of Getting Involved—

Easy for Frank Minirth to say. He can sing well. Charles Mayer was just plain embarrassed by his singing voice, or lack thereof. Not even in the echo chamber of a shower stall did it sound like anything. But he did a great Arte Johnson imitation, with a phony, funny, middle European accent. So although Meghan sang to infant Sean Michael, he never did. He joked. He spoke falsetto, and he spoke rumbly and deep. "Ach! Vass iss dis?" he would ask when he encountered a full diaper.

When Charles took his newborn out for walks, he didn't bother with a stroller or a baby sling. He hauled Sean Michael around in the crook of his arm, yakking with the neighbors, rubbing the stiff, velvet nose of the horse in the pasture behind Bill's place, stopping for bread or milk at the minimart on the corner of 45th Street. Charles did the things he enjoyed doing, and he included his baby boy.

In short, Charles was having a ball with his tiny kid. And that is the whole idea, the bottom line. To follow guidelines by rote is not the key to fathering success. Building a happy relationship is. If Dad's having a good time, so will the child. Already Charles and his little Sean were well along the road to a lifetime of happiness together.

To Think About

As I think of friends and acquaintances—men at work, church members, neighbors—I would most like to emulate the fathering techniques of:

1. _____
2. _____
3. _____

because:

_____ Their kids turned out well.

_____ They seem to enjoy being fathers.

_____ They're the kind of people who get things done.

_____ They don't let fathering get in the way of other important things. They seem to juggle their responsibilities successfully.

_____ Their kids really admire them.

_____ Other people's kids admire them.

_____ Other _____

—Here Comes a Two-Year-Old!—

Tiny Sean Michael Mayer did not stay tiny forever. In fact, within a year or so he was walking and therefore no longer qualified as an infant. Sean was moving from good-natured comic-strip baby *Marvin* to *Dennis the Menace,* in one fell swoop.

How is Dad going to deal with the walking Death Star that preschoolers are reputed to be? Let's talk about that.

FOUR

Dad and His Preschooler

Because he spent so much time on the road driving for the moving company, Elgin Mayer found himself in a lot of motel rooms with nothing to do. Frankly, television got old in a hurry. He never was much for TV anyway. Even if the motel had a pool and Jacuzzi™, there wasn't much besides TV for a weary driver. So Elgin Mayer had long ago taken up the hobby of wood carving.

It fit his lifestyle perfectly. When he went out on the road, he made sure he took a couple projects along in a big canvas tote. His carving tools all fit nicely in a folding suede case Jean had made for him. On the lonely evenings away from home he would get out a three-dimensional carving or perhaps a plaque, unroll his tool case, and chip away.

Tonight, halfway between Baltimore and Moline with a full load, Elgin settled himself into a motel room chair, falsely called an "easy chair." From his canvas bag he pulled the infant he was carving in cherry wood. He smiled. The sleeping baby lay on its ear, tummy down, with its legs pulled in under it. The draped flutes of its little nightie looked very natural; Elgin was proud of his job so far. He unrolled his tool case onto the Formica™ table by his elbow and chose the veiner. He'd free up the little guy's chin by undercutting from below.

Little guy? Not just any little guy. This was his grandson, Sean Michael; the babe's infancy immortalized in clear cherry. Elgin laid out the reference photos he'd taken of his sleeping grandson, pictures he had snapped from every conceivable angle. He picked up his favorite snapshot and studied it. He had an easy job; carve a likeness out of a formless block of cherry wood.

Charles had the difficult job: shape a worthwhile human being out of an innocent newborn baby.

—Shaping the Whole Little Person—

Charles had it even harder than Elgin realized, for several reasons. Sean Michael would mature so rapidly that the methods of shaping were bound to change from year to year. As Sean grew, Charles would have to play with him in different ways, relate to him in different ways, teach him in different ways. All Elgin had to do was whittle.

Consider this brief summary of how the child's development affects Dad's fathering techniques:

Child at years:	Learns by:	Father's best method of relating:
0 to 2	Feeling Hearing Seeing	Handle, snuggle skin to skin, talk and make faces.
2 to 6	Imagination Pretend play Symbolic play	Play pretend, tell stories, read with child in lap.
Grade school	Activity Realistic play Some talking	Do things; ride bikes, shoot baskets, take hikes; build models and real things (a birdhouse, a scooter); play competitive games.
Junior and senior high school	Talking and abstract discussion	Do adult things; fishing, hiking, working on the car, cooking, home improvement projects, etc.

Too, Elgin's block of clear cherry was predictable. Press a sharp gouge into the wood at a particular angle and a particular sized chip would come away. Then the block would just sit there until Elgin chose to make another cut, another shaving. Children are not by any measure predictable. Try to shape them to your liking and they are quite liable to assume some different shape you did not expect.

Charles's task as a father, moreover, was not simply to raise a worthwhile child but to raise a worthwhile servant of God. That is every father's ultimate responsibility. Let us therefore pay particular attention throughout this book to ways in which fathers can help their children grow spiritually as well as physically and psychologically.

How would Charles shape his baby, Sean Michael, during the preschool years? Let's look at the tools and techniques he will be using, and also at the material to be shaped.

Preschooler's Traits	Dad's Best Response
Physical, learning about self through activity. Testing limits.	Active, hands-on play. Build simple things. Roughhouse.
Timid about new things, fearful.	Take lead in exploring. Remember that adults' everyday world is new to the child. Recognize legitimacy of fear. Help child cope; walk with child in scary circumstance.
Just learning to communicate.	Talk, read aloud, simply make sounds and noises in play.
Symbolic in thinking.	Play symbolically, "waste" time, play-act, give play to imagination.

Preschooler's Traits, *cont.*	Dad's Best Response, *cont.*
Just beginning to understand sexuality and its differences.	Model respect for both sexes.
Mommy and Daddy *are* God.	Model a just, loving God.

How Father Teaches

Charles will shape his new little person in two ways: by hands-on playing with Sean (which includes reading stories to him) and by modeling various behaviors. Those ways boil down to one simple precept: Spend time with the child.

"I always spend time with my daughters," says Frank Minirth, and he's not boasting as he says it. Time is not an "extra"; it's the bare minimum. "Especially Alicia, a year and a half old. She loves to go four-wheeling. So do I. You find then, as they get older, you spend less time. They do more things with other people, with friends. School schedules get heavy.

"You have to spend time with them when they're young. This is the reverse of what too many men do when relating to their children. They usually wait until the kids are fifteen to talk to them. By then they don't know their children."

How do you get to know a two- or three-year-old who stands not nose-to-nose but head-to-knee, can't speak English properly, and doesn't comprehend any instruction more elaborate than "no, no!"? You do it the same way Mom does it. You goof off with your kids (they think it's playing) and read to them a lot. You draw pictures with them, strange pictures with sky that ends just above everybody's head. You pretend. Hands on. Active. Fathers might not think to do that stuff; that's Mommy stuff. But that's the stuff that works.

Remember that small children bond with their father through the senses of touching, hearing, and seeing. They learn in that manner also. Most fathers aren't very comfortable playing with a two-year-old, carrying the child on their shoulders, rolling around with him or her—her especially. A preschooler is so tiny. Fragile. Romp with a toy female person who can shatter at a touch? No way! And yet, that is the physical touching to which children relate. Dad must overcome his own reluctance—without, of course, abandoning gentleness.

Preschoolers are learning identity—who they are, and what their bodies can and cannot do. They run and jump and climb, testing their limits and resources. Now is the perfect time for Dad to encourage climbing on the jungle gym and to push them on the swings. Although it's old hat to Dad, who may have chipped a tooth or two on playground equipment in his own youth, to the child it is a new and immensely important way of relating.

From the child's unarticulated perspective, Dad is providing a sense of bonding through action. Motion and activity are the kids' currency at this age. Dad is simply tapping into it by taking part.

Because these are crucial years for separation and individuation—that's a fancy way of saying, "I am learning who I am"—it is important for children that the parents go and return. It works like this:

The child, always in Mommy's company, considers itself little more than an extension of Mommy. But then Mommy leaves the room. Mommy returns. Mommy drops the child at the baby-sitter's to go to the dentist. Mommy returns. Daddy goes to work. Daddy returns.

The pattern repeats over and over. The child realizes (again, without actually articulating it at a conscious level), "I exist whether Mommy is here or not. I am me, even when Mommy and Daddy are gone."

If Dad and Mom do not leave and faithfully return, that essential lesson of individuation goes unlearned, with serious consequences later. The child always will have difficulty defining himself or herself as an individual, an entity.

Daddy should take the initiative here, especially when

Mom is sometimes reluctant to leave a small child with others. He sees to it that Mommy gets away now and then, and that from time to time they both go somewhere without the child. He thus ensures that the important lesson of individuation goes smoothly.

Charles will teach Sean by example, as well. We also call it modeling.

"I think that fathers intuitively realize that they reproduce after their own kind," says Frank Minirth. "Their kids will copy them. Their children can't read thoughts or exact feelings, although they're very, very good at sensing feelings, especially anger. What they read best is behavior. It's the first thing kids analyze because it's so obvious, so overt."

Dad, then, has to set the right example. But it's more than that. When Sean observes Charles doing something, or reading, or relating to family members and others, Sean perceives, "This must be important because it's important to Daddy." With his own behavior, Charles will shape not just Sean's behavior but his attitude toward life.

Charles will teach Sean other, more specific, things as well.

What Father Teaches

Charles and Meghan weren't starting out from scratch with Sean exactly. They had first practiced somewhat by raising a black Labrador retriever. A lot of young couples these days do that.

The lab, named Cowboy, treated the living room carpet with the same disdain Hell's Angels bikers hold for neckties. Cowboy considered "Here, boy!" an option, not an order. The Ten Commandments? They were the Ten Suggestions. He chewed Charles's running shoes into running shreds and dug so many holes that the Mayers called their back yard, "The Bomb Zone." After some months of attempting in vain to civilize Cowboy, they dragged him off to dog obedience school. There the Mayers learned a lot of useful things.

They learned to be firm and to expect—nay, demand—

prompt obedience. They learned to reward not with a bribe but with affection and a relational gesture—a pat, a hug, a happy scratch behind the ears. They learned that to discipline Cowboy well they had to have a close personal relationship with him. All that would apply to kids, too.

The Mayers were taught, among many other things, to employ deliberate voice inflections when addressing Cowboy. They were to use a deep, low voice when correcting the pooch and a higher, livelier voice when praising him.

• Communications Skills

Along came Sean. As the baby entered his second year, toddling full tilt from adventure to adventure, bouncing off the walls (literally at times), they found themselves using a low voice in a corrective manner, such as "Don't you do that!" rumbled in baritone. And as they romped with him, they often employed a high, even falsetto, voice. "Let me tickle you! Tee hee hee!" This variation of tone and inflection came pretty much naturally, and both Charles and Meghan did it. That was good.

"So very often, young children tend to associate the male voice with fear and punishment only. Dad yells at the kid and corrects, and then lets Mom take over. It's sad," says Dr. Warren, nodding toward a photo of his own son. "Children need to hear nurturing, supportive conversation from a male voice too. . . . How much their father loves them; 'You're my favorite boy in all the world.'"

Because most men's voices are lower and deeper than most women's voices, and because most men are physically larger than most women, children pay more attention to males' correction. The dog-training rule comes into play, somewhat—not because kids are anything like dogs, but because of a universal caution about angering someone or something much bigger than you (across the board in the animal kingdom a lower, deeper sound is recognized as coming from a larger sound-maker). This gives Dad an extra dollop of power, and that in turn requires additional responsibility.

Because of Dad's special attributes—size and voice—as a corrector, we will devote the next chapter to Dad's role in discipline.

Since this is the age when communication skills are so rapidly expanding, Sean needs lots of conversation with his father. If he primarily hears only Meghan talking, he will miss out on the variation Charles would provide. For men say things differently and use different tones of voice.

"These variations, and the necessity of hearing them, are one of the many advantages of a daddy reading to his child," Dr. Warren continues. "Just to hear Dad's voice with its unique inflections . . . Dad's voice making the voices for Mama Bear and Papa Bear and Baby Bear; the kid hears that from Daddy too. It helps the child learn what male is, and it helps immensely with language skills."

• Socialization and the Outside World

But that's merely one small portion of the learning process. Kids will spend a lifetime sorting out personal relationships. At the beginning of this process, small children cannot take for granted the fact they are loved. It is something they must learn through oft-repeated lessons.

"Children need physical affection from their fathers," Frank Minirth says, "boys and girls both. They need to learn they are cared about through all their senses, not just the voice. Certainly you tell them you love them, and they're special. But a side-to-side hug speaks it too. So does a smile and a wave."

And this preschool time is when Dad first steps into his role as skills-enabler.

Two-year-olds assume themselves to be the center of the universe. By three, toddlers make a horrible discovery: they're not. Not only that, the universe can be a threatening, very hostile place, and they are powerless to control it. Fathers, who have a little better handle on what the universe is like, have a lot to teach horrified little three-year-olds about the alien cosmos.

"Either socialization happens here, or it will be very difficult for it to happen later," says Dr. Warren. "The child is starting to walk, to explore the world around. This fact works on a symbolic level as well. Kids are very symbolic-minded. The child is coming into his or her first contact with the universe beyond Mommy. Daddy has a crucial task—to be involved with his child; to accompany the child into this hostile wide world. Remember, symbolically, Daddy represents the outside world."

Charles commenced that role when he'd carry the infant Sean around on his arm, patting the horse, and talking over the back fence with Bill.

As baby Sean started scuffing the soles of his shoes instead of their toes, Charles took him along just as before, but permitted Sean to explore abroad as they went. Going for a walk seems such a simple, relaxing thing for an adult. To a two- or three-year-old, it's high adventure.

In fact, old Cowboy loved it too.

A puddle, a gum wrapper, a loose stone, things delicate (a flower, a butterfly) and indelicate (the land mines deposited by dogs, oil from a leaking crankcase) . . . all demand attention. By talking, by ignoring, by pointing out, Daddy teaches his child about the millions of new and wonderful things out there.

And indeed, children need a man's point of view toward the world as well as a woman's. When Sean is exposed both to his father's understanding of the world and to his mother's, he learns about life in the round, as it were. He is introduced symbolically to the three dimensions of life, just as you would view a statue or other free-standing sculpture from more than one perspective. Children think symbolically in just that way.

Children also learn about the world through imagination. Again because the father is the symbolic representative of the outside world, he becomes the ideal person to teach about the real world by means of imagination.

When Charles sits in the sandbox with Sean, running toy trucks all over the "roads," Sean is processing the real world symbolically. You don't go out in the real street where real trucks roar. You figure the whole thing out here in the safety of the sandbox with Daddy.

When Charles sits in a chaise lounge while Sean "fixes" his shoe soles with a colorful plastic hammer, Sean is coming to terms with tools, to an extent even with career options on a very, very rudimentary level.

Daddy, as the child's first exposure to the world, represents the fact that people do a lot of things out there—fire fighters, cowboys, waiters, barbers, astronauts, gardeners, preachers, flaggers at construction sites, male and female, base and noble. The child begins processing all that by playing pretend, and pretend play is best done with Daddy, the universal rep.

"Let's pretend you're the customer and I'm the waiter."

"Pretend you just saw me, and I'm a cow."

"Pretend I'm a tugboat and you're a ship like we saw on the video this morning."

Daddy, you assume this role and I shall assume that one, that I might work out how they go together.

Again, reading, with the child in Daddy's lap, plays a key role in the learning process, and again that role takes many dimensions.

• Trust

"Children come with a built-in fear of the power of those huge, unpredictable adults," Dr. Warren explains. "When Daddy takes the child up in his lap and reads a story, in addition to all the benefits we talked about regarding language skills and lessons about the greater world, the child learns that this huge, powerful adult can be trusted. It's safe. It's cozy. It's a personal relationship. That means so much to the child, especially on the symbolic level."

• **Feelings**

The year is 1845. You put everything you owned into this huge, clumsy Conestoga wagon, the best overland vehicle money can buy. You stocked it with flour and other staples, nails, tools, seed, and dry goods. You were admonished that "one pound in St. Louis is ten pounds out on the trail," and you thought you had pared the number of your possessions to a minimum. Still you're abandoning treasured items along the way, quite literally in the middle of nowhere.

You have lost contact with all your friends and relatives back in the states. You are risking absolutely everything because you heard that the Oregon country is the next best thing to paradise. If you can just succeed as a farmer in those distant, fertile valleys, your children will have a better life than yours.

You are trusting, then, your life, your family, your fortune, and your future to . . .

. . . a wagon scout, a guide you never met until the train began its westward roll.

He travels ahead of the train, finding suitable campsites and water, grass for the livestock. He watches for signs of Indians and advises the wagon master accordingly. He knows the best routes because he's been through the area before. Snow? Floods? He understands weather patterns in mountains and on prairies, and how they affect the party. He's the advance man, likely to ride thirty miles a day and be gone days at a time. The wagons complete twelve miles a day.

Without the expertise of the guide scouting ahead, most of the wagons would fail to complete the trip. Those that made it would suffer great hardship unnecessarily.

In a remarkably exact analogy, Daddy is the guide and scout for his preschooler on the trail through life. As his children mature, Dad's role will change somewhat, from the Daddy-who-knows-all to the wise mentor. But throughout, he will fill a need no one else in the child's life can fill.

Sure, perhaps his preschooler might make it into adulthood without him, but at what cost?

The most perilous of the unknown territory that Dad will guide his child through is feelings. Dad has experienced the different feelings and emotions many times and has learned to cope with them. Most important, he learned that you will eventually get over most of them.

His child knows none of these things about feelings, and the kid is terrified. Moreover, now is when children learn about empathy, the sense that other people have different points of view and feel and experience different things. Pre-school is the time to develop that important understanding.

Dad can do that in three ways.

He may simply explain in so many words that others have a different approach. "Your mom doesn't feel this way. Your sister prefers . . . ."

Secondly, he can help his kids begin to understand there's a reason for rules and for the differences within us. He need do nothing more than drop little comments in, such as "You have to go to bed at eight because tomorrow we're going to Grandma's." "You have to go to bed because I told you to" is definitely out-of-style.

Thirdly, the child senses that Daddy has respect for his or her feelings. Daddy pulls this off by respecting the child's feelings. Nothing less will do it. Kids know.

These preschool years are a crucial age for fathers to empathize with kids' thoughts and understanding, and to themselves appreciate the differences between kids' feelings and their own. Here's the age when devastating damage can occur should Dad say, "Boys don't cry." He's saying, "Boys don't have feelings."

If I am a preschooler, I discover myself experiencing strong, gripping feelings I didn't recognize before. I can't explain them. As my individual identity emerges and grows, I get extremely angry. Extremely sad. Extremely scared. This is all very new and beyond my control. I need a guide to help me learn to deal with feelings.

The very best guide for me at this age is Dad. He's been there. He can comfort me and reassure me in specific ways.

First, he can guide simply by listening to my fears and to my feelings. The very fact that someone big acknowledges them will help me understand that they are real. By admitting they're there, he validates them, and the validation of feelings is a powerful, powerful need in small children. Remember, I have a limited ability to discern between real and imaginary.

Dad will therefore avoid saying, "Don't be frightened!" "Don't cry." Instead he will comfort me without denying that my feelings have a right to exist. Put another way, Dad is tacitly giving me permission to have the feelings natural to a little kid like me.

He will guide me into the realization (taken for granted by grown-ups for so long that they forget it's new to me) that I'll get over my feelings. I will not be angry forever. Sadness doesn't last the rest of my life. This realization doesn't come right away. Dad will guide me through this by telling me, "I understand. I've been angry before." "I've been sad like that." Dad isn't always angry, or always sad. Therefore, the feelings must be temporary. I will make the logical inference even if I can't work it out consciously, in words. I desperately need that reassurance that I can get through it, and that it won't last forever, or feelings will forever terrify me.

By acknowledging my feelings and admitting to feelings of his own, Dad will guide me into the realization that he himself possesses more feelings than just anger. His deep voice, remember, frightens me, especially when he's angry, and his anger makes a particularly strong impression on me. If he's one of those men who usually doesn't pay attention to small children unless he's disciplining them, I'm justified in thinking anger is his only feeling.

Besides, these preschool years are my Age of Reproachment. I figured out that I'm probably not the center of the universe anymore, but I still assume a lot of weird things happen because of me. I think everything's my fault. If Daddy is angry, it must be my fault. If Daddy comes home from work mad, it must be my fault. I need him to repeatedly reinforce the lesson that anger comes from lots of places, not just me. And I need him to reaffirm his unconditional love.

• **Sexuality**

Sex ed? For a preschooler? You bet. A lot goes on now that provides the foundation for all the child's future attitudes about sexuality. And we have found that the father is teaching sexual attitudes whether he deliberately tries to or not. Noninvolvement is also a lesson, though not a good one. Dad teaches his kids about sexuality in several ways.

One way is simply by being comfortable with his own maleness. If a father does not feel good about his own manhood, the child will not feel good about being a boy or girl. Children closely mirror parents' attitudes, and this is one area in which the unspoken speaks loudly.

A part of this is practicing respect for the father's own body and for the child's. Daddy will do that not by displaying prudishness but by using restraint and modesty. He will respect his own modesty, and when the time comes, his child's. The time usually comes around age five when kids start to get bashful about nudity. Until then, running around naked and running around in a snowmobile suit are one and the same to the little tyke. Daddy of course will not behave in any abusive way, ever.

An immensely important way Dad influences his child's understanding of sexuality is in his relationship with the child's mother. Does he treat Mom respectfully? Affectionately? Let us hope so, because as he symbolically represents the world and All Men, Mom stands for All Women. What observation does the small child make—what lessons does he or she intuit—by All Men's behavior toward All Women?

Too, Dad will demonstrate respect for the opposite sex generally. He'll not be disparaging of women (nor will Mom of men, for that matter). He will search himself for attitudes demeaning to the opposite sex and modify them, knowing his child is going to blot them up and claim them as his or her own. The definitions and terms of sexual harassment, of inappropriate sexual comment or innuendo, change daily. The attitudes toward sexuality that Dad's dad entertained won't serve children growing up now. Dads today, being the link between the old and the new, must take care that their kids pick up healthy attitudes.

Then, there is that Oedipal complex everyone hears about. It occurs with boys at about three years of age and will deeply influence their whole lives. We think it works about this way:

The small boy, just now getting a handle on this man-woman business, falls in love with Mommy. It's certainly not a sexual attraction of the sort we usually associate with "falling in love." It is at once much more naive and much more profound than that. Daddy becomes a dangerous rival. The lad may push Daddy away from Mommy, or insinuate himself between them. He will demand Mommy's full attention, drawing her away from the rival. When he grows up, he will marry Mommy.

Then a curious, subtle shift happens. He observes that the bond between Mommy and Daddy is a strong one. They are well wedded to each other. He cannot marry Mommy. Rather, he will marry a lady like Mommy. In the child's heart, the relationships in this family fall gracefully into line. Mommy is Mommy, wed to Daddy who is Daddy, and the child is free to be a little child. The child has no emotional responsibility save to be loved and to grow. It is a very liberating realization.

In little girls, a similar experience is called the Electra complex.

And finally, Dad is involved directly in his child's education about sex. This is the spoken rather than unspoken lesson of life. Preschoolers need information appropriate to their age. That means: Dad answers what's asked, and not what's not asked. How do you know what's appropriate? We suggest that you listen carefully. Weigh the words you hear not from your position of knowing a lot about the subject but from your child's position of knowing nothing. Answer the question briefly in its simplest, most innocent meaning. Adults are quick to pick up sexual innuendo. To a small child there is no such thing as innuendo. The child may not even be asking what you think he or she is asking.

"Daddy, where did I come from?"

"Well, uh, that's a difficult question to answer quickly and it's going to be suppertime soon."

"Raul says he came from Mexico."

On the other hand, your child may well be asking the question.

"Where did Mrs. Majors get her new baby, Daddy?"

"She went to the hospital and had it."

"How?"

"Remember how big her tummy used to be? The baby started in there."

"That's silly."

"I think so, too. Let's go read about Peter Rabbit until supper's ready."

It is perfectly appropriate to take the quickest way out. Also, when it comes to verbal explanations, a small child's attention span can be measured in nanoseconds, so don't bother dwelling on anything.

We do recommend you avoid being cute. Small kids take answers very literally. Their sense of humor is not well developed (for that matter, analyze a ten-year-old's; it hasn't improved much).

"Daddy, where do babies come from?"

"Pittsburgh, usually," is not a good response.

Daddy is not just a font of learning, the Teacher About the World. Another of his primary roles is Protector.

—Protecting the Whole Little Person—

Harley Turner's daddy is a state highway patrol trooper. He rides a huge, noisy, very impressive motorcycle. He wears all the uniform and accoutrements of his office. Harley, age four, idolizes Daddy at home. That's when Daddy wears blue jeans and T-shirts and he's . . . well, he's Daddy. But when Harley's daddy puts on his uniform—the white, visored helmet; the boots and gloves; the belt with weapon, baton, flashlight, and cuff case—Harley's daddy isn't Daddy anymore. He's bigger than life, awesome, and more than a little scary.

Harley can watch Daddy put on his uniform, item by item; Harley can watch the visual transformation from blue jeans to class A's and know who's inside the visored helmet; but that makes no difference at age four. Harley believes only the externals which his eyes see, and his eyes do not see comfortable old Daddy anymore.

Like Harley, all preschoolers take life at face value. What you see is what you get. They cannot perceive things figuratively enough yet to understand that there might be a different person behind the visual image. Rephrased, they approach life in concrete terms and cannot deal with abstractions. Moreover, preschoolers draw a very fine line between the real and imaginary, or perhaps no line at all. All this works both for and against the dads who would protect their little Harleys.

Protect from the Imaginary

Nearly all kids go through the stage celebrated in *Calvin and Hobbes* cartoons, the monster under the bed or in the closet. That monster lurks there, man, and don't you question it.

When Harley envisioned huge insectoid things beneath his bed, his daddy (in blue jeans) borrowed the pump squirter Mommy used to wash the windows. Together, Dad and Son mixed up some Monster Killer Juice, put it in the bottle, and spritzed under the bed. End of problem. Harley's dad was able to fight fire (imagination) with fire (imagination). This sort of protection works only during a brief window of age: three- or four-years-old. The five-year-old will see through it, and the two-year-old isn't sophisticated enough yet to appreciate it.

There's the wagon scout again. He is the train's primary protector. He does his best to ensure that the travelers don't get into any situation they can't handle. So does Dad.

All children, though, fear things, and there are a few specific steps Dad can follow to ease those fears.

• Acknowledge the Validity of the Fear

Dad can provide that necessary permission to be afraid with a simple, "I understand you're scared. It's okay." Or, "It's no fun being afraid, is it? I used to be afraid like that when I was very small."

Is it nonsense? Quite possibly, to an adult. Not to a preschooler who still doesn't know truth from fiction, let alone what life is all about.

• Balance the Fear with Facts

What are the salient facts? "I am here. I won't abandon you to danger. You're not alone in this. I won't let it hurt you," whatever it is.

Notice that what Dad will be doing is investing himself in the child by using a lot of "You and I" talk. He's sympathizing with the child's feelings, validating them. Over and over, in dozens of different dimensions, we find that the key to fathering lies in one word, relationship.

Protect from Real Danger

Nobody but nobody comes between a she-bear and her cub. Or a sow and her piglets. That's woodlore from the beginning of time. It's scriptural. An up-in-arms mom defending her kids is not a lady to mess around with. Still, traditionally, Dad is seen as the primary protector. That's not sexist; he's probably bigger and stronger, and when it comes to defense, power wins the day.

Too, Dad becomes a child's best defender because he represents the world and therefore knows its dangers. In his classic role as leader, Dad should assume the lead in protecting his children from preventable harm.

- Childproof the home, paying attention to poisons and medicines a child can reach, dangerous stairwells, plumbing fixtures (including bathtubs), and the like.
- Install smoke detectors and conduct periodic fire drills. Even the smallest child should know what to do in an emergency. The drills will mean far more if Dad takes part.
- Teach the child what to do if approached by a stranger. Play-act and rehearse the options. The child doesn't learn by preaching, remember, but by doing. Action.
- Teach the child what is appropriate and inappropriate behavior on the part of others. Again, hands-on (judiciously, of course) activity is the key, Daddy to kid.
- Make absolutely certain the child is appropriately supervised every minute of the day. The level and nature of supervision, of course, will vary as the child matures.

Protect Innocence

"Small children can be robbed of their innocence through television and videos—that kind of thing." Dr. Minirth speaks of desensitization. "That's a long word for a very sad principle: When little children see those acts of violence, especially cartoonish violence and the very realistic stuff you get in some of these movies and TV—they lose sensitivity to it. They even take part in it, in a way. We call it vicarious experience. It's when your imagination participates but not your physical person."

To the desensitized child, hurting people isn't all that terrible. Kick the coyote and he'll get up unscathed and formulate another dastardly plot against the roadrunner.

We are talking about small children here, little people who have no definite boundaries yet between real and make--believe. As children get older, and more mature, and they come to understand clearly the difference between pretense and reality, desensitization becomes less and less an issue.

Children are also robbed of innocence through abuse, and not just the horror of sexual abuse you hear about. Explosive anger; emotional abuse; neglect; there are many. We recommend you peruse books on codependency issues, such as *Love Is a Choice* or *Kids Who Carry Our Pain*, simply to educate yourself on what abuse is and how it damages children. To protect a child you must know where the danger lies.

"There were two times in biblical history that were an all-out attack on kids; a slaughter of innocents—the birth of Moses when Egyptians killed the Hebrews' male babies, and the birth of Jesus when Herod did it," says Brian Newman. "In both cases, the motive involved a threat to rulers. There is an interesting opinion these days that Satan, the ruler of this age, feels threatened because this generation is ushering in the kingdom of God. He's killing kids' innocence, taking away their godly sensitivity. God cares acutely. The desensitized person does not."

Protecting and teaching are immensely awarding endeavors. Satisfying. Ideally, every dad would jump right in and get wrapped up in the job of shaping his kids. Unfortunately, it's not always that easy. He harbors a few natural inclinations that hinder his participation.

—What Hinders Dad in His Role—

"I hate to waste time." Brian Newman wags his head.

"I hate to waste time." Paul Warren grimaces. "I grew up under a very task-centered father. Redeem every moment. It's still with me."

"I hate to waste time." Frank Minirth begins his day in fourth gear and rarely drops to third before nightfall.

"I hate to waste time." That's probably you speaking.

"Most men are into task completion. Finish that job. Achieve that goal. It's built into us. Preschoolers definitely are not," says Dr. Warren about why fathers have trouble relating to their preschoolers. "Dad's so much into task completion, and that's okay in grade school. Grade schoolers are too. We dads teach, 'Here's how we do it, start to finish.' Our joy is in the accomplishment, not the process of doing it."

This yearning to redeem the moment and complete the task serves men splendidly as they reach for success. There's not a thing wrong with it. But the daddy who would bond with his preschooler, who would guide the child effectively, has to forget all that adult male task completion stuff. He must simply steel himself and prepare to waste time.

Play without a purpose. Do things without a reason. Play-act idle stories with no beginnings and no endings. To Daddy, it's mind-numbing. To the preschooler, it is the most important thing in the world Daddy can do—far, far more important than undertaking a task together and completing it. Obviously, then the time is not truly wasted. Not a bit.

"It doesn't come naturally," Brian Newman explains. "At first I had to deliberately think about wasting time. My temperament especially is such that just messing around at something goes against the grain. Before Rachel, I couldn't imagine playing to no end. I had to learn."

Learn he did.

"Daddy? Look at that on TV! What's it like to have a pie thrown in your face?" Rachel's question tickled Brian's fancy.

"Let's find out, Rachel."

The two of them bought disposable pie tins and whipping cream.

Brian pauses, a bit abashed. "Even here, I couldn't really let go. Instead of letting her squirt the whipped stuff into the pie pan, I had to do it, so it would be done right. I'm getting better now at holding myself back and letting her do it, though."

"Daddy?" she said in her I've-got-Daddy-twisted-around-my-finger voice, "Can I put a pie in your face first?"

"All right," Brian conceded with just a bit of trepidation. What laughter! What pure delight! Rachel's sheer joy repaid every bit of messy discomfort and whipped cream up the nose.

Gently Brian squashed a pie into her face.

Again that joyous laugh. "It kind of tickles!" She stood there with sticky fluff dribbling down her face, her shoulders, her hair, her clothes, her whole ecstatic little being.

Brian completes his narrative. "Okay, I was finished. End of experiment. I was ready to clean it up and do something else. Rachel, though, wanted to play in it, mess with it. She was still just as enthralled with the whole notion as ever. She didn't want the experience to end, and for her, at age four, there was no reason it ought to. It took every bit of effort I had to just let her go awhile. I had to consciously think about it and tell myself to cool it."

How do you, like Brian, waste time with a small child? First, you deliberately remind yourself over and over that no matter how this mindless activity seems to you, it is not wasted. The child is working on things, processing the world. And that child is letting you be the guide. It's necessary, and it's an honor.

Secondly, you deliberately put the clock on hold. Time is relative (nonexistent to the child), and the time you are spending now will be repaid manyfold as the child grows. You're not baby-sitting. You're building a relationship.

Relationships come first.

Dennis Rainey, whose ministry is to families, cites this incident. Charles Francis Adams, son of President John Quincy Adams and like his father and grandfather a United States diplomat to Great Britain, wrote this in his diary:

"Went fishing with my son today—a day wasted."

His son Brooks's entry for that same day:

"Went fishing with my father—the most wonderful day of my life."

How About You?

If possible, list some memories of doing things with your dad (they may be the same things you listed at the end of Chapter Two, or other activities, such as sporting events, hunting or fishing, family outings, goofing-off times that you recall fondly):

1. _____
2. _____
3. _____

Was Dad doing those activities out of a duty ("That's what fathers are supposed to do with their families") or because he really enjoyed it as well? Clues that might make you think he did or did not enjoy it may include:

His general attitude:

_____ Grumpy
_____ Eager
_____ Bored

The time we spent at it:

_____ Lingered
_____ Rushed

His comments and attitude after we returned:

_____ "We spend too much money on this stuff."
_____ "Now maybe I can sit and relax a little, all right?"
_____ "Let's plan another outing like this soon."
_____ "This [event] gave me an idea. Let's [do something similar] soon."
_____ "I enjoyed it."
_____ "I hope you [kids] [Mom] are satisfied now."

As I think about it, Dad's attitude toward special family events and outings [is] [is not] affecting the way I look at them.

Of the memories I have of my childhood, I would most like to repeat these times with my own child:

1. _____
2. _____
3. _____

If I had a four-hour chunk of time with nothing pressing, I would most like to:

_____ Read
_____ Sleep or goof off
_____ Work on the car
_____ Work at my hobby of _____
_____ Drive to _____
_____ Mess around in the kitchen
_____ Other _____

Now think of a way in which you could include your child (girl or boy) in that activity.

Within half an hour's drive of my home, there are these places to go, attractions or opportunities to explore that interest me (natural park areas, museums, amusement parks, tourist attractions, unusual stores, zoos, or refuges . . .):

1. _____
2. _____
3. _____

Were I to take a small child to these places, special things we could do there, especially physically active things, would be:

1. _____
2. _____
3. _____

—The Discipline Dilemma—

Children do not grow in tidy ways. They grow by testing the limits. Your limits. Before we get much farther into the development of your children, let's look at the problem so many fathers find vexing: how to administer effective discipline.

FIVE

Dad and Discipline

J ohn Brubaker was in love. He didn't say so. At age fourteen you don't ever admit something like that. But he was.

Her name was Shannon, and she had invited him and his best friend Maxy to her folks' house for Sunday dinner. John was sweating, and not because it was humid out. These people were fancy. Big house, thick rugs, cars that cost more than a fighter plane, a Doberman in the back yard that could take out a sumo wrestler. They served dinner one part at a time. And he didn't know which fork to use or how to hold it. Maxy, the bum, was sure no help. He and Shannon's sister, who was only a year younger than Shannon, were flipping peas at each other when no one was looking.

How John got through the evening, and whether his social reputation survived it, he had no idea. He did realize though, as they left Shannon's just after dark, that if they ran they could just barely catch the last bus home. If they missed that bus the evening would really be a total disaster. He and Maxy took off across town at full gallop.

They ran the length of the alley east of 154th, with dogs barking behind high fences all the way, and popped out onto the main drag half a block from the bus stop. . . . And just about collided with a police cruiser, its blue lights flashing.

"You boys wouldn't be up to no good, now, would you?" the officer sneered. He must've got that line from a grade B movie.

Monday evening John told the story to his grandfather,

and it was so weird he didn't have to embellish the truth at all. "So Maxy, the dimwit, says 'No sir, we always run through alleys. We like to hear the dogs bark.' That's when he hauled us in. The cops called up Dad and said, "We're holding your son.' And Dad, all cheery, says, "Well, you can have him,' and hung up."

Grampa Brubaker chuckled, nodding. "Yep. Yep. Bet your dad thought it was one of his buddies down at the air conditioning plant playing another joke on him."

"You got it. The cops had to call up Maxy's dad. Maxy's dad believed them right away."

John Brubaker wouldn't admit being in love, and he wouldn't admit being proud of his dad, either. But he was. And of himself. His dad had complete confidence in him. His dad never for a moment guessed the cops might really have picked him up.

And John felt a little sorry for Maxy.

Jack Brubaker's confidence in his son did not emerge overnight when the boy entered his teens. It was based on a foundation that Jack had established right in the very beginning, the preschool years. Jack didn't realize he had done so. Indeed, he didn't begin to appreciate how well he had succeeded in building a solid, working relationship with his kids. Now, though, he was enjoying the fruit of it. They were exasperating at times, his four kids, but they were good kids, really, with plenty of healthy self-confidence.

Let us analyze that relationship and the varied blocks that built it. The centerpiece, the building stone easiest to recognize, is good discipline. Fortunately, Jack Brubaker was not an eagle.

—Look Out! It's the Swooping Eagle!—

"In my practice I see swooping eagles so often," Paul Warren laments. "I'll bet you have too. Mommy handles the day-to-day discipline. She keeps the kids in line. In a lot of households it's her job to keep them quiet. When things get out of hand, or Daddy sees a problem, he comes swooping down like an eagle out of the sky. Fwooosh!" Dr. Warren zooms his flat hand down, from high to low.

"Dad sets it right with a few thunderous pronouncements, and he goes back up to his aerie. Then he'll sit there with his head in the clouds, all wrapped up in his own world, until something annoys him or looks wrong and it's time to swoop down again. Often he may not even handle the disciplinary measure himself. He mandates the discipline and expects Mom to carry it out."

Mom unwittingly abets the eagle when she avoids major disciplinary moves herself with a dire, "You just wait 'til Daddy gets home."

The swooping eagle is a colorful model, and very common, but there are a few little details wrong with it.

The Eagle Is One-Dimensional

One major problem is that the eaglet sees his or her dad in no role other than that of disciplinarian. You recall how Dad can guide his preschooler through the wilderness of feelings. The swooping eagle cannot. The child sees only Dad's anger and hears only Dad's angry voice. Dad is either noncommunicative or mad. The child, who always assumes that somehow he or she has generated all anger anyway, has no opportunity to know that anger does not last forever in a daddy, or that Daddy might have a more tender side.

The Eagle Is One-Directional

Another problem with the swooping eagle is that he is not really disciplining. He's merely controlling. He stops a particular behavior, or tries to. That's all. Real discipline is infinitely more than simply making a kid less annoying. Good discipline consists of correction plus redirection. Good discipline is aimed at the child's best interests, physically and emotionally.

Remember that a small child blots up the world by touching, hearing, and feeling. This is how the child learns, and good discipline is nothing more than learning. The wise dad will encourage bonding through these three means even as he changes the child's direction.

He verbally conveys the message—"You can't do that, but you can do this." Then he picks the little one up and physically changes the child's direction. It's all very symbolic, this physical change of direction, and the child, being symbolic-minded, picks up on it right away. Even when the child goes right back to the forbidden activity, testing the limit, the symbolic lesson has found its mark.

A loud voice and a pat on the bottom does none of that.

The Eagle Is Inconsistent

Consistency. The parent makes a request or issues an instruction. The child understands the order and chooses deliberately to either obey or disobey. The parent then responds accordingly. Action precipitates reaction. Cause and effect. Truth or consequences. Obedience thrives through consistency.

Eagles foster inconsistency. If Dad's in the habit of swooping, he usually lets the kids get away with more between swoops, simply because he doesn't want to bother taking the time and trouble for the small stuff. Besides, it's Mom's job to keep the lid on, isn't it? When the eagle finally does bestir himself, he'll come down harder. He's likely to overreact because his patience has just been tried. Like a rubber band, he's been stretched out, and now he's snapping back. He's harsher and more inflexible. He'll provide less leeway in situations that may demand some flexibility.

Kids aren't dumb. The child thinks, and not unfairly, "If I just don't tip Dad too far—if I don't get caught by Dad—it doesn't matter what I do." That sort of attitude does not build conscience.

As we will see as we look at older children, conscience grows when the child takes the rules imposed from the outside—which is what Dad is doing with his preschooler—and internalizes them. The tiny child thinks, "I ought not do this because Mommy and Daddy say 'no.'" The reason for behavior lies outside the child. The older child thinks, "I ought not do this because it's wrong." The reason for behavior lies inside. That's conscience.

That extremely important shift, that internalization, will determine the child's deepest character. It will help keep your child out of trouble and danger (one of a guide's biggest responsibilities) if the sense of right and wrong are firmly planted deep within. How many people that you know have never worked past the elemental stage, *if I don't get caught, it doesn't matter what I do?* Is that what you want for your children?

Consistency also requires self-discipline on both parents' part. If it's not worth it to the parents to go to the line on something, they cannot expect the child to. A rule enforced at this time because it's convenient, and not enforced the next time because Mom or Dad are too busy or tired to handle it, is not consistency. Therefore Dad in his role as family leader will step forward and set a reasonable limit, and he will be consistent and constant in seeing that those limits are met, even if he's busy or tired.

The Eagle Is Wrong

Probably. Too often, at least. Because the eagle never really gets to know his kids intimately, he's not likely to come through with an appropriate discipline. Children's personalities differ as widely as do adults'. What is appropriate for one child may not be at all what's best for another. Because good discipline serves the child's best interests, it must be tailored to that child. What tailor can fit a suit of clothes if he does not know his client's measurements?

The Eagle Is Probably Angry

The swooping eagle is particularly subject to discipline from anger. Because his only connection to his child is discipline and not relationship, he sees only the externals. He doesn't know what's going on inside and therefore doesn't react to it. The outside, then, either pleases him or angers him. When it angers him, *swoop*.

Because of their focus on task completion, fathers are easily frustrated by kids, especially small ones, because the kids' focus is on the doing, not the completion. *Swoop*. Besides, dads tend to be more aggressive than moms in a lot of situations. They're easier to irritate and anger than Mom is, especially when they're not really involved with kids.

Ultimately, the Eagle Is Ineffective

The eagle has forgotten, or has never realized, that there cannot be discipline until there first is a relationship.

As Brian Newman points out, "God gave the Ten Commandments to the Israelites only after He attended to their needs and spent time with them. That was no stranger uttering pronouncements to strangers."

A baby squirming on its tummy in a playpen does not need a lot of correction. About age two, as the toddler becomes ambulatory and starts getting into stuff and going places, discipline begins in earnest. This, too, is the time when it is so important for Daddy to develop a relationship with his little one. Therefore, right here is where you can nip that tendency to be a swooping eagle in the bud.

When a child is very small, Daddy derives his authority simply from being big. The wise weakling does not intentionally rile Arnold Schwarzenegger. As the child grows both physically and in understanding, however, Dad can no longer rely on mere size. Increasingly, his authority comes from his relationship as a father, not just because he happens to be the father.

Someday, the kid will come home with a pony, or a hairstyle created by aliens, as Jack Brubaker's fourteen-year-old did one day, or a weird girlfriend in biker leather with a ring through her nose. At that dreaded time, behavior, things, gadgets, music, and hairstyle will not be the issue. Relationship will be the issue. Always.

—Anger's Ugly Fallout—

Miles and his dad, Arnold, sat in Paul Warren's office scowling at each other. The arms of both were folded tightly across their chests. If glares were thermal, they both would have fried like potato chips.

"The kid's got no reason to be acting like this." Arnold appeared wound as tight as a garage door spring.

"Miles's mother explained in part; something about a peacock," Dr. Warren began, "but I'd like to hear it first-hand." He looked directly at Miles.

Arnold answered. "What's to hear? The kid and his weird pals pounded one of the Herrons's peacocks to death. Now the Herrons are talking about suing. We'll fight it, of course, but I can see their point. A gang of little thugs beat one of their stupid birds to death for absolutely no reason."

Miles sat silent, sullen.

Arnold, still so irate his voice cracked, described a Sunday afternoon gathering at the home of friends. The friends kept several peafowl in a spacious garden on their property. As the adults lounged inside, four teen and preteen boys went exploring. They found the peacock, harassed it, and eventually bludgeoned it. They kept some of the feathers and tried to hide the remains in a stack of wood. The family dog dug it out.

Arnold listed the punitive measures he'd initiated, a polite way of saying that in his fury he really pounded on Miles. He grounded the kid. He cut off the phone. He suspended television and Nintendo®. He put a dozen restrictive rules in place about where Miles could eat, what rooms he could be found in, and when he could join the family (hardly ever).

Arnold was clearly reacting instantly and violently out of anger. And yet, he was quite correct that this was no matter of stealing penny candy. This was a serious infraction, a brutal, needless, and unjust death.

Arnold excused himself from the office shortly thereafter,

taking a palpable cloud of bitter fury. Miles and Paul Warren sat awhile in silence. Now what?

"I'd like it if you'd tell me what happened," Dr. Warren suggested.

"You already heard it."

"One side, filtered through anger."

"There isn't any other side. We did it." Miles shrugged heavily. All his gestures were exaggerated, it seemed.

"Your father doesn't know all the details. The motives. He can't; he wasn't there. What would you like to fill in what he didn't mention? What went on inside you? That's the important part."

That heavy, heavy shrug again, but this time it was accompanied by a sigh. "We were bored and sort of clowning around. There's nothing to do at the Herrons'. Their place is all show. I hate it when we have to go there." He brightened a bit. "Guess we won't anymore, huh?"

The brightness faded. "I know what we did was wrong. Real wrong. The dumb peacock didn't attack us or anything. We just started messing around, throwing things at it, and it got out of hand, you know? One thing after another. And then it was hurt and couldn't fly or hop right, and we got scared and finished it."

"Why did you start messing around?"

"I don't know." And Miles really didn't.

"Angry at the bird?"

"No. But Dad's sure angry at me." And fear as well as defiance haunted Miles's eyes.

The father's fury engendered fear in his son, not just after the fact but before, when that peacock was still alive. "We got scared." And Arnold indeed reacted out of anger. Just what, specifically, did Arnold's fury do in this case?

The Negative Impact of Dad's Anger

An indirect impact is that anger in men influences how they treat their wives. Unfortunately for the kids, these childhood years are when they are learning sexuality, husbanding, nurturing. And they're blotting it up from dad. Animal husbandry is the considered nurturing and care of animals. Wife husbandry can be no less. "Of course," says Brian Newman with a twinkle in his eye, "in this Texas cowboy culture, it's macho to nurture a cow but not your wife."

The direct impacts are even more devastating.

A patient told Brian Newman of a memorable quote from a *Leave it to Beaver* episode. According to the lady, Ward blew up and chewed the boys out. The boys opined, "We wish you had spanked us. The hurt from the spanking is temporary. Hurt from words lasts a lifetime."

And it's true.

Angry words can damage kids more so than physical disciplining measures. Kids, particularly small kids, take in harsh words unedited. "You're a jerk!" means "You're a jerk!" and it's emblazoned on their hearts. The fact that Dad is coming off a bad day at work, and his new shoes pinch, and he is upset at Mom for some unrelated reason, makes no difference. The anger and the words speak, unmodified.

Not only are his words and the fears they engender having a negative impact, so is the way he is modeling low self-esteem.

"Here we are back at that issue of adequacy," says Brian Newman. "Men don't always feel good about themselves, and when they don't, their kids get burned. A man who's got his own problems is likely to be short-tempered. He'll probably degrade and shame the people around him, people he loves, without realizing or thinking about what he's doing."

Because a father's anger is so destructive in his child's life, it is imperative that he learn its true source (which is rarely the child's behavior) and learn to control it. "Dad's gotta get a handle on it." There are ways to do that.

—Controlling Anger in Discipline—

Arnold might be having trouble with Miles now, but he had two more kids coming up through the ranks, aged eight and ten. Obviously they were already too old for Arnold to begin a Daddy-preschooler relationship, even if he were prepared to do so. What are Arnold's options?

Steps to Consider When Anger Is Not Actually Upon You

One of the reasons Miles got into such deep water was his fear of his father's explosive anger. Arnold agreed he tended to lose his temper on those occasions when the kids messed up even though they knew better—or sometimes, even if they didn't know any better and messed up, child-style. Arnold could take these steps to avoid disciplining in anger:

1. Commit himself to finding where this anger really comes from. The reason for the anger is probably not the kid," Paul Warren claims. "Dad can separate out the anger source by sitting himself down and exploring what triggers his reactions. What is his history of anger? What was his father's? His grandfather's, for that matter? Is anger the family tradition?

"Professional counseling would be very helpful for finding unresolved problems down below his conscious level, and we normally recommend it."

2. Practice accountability to another person. Arnold's wife, a support group, a trusted male friend, a counselor or pastor can act as a warden, a watchdog, a concerned other person to whom Arnold would voluntarily be accountable. Arnold would keep in regular touch with that person (a phone call several times weekly, perhaps), reporting success, failure, feelings, and situations. And being honest in the reports.

Can God be the other person? Certainly. Remember,

however, that Arnold's primary contact with God would be through prayer and Bible reading, and anger normally puts the brakes on both. The other person can phone Arnold if he fails to check in. When God calls, Arnold can block Him out. Ideally, Arnold will render himself accountable both to God and to a human being.

Arnold would also be accountable to his children, the other people who take the brunt of his anger. He is called by God to raise them in nurture and admonition, and that means to raise them to follow God's rules. His godly purpose for his children is not to make Daddy look good. Face it, when Arnold blew up at Miles, it wasn't because he was fond of peacocks; it was because Miles had made him look bad. Miles had committed a severe sin, killing. Unfortunately, killing was not the bad deed that bothered Arnold; tooting off the Herrons was.

3. Arnold would have to ask for forgiveness for his present rage and for past rages. This third step is probably harder than steps 1 or 2.

"Men are all going to blow it when it comes to anger with kids," Paul Warren insists. "We will at times inappropriately express our anger. Even when it's appropriate we'll over-react. We must be willing to face that mistake, hopefully to repent of it to God, and ask forgiveness from those concerned; horizontally to the children and vertically to God Himself."

Forgiveness is not without price. Arnold must first repent. That means challenging himself to get control of his anger and accept accountability. Only then is he prepared to go to his child and ask forgiveness.

Forgiveness pays huge benefits, however. Forgiveness sets up a positive example in the child's life. Particularly, when Daddy asks God's forgiveness the child comes to understand the vertical component. Daddy has just taught a valuable lesson in a way—by sincere example—that will stick with his child.

Forgiveness for the older child carries a powerful second message. Daddy does not claim to be perfect. Never mind that until age twelve or so the child considers Daddy to be without error (Mommy, too). Daddy is not painting himself thus. It's an important difference.

Arnold found it particularly difficult to ask anyone's forgiveness, especially Miles's. He phrased it well in an interview with Dr. Warren. "Miles is my kid. I'm supposed to be in control. If I say 'Hey, I messed up. I need you to forgive me,' Miles is going to lose confidence in me. I'll lose respect. I can't do it."

"Does Miles respect you now?" Dr. Warren asked.

"He has to. I'm his father."

"Does he?"

"He's afraid of me."

"Is that respect?"

"He knows that when I say something, it's the law."

"But is that respect?"

No, it's not, though Arnold never did make the distinction.

Forgiveness. It is a bitter pill to swallow. Curiously enough, we find that when Dad admits occasional human frailty and failure, his kids' respect goes up dramatically, not down. Heroes are allowed to fail, so long as they display the honesty of admitting their failure. Asking forgiveness does that. If Arnold can bring himself to this important step, he will see in his son a new respect that was not there before.

It will probably surprise him.

These three steps work fine in the cool of the moment. They are points to be considered at leisure. However, nobody seized by rage is going to think of these things in the heat of the moment. There are, fortunately, immediate things Arnold can do when fury strikes.

Emergency Steps at the Moment of Anger

Your kid, that stupid kid who's suddenly taking after his mother's side, has really blown it. Let's say he took part in the peacock debacle. Or your five-year-old got caught stealing nickels from the church collection plate—by the church's biggest gossip. You feel your anger rising. You're livid. That crazy kid! A moment ago you were bent on discipline. Now you're thinking about murder. Flaying. Something.

Even as you sense that you're getting out of control, you pause, and do the following.

1. Get Mom or another care-giver involved, now! Step back. Give the kid to another person for a short time. Go into another room, or outside. Cool down. Before you can discipline anyone, you must have your own discipline firmly under your thumb. That means controlling your anger first, regardless of its ultimate source.

Sure, you're going to examine the real reasons for your anger under the magnifying glass of introspection, but that's later. This is now.

2. Focus on the discipline aspect. You never, never, never discipline a child in anger. If you're going to handle this situation wisely (and wisdom is expected of a father), you're going to have to take an objective view of what the discipline ought to be. Not what feels good to you. Determine what the discipline would be if it were someone else's kid and that someone else were asking your advice, and you had no emotional investment in the situation.

What's going to build your child's character? What's going to teach him to do right? Here we go again into profit and loss. Your child is supposed to profit from this discipline. How can you maximize that profit?

When the peacock incident came to light, just before the party at the Herrons' broke up that day, Arnold apologized profusely to the hosts and promised no end of mayhem to his little perpetrator. So far, so good. He told Miles to apologize, and Miles did. Still good.

From that point, Arnold might have acted somewhat along these lines:

- Turn the driving over to his wife because he was too boiled to drive safely. Safety is always a consideration where anger is involved, safety for kids and parents both. Were they home, the kid's safety would still be a factor if Arnold felt like beating the tar out of Miles. Safety for infants is a special concern. They are so easily hurt, and permanently, by hitting or shaking.

- Keep silence in the car. "If you can't say something nice, don't say anything at all." Anything either Miles or Arnold said, with the temper of the moment so heated, would ignite the situation (in fact, it did. Arnold ranted nonstop for twenty-two miles). Don't invite an explosion.

- Declare a regrouping period. Arnold might banish Miles to his room for twenty-four hours, except for meals and school attendance. Whatever Arnold did at this juncture, its purpose would be to put some distance between himself and the situation, between himself and the perpetrator. You can't think about what you're going to do in the bullring when the bull is staring at you with its beady, bloodshot eyes. You plan your moves first and then face the bull. Arnold was going to have to vanquish a very dangerous bull—a serious situation intensified by his own emotions—and he needed time to decide on a plan of action.

- Examine what avenues of discipline he would pursue were this someone else's son. What would his father have done if he were the errant kid? Would it have been appropriate? Arnold would take the time, having given himself the time, to study the discipline aspect itself. Maybe twenty-four hours wouldn't be long enough. Maybe forty-eight is more realistic. No matter. Miles would know the axe was going to fall, and he would know approximately when. That in itself would be a potent punishment.

3. Examine the source of sadness. Not the source of the anger. The sadness. Arnold was really ripped up that this happened. Was he sad because now the Herrons thought his whole family were dangerous creeps? Was he sad that a good peacock was no more? Or was he sad because Miles had just done a very bad thing? Good discipline involves grief in the father's heart that his child has done wrong. Genuine sadness, for the child's sake.

Another possible source of sadness might be remorse for overdoing the discipline, for overreacting. That's not the sadness we mean here. We mean here that Arnold should be experiencing and identifying sadness about his child's behavior, not his.

4. Ensure that the aim of this discipline is teaching, not payback. Always. Miles delivered a painful blow to Arnold's reputation and cast doubt on his effectiveness as a father. The urge to lash back was strong. Every father feels that way when his own kid casts him in a bad light, even if no one but he himself knows about it.

Every father, therefore, must take some time to think about it: How much of my feelings just now are retribution? Am I correcting or retaliating?

5. Make sure the discipline is appropriate. There are two kinds of appropriateness at work here, discipline to fit the age of the child and discipline to suit the nature of the infraction.

Discipline tailored to the infraction should be designed on a case-by-case basis. The best discipline will include a memorable lesson, a deterrent, and some form of restitution. One of the primary facets of Miles's discipline ought to have been his part in replacing the Herrons' peacock.

6. When you discipline any child, communicate love also. "This hurts me worse than it hurts you" will fall on deaf ears, even though it is quite true. Verbally telling them, physically telling them with a hug or a snuggle, all help them understand the difference between the transgression and the transgressor. You are correcting the transgression. It's just as important to a seventeen-year-old as to a four-year-old to know that the child is not being rejected. It is only the behavior that is not tolerated.

Can kids pick up the distinction? Yes. They also know when you're mad at them, not their deeds.

Exactly What Is Appropriate?

Arnold was more than ready to cuff his errant son alongside the head. Or spank him within an inch of his life. Or shake him until his teeth rattled. Arnold was mad at the deed, and he was mad at the kid as well. What was Arnold to do? And not do?

"We're not against spanking, as such," claim all three men. Paul Warren articulates their position. "We feel it's effective only within an age range of from two to, at most, nine, and then it is only one trick in an extensive bag of tricks. In fact," he adds, "it's not even the first trick out of the bag. It has its place, we feel, but that place is very limited."

Brian Newman says, "We see so many Christian parents who consider spanking to be the only God-ordained, biblical form of discipline. We need to deglorify spanking. Incidentally, the Bible does not say, 'Spare the rod and spoil the child.' That's folklore.

"The concept of spanking as God's approved means of discipline comes from Proverbs 13:24, 'He who spares his rod hates his son, / But he who loves him disciplines him promptly.' Hebrews 12:3–11 expands on that, pointing out that when we are chastised that proves we're God's own children. "Whom the LORD loves He chastens.'

"What purpose did the rod serve a thousand years before Christ, when Proverbs was put into written form? It was a shepherd's tool used for far more than just discipline. The

AGE APPROPRIATE DISCIPLINE	
INFANT Everything relates to self. Easily injured. No concept of rules.	A simple "no" with voice sharp but not raised. NEVER shaking. NEVER striking or spanking.
TODDLER Everything relates to self. Conscience and rules all external.	Clear, one-word commands; nothing complex. Physically redirect child to a permissible activity. Time out.
PRESCHOOLER Beginning to internalize conscience. Big on fair play and justice.	Simple explanations for the why's of rules and no-no's as well as actual discipline. Physical punishment controlled, restrained. Always convey love along with correction. Time out.
GRADE SCHOOLER Competitive, into winning. Conscience internalizing.	Limited physical punishment. Simple grounding (no play at neighbors'). Restriction of privileges. Restrictions, groundings brief—few days at most. Restitution included in correction.
JUNIOR AND SENIOR HIGH SCHOOLER Starting to reason as an adult. Conscience level that of adult. Abstract in thinking.	No more physical correction (spanking inappropriate). More elaborate grounding and restrictions. Restrictions can extend over longer period of time; weeks. Restitution a major part of correction.

shepherd used it to guide his sheep and protect them; get them out of jams and keep them on the straight and narrow. 'Thy rod and thy staff, they comfort me.' Comfort. Guide and protect. There's Dad's primary role, right there.

"So when you understand what the biblical rod is in its full context, and what it does, you come to understand that it's not just a swat. 'The rod' is everything you do to shape your child."

He pauses, and adds, "I've had dads tell me that they insist on spanking until the child is crying. That is, until you can see the repentance. If the child isn't repentant, you didn't spank long enough." He shakes his head. "Hey, if it's not working, don't keep doing it. Clearly, if your child is still defiant, it's not working."

Suggests Paul Warren, "Spanking—a few firm swats—is one of your options for handling defiant behavior. Never for handling human error. Children are even more prone to mistakes in some ways than adults are. They have very few lessons of experience yet, and their powers of judgment are rudimentary. A spanking is never the response to a childish error. And absolutely never for an infraction the child didn't know about until he or she committed it.

"And of course, you're going to be certain you're fully under control yourself before administering any sort of physical measures."

As Frank Minirth phrases it, "You want to follow up right away, as soon after the infraction as you can. But it's even more important that the parent be under control first.

"And accountability between the two parents—that's so important; that's first. Accountability means that they're handling discipline with the same mind-set in the same way. Dad's not letting junior off for something Mom is disciplining him for. So often parents don't talk about discipline. It's not that they're disagreeing, it's that they're not sitting down and discussing it, specific situations, what they'll do."

We suggest that the father initiate a sit-down discussion with Mom, without little ears listening, of course. Brainstorm the situations you'll most likely encounter—mild disobedience, dangerous disobedience, forgetfulness, impertinence or rudeness, accidents, errors of judgment, a moral misstep, lying, neglecting homework—the list goes on. You know your kids best. What's likely?

Treat each prospect you think of with these questions:

- How shall we handle this situation? Think of four or five possible responses. Have a quiver full of choices ready in advance.
- Keep in mind the behavior and level of obedience you should expect of a child at this age.

For example, consider the fault of lying. A child telling a lie at age two is correctable but not punishable. The child still does not discern between fact and fancy and will tell whatever he or she thinks you ought to hear.

A child telling a lie at age six should know better. But remember that this is still a very small person in a very big, hostile world. To that child, a lie may well seem the best refuge and protection from harm. Safety and expedience will win out over truth, justice, and the American way every time.

By nine, the child should have an internalized conscience well enough developed to know that lying is wrong. Ideally, the child of nine or older also knows the consequences of lying.

By twelve, the child is essentially an adult, in conscience, in understanding, in the ability to sort fact from fantasy. The response of parents to a lying twelve-year-old would therefore be harsher than to a small child. But the twelve-year-old is also still naive enough, and tender enough, that mercy should be dispensed generously. Into early adulthood, children still lack the practice that strengthens them to consistently make good choices. The mind is willing but . . . .

Discipline, then, is executing a plan of action, not simply reacting to the sudden shocking revelation that your kid's not perfect. Husband and wife together should have already developed their flexible plan of action for when the revelation arrives.

Devising the Restitution

"Somehow, somewhere," Paul Warren philosophizes, "we got away from restitution in this country. There is great power in restitution for shaping a child in positive ways.

"We encourage parents to require their child to offer restitution as a learning experience. Negative consequences usually extinguish negative behaviors, but they don't teach anything new. They don't teach positive behaviors. Restitution is a positive response to a situation that teaches positive behavior."

Ideally Arnold would require Miles to either replace the lost peacock or pay for it, and to earn the money for the act of restitution himself. By so doing, Arnold would neither be bailing Miles out nor leaving him hanging. Arnold would stand by his child even as his child stood by himself.

But what if it's not something the child can repay or replace? Restitution still can work. As an example, we can cite the wise actions of a father we all know, Dave. Dave's daughter Camille, a high school freshman, tried to cheat on a test at school and was caught at it. For starters, her parents grounded her for three weeks.

Dave was smart enough to say, "The first thing we need is to help you understand how you got into the situation where you felt you had to cheat. Punishing you without helping you understand why you did what you did isn't going to help you." That meant talking it out with Camille. A lot of talking. Introspection. Kids like to talk about themselves and their motives. It wasn't too hard for Dave to open his daughter up.

Dave also insisted that Camille had to deal with her school. A part of restitution is dealing with the injured party. Discussing the situation together, Camille's mom and dad together decided on what would be an appropriate and acceptable restitution. Camille was given a choice during her grounding. She could, if she wished, go talk to her teacher and work out some sort of arrangement with her. Retaking the test, doing extra assignments, writing extra papers or reports might be some options. If Camille did so and completed the arrangement to the teacher's satisfaction, the teacher could call the father, and he would reduce the time of grounding by one week. But the fourteen-year-old had to take the initiative.

Dave and Mom never brought it up again. They didn't nag Camille to go talk to her teacher. She had to do it on her own or not. And she was given to understand that restitution might reduce punishment but it could not replace it.

"As a rule of thumb," Paul Warren suggests, "the restitution should never reduce the original sentence by more than half. The best Camille could get, for instance, would be ten days off or so. You still need some measure of consequence. The child has to experience firsthand the consequences of his or her actions, or the discipline lesson is largely lost."

Dave's approach served another extremely important function. It taught Camille that she had some power in the situation. Remember that as children get older, and begin individuation in earnest, they need a feeling of control, of some ability to direct their own lives. Camille's discipline was not just something her parents inflicted upon her. She could act to alter her situation favorably. That small opportunity for the power to control what happened would teach Camille a great deal about personal responsibility. That sort of thing is not always possible. Often, though, it is.

"Remember that restitution doesn't always produce perfect results," Paul Warren concludes. "Arnold and Miles still had to deal with a dead peacock. Miles learned you simply cannot undo some things. Irreversible consequences. That in itself is an important cautionary lesson. Basically, I'd say, effective restitution is only effective from age eight or nine or above. Although in mild ways, simple ways, it can sometimes work with younger kids."

Miles was not a younger kid. And Arnold, poor beleaguered Arnold, was having no luck at all with his swooping
eagle tactics. And the worst of his feelings as he sat in Paul
Warren's office was the gnawing fear that it was too late to
change anything. The eagle was at sea.

—Starting in the Middle—

Arnold could not start at the beginning of Miles's life.
Miles was big now. Arnold's other kids also were past infancy. He could no longer shape them or shape his image.
What hope had he for change at this late date? Arnold could
work on two aspects, both interconnected.

1. Start Building a Relationship

The sooner the better, but, literally, it is never too late.
This would mean spending time with the kids. Spend time
with the family as a group, spend time with the kids individually.

"I don't have that kind of time," Arnold grumbled.

No father does.

As you read through this book, continually apply what
you're reading to your own circumstance, or to the circumstance you hope to be in someday if you are a new father.
Think specifically about ways you can carve out bits of time
with your child, as we discussed in the preceding chapter.
If Arnold learned nothing else from the peacock incident,
he learned, we hope: The relationship is all-important.

2. Shoot the Swooping Eagle

Okay, okay. It's an endangered species. So is bubonic
plague. Let's endanger it further. You now know what the
swooping eagle does and fails to do. When the eagle croaks
at any stage of a child's life, right through adulthood, prog-
ress occurs. Again, it's never too late, although the quicker
you improve matters, the better.

We went down through Arnold's disciplining repertoire
item by item, talking about his methods from the swooping

eagle viewpoint. He himself was able to suggest ways the eagle, when applied to himself, proved insufficient.

So we suggest you, too, look at your methods. Think about the last time you disciplined a child. It could be for a simple infraction or a serious one. Check the statements below that apply to that situation.

_____ It was a situation you had known about and let coast awhile, hoping Mom would take care of it, or it would just go away. Eagles do that.

_____ You really got annoyed at the behavior, or at the child. This item takes some thinking about. Be honest.

_____ If you had done that to someone else's child, the other parent or a bystander would have complained it was too punitive . . . complained it was too lenient.

_____ The disciplinary measure fit comfortably in the Appropriateness Chart.

_____ Your actions provided a character-building lesson for the child. They helped internalize the rule and improve the child's conscience.

_____ Your dad/stepdad was a swooping eagle.

—School Daze—

As discipline changes with the child's age, so does everything else. Here comes school, and there will be teachers disciplining your kid now too. Ideally, the child has you for backup, but he or she is stepping out into the real world alone for the first time.

When your child climbs aboard the school bus for that very first day of school, your wife may possibly shed a tear. Her baby is grown up now. So if you are tactful, you'll hide that big silly grin on your face. Your kid is growing up! Everyday, he or she is more fun to talk to, to be with, to do things with.

And it will be even more fun as your little one takes the giant step forward into the big, wide world.

But, be honest: It's sad, too. This wagon guide stuff was rewarding as you led the little one into life. You'll hate to see it end. You may think your wagon scout days are about over.

They're just beginning.

SIX

Dad's Kid Goes to School

Carl Jefferson sold mud.

"It's a dirty job, but somebody's gotta do it," he loved to say, of course.

Jefferson Mud was his one-man company's name. Carl's mud was expensive, as dirt goes. It was the specially formulated flux that petroleum drillers pump down oil wells. Carl traveled widely, prowled well sites, hobnobbed with roughnecks, and bandied about such arcane terms as fishtails, kellies, cuttings, and monkey boards. He was occasionally called as a consultant to oil fields in Australia, South America, and Asia. For a guy who grew up making mud pies, his was a wonderful life.

His wife, Ivy, sold weeds.

Weeds and Ivy, she called her sole proprietorship. She provided dried plant materials such as teasel and pearly everlasting to florists and others who used them in arrangements, decorations, and parade floats. She maintained a stock of over two hundred varieties, nearly a hundred of which she raised herself. For a kid who picked dandelion bouquets for Mom, hers was a wonderful life.

Their girls, Cathy, four, and Janey, eight, were just precious. Everybody said so, and Carl was proud as a peacock. A local college student baby-sat part-time, permitting Ivy and Carl a lot of freedom and flexibility. Carl and Ivy Jefferson had it made.

Well, not exactly. They used to have it made, until Ivy was stricken by peritonitis. She spent over nine weeks in the hospital, at a time when Carl's business particularly demanded his attention. The college student could help, but not nearly enough. Carl had to quit traveling. He had to give up a lot of his field work, and with it went a lot of his income.

Carl chafed. His was not the only mud in the world, and with the petroleum industry in a major slump, he had to hustle if he were to stave off the competition and make a buck. But here he sat around the house, coloring pictures with the preschool Cathy and waiting for Janey to walk in the door from second grade. And Ivy so sick . . . Life had turned gray.

Here Janey came up the sidewalk. She slammed the front door. Carl had pulled her fine, dark hair up into a neat ponytail this morning. Now the ponytail hung in disarray, with flyaway wispies sticking out all over. Her clothes were a disaster too—a big smudge on her shirt, grass stains, and a rip in the knees of her jeans. Another successful day at school, obviously.

"Is Mommy home yet?"

"Not yet, Sugar. Next week maybe." Carl gave her a hug and thought about all the mud he could be selling now.

She clung, so he clung. "Promise you won't get mad at me, Daddy?"

"What kind of question is that? Okay. I promise."

"Don't get mad at me for saying this, okay? I'm sorry Mommy's sick. I don't mean I like Mommy being sick. But I'm glad you're home. It's so great! This is the best time I ever had in my life."

—The New Child of the World—

Janey Jefferson wasn't overstating anything. Certainly she loved her daddy, but it was more than that. By having her daddy home, she literally had her wagon guide waiting in the house for her as she returned from the outside world. His role as scout was not diminishing in the least.

A few years ago, he had colored with Janey as he was coloring with Cathy now. They drew pictures and crayoned in coloring books, talking about the flowers and animals and scenes, discussing dreams, and telling stories. Through that seemingly inane process, Carl was actually introducing Janey to the world beyond the front door. When she went off to kindergarten she entered that world. For several hours a day she was not with Mommy; she was not with Daddy; she was not with Melody, the baby-sitter.

She came under the discipline and guidance of a total stranger who became another god in her life, Mrs. Bromley, her teacher. Then Mr. Matthews in first grade. And now Mrs. Stitt in second. People not related to the family. People carrying just as much authority as her parents. When you think about it, these were giant steps for Janey.

The preschooler is curious about the outside world; the grade schooler is beginning to actually experience it. In between lies an important transition stage: The kindergartner learns and prepares to do things away from home.

My, How the Child Has Grown!

How specifically does a grade schooler differ from the preschooler? Were Carl to compare his Cathy with his Janey, he'd see these differences:

Preschooler	Grade Schooler
Activity is random; movement and play may seem without purpose to adults.	Purposeful activity; play a game, do something, build, explore.
Play symbolic; play items can be symbols (a stick for a person, Playskool people; a block may represent an iron).	Play becomes increasingly realistic; play items must look like what they represent (Tonka Toys, mini animals, Lego and Lincoln Logs, Barbie dolls).
Playmates optional. Child plays in company of other children but often independently.	Playmates very important; "best friends." Group games and activities flourish.

Preschooler, *cont*.	Grade Schooler, *cont*.
Play is fairly selfish; not much cooperation or competition.	Play, even when cooperative, is highly competitive. Child constantly compares self to others.
Child needs Mommy and Daddy's approval.	Child needs approval of peers, of parents, of other adults. Achievement and recognition immensely important.

Carl would probably respond to these differences instinctively, as do you. It pays, though, to understand the way a child is changing, the better to communicate and guide.

As his little one becomes a child of the world, Daddy's role shifts considerably. Mommy has a special place. But even when he's filling Mommy's role, as Carl did temporarily, Daddy has a special place that is not Mommy's. He will, as before, model maleness. He will, as before, serve as protector and skills-enabler. He will, as before, encourage and affirm. But he'll do all this in new dimensions.

—The Great Protector—

At this age, protecting and skills-enabling go hand in hand. Even as Dad the protector encourages his little one to make friends and play sports and games, he will supervise. His supervision may be obvious and direct, as when he becomes a Scout leader, a coach, a Sunday school teacher. It may be surreptitious and indirect, as when he simply looks up from his work now and then to make sure the kids aren't drawing blood.

For hours of each day, Mom and Dad have no supervision over their children. The school assumes part of that responsibility. And frankly, Dad the protector will keep an eye on the school. When something blows up between his kid and the teacher, he will monitor. He will make himself the child's backup support, but not the child's alibi.

The swooping eagle tends to respond badly in those situations of discord between child and school. For example, when Miles was in the fourth grade, he and two buddies were found out in a certain matter concerning a stink bomb. In his school, a stink bomb automatically bought you a three-day suspension, no ifs, ands, or buts, and a five-percent grade reduction.

Arnold swooped down on the school, going from teacher through principal to superintendent to get his kid off the hook. He pulled every string he could grab. When he got home, he swooped on Miles as well, with a spanking, a grounding, and a loss of privileges.

Arnold, typical of swooping eagles, did not let cause and effect play out. As a result, his son Miles lost the opportunity to learn a valuable lesson in personal responsibility. Arnold had only to hold Miles accountable, and the lesson would have been made effectively.

The swooping eagle, because he is not well-connected with his children, tends to stick bandages on problems; it's all he knows to do. Too, appearance means much. The eagle is very concerned about whether the child is making him look good. He is desperate to fix it before someone notices it was broken, be "it" his reputation as a father or the light in which his child has cast the family. The eagle does not know his child well enough to be concerned about whether the child is internalizing the necessary lessons of life.

Thus, the eagle works hard to avert the school's penalty, lest his child's infraction be made glaringly public and he himself be cast in a dubious light. Then, because he is humiliated and angry, the eagle will probably turn around and overdo the punishment. Not only does the child lose out on the lesson of natural cause and effect, he or she is subjected to a more severe discipline than the case warrants. That's not good protection, for it does not prepare the child for the future.

How could the eagle use the incident to better value?

"The penalty, smart boy, is suspension and grade slash. You knew that. You broke the rule and tried to pull a funny anyway. Now you can suffer the consequences."

Action. Consequence. That the kid understands.

Increasingly now as the grade schooler goes out and about, he or she spends blocks of time essentially unsupervised. And that is as it should be. The child is becoming more independent. The child wanders farther afield, secure in the knowledge that home is still the haven, still available.

If Dad is to protect this increasingly independent little person, he must help his child internalize the protection, just as an internalized conscience works when external guidance is absent. What should the child do, exactly, if a stranger approaches or tries to entice him or her into a car? No theory, here. The child is not yet into blotting up theory and putting it into practice when needed. He or she needs exact, clear courses of action. Dad should rehearse the child through specific actions.

These true incidents were taken from the police blotter of a major western city over a three-month period. We do not include them here to scare you or point a finger of blame should your child be victimized. We believe they offer some interesting and useful instruction.

- **On a weekday after school:** A boy, seven, was crossing a parking lot on the way home from school. A man in his forties snatched the boy up and carried him quickly toward a car. The boy began instantly to scream and flail. The man told an approaching teen male that this was his son, about to be punished for disobeying. The child fought harder and begged help. Wisely, the teen intervened. The man dropped the child, bolted to his car, and drove away.

   The boy's father had taught him to make a noise if any person frightened him—the louder and more boisterous the ruckus, the better.

- **On a Saturday afternoon:** A man claimed to have lost a puppy in a dense woodlot near the home of a boy, also seven. The child followed him into the thickets to help locate the dog. Under the cover of the woods, he mutilated and sodomized the boy and left him to wander out on his own.

    The child had been told, "never talk to strangers," but because of the puppy angle, he thought this was different. He had never play-acted a safety lesson.

- **On the way to school:** About eight A.M., two men in their twenties stopped a car beside a thirteen-year-old girl and asked directions. When she turned away from them they made lewd and obscene requests. She dropped her books and ran back home. The mother called the police immediately, and the girl was able to provide enough description that the young men were apprehended twenty minutes later. They were held on previous charges.

    Mom and Dad had both impressed safety rules upon her.

- **During an early morning house fire:** A boy, twelve, led his three younger siblings to safety by crawling the length of a hall on hands and knees with the youngest riding piggyback. They gathered at a prearranged place of safety. Their parents barely escaped from a second-floor window.

    Dad had led the family in rehearsed fire drills.

- **Early morning while the mother and an uncle still slept:** Playing with a butane lighter, a girl, three, accidentally set fire to a living room chair. When the blaze spread, she and her sister, four, hid in a closet. Both died of smoke inhalation.

    What else can be said?

- **In a wooded county park:** A boy, nine, playing near his family's campsite, became disoriented and wandered away. He sat down on a stump and was found two hours later. (Police were involved from the outset because of foul play in the area a few days earlier. The parents, however, made the find.)

The child had received his school district's "hug a tree" training. His father reinforced the lessons with play-acting at home. The boy was embarrassed by the childish play-acting, but participated.

In that same city within a span of three years, grade school-aged children won heroism medals for rescuing playmates, for resisting persons with alleged criminal intent, and in the case of one eleven-year-old, for performing resuscitation on a near-drowning victim. (The child had tagged along with Dad, a volunteer fire fighter, to Dad's annual CPR recertification course, picking up enough knowledge to be able to assist the person's breathing.)

Certainly, we know that not every incident is going to have a happy ending simply because the child was instructed on what to do. Tragedy happens despite the best teaching, for even with all the training in the world, children are still essentially helpless, totally vulnerable. And a good many well-trained children will never encounter a situation in which such training is needed. Still, by exercising his role as protector, Dad can raise the chances that, should his child encounter difficulties when he or she is outside of Dad's supervision, that child will be able to act wisely in a positive manner.

Some Things to Do with Your Child

Talk about these generalized situations and play-act various actions and responses. Talk about responses. Talk about the child's capabilities and strong points (speed, agility) and short points (lack of strength, size).

Are you going to unnecessarily terrify your kid? Not as much now as if the child were still a preschooler. Preschoolers' imaginations, untrammeled by reality, are likely to build wrong pictures. By grade school, kids have a more accurate understanding of the world. Their imaginations are more disciplined because they have a broader base of factual knowledge with which to build mental pictures. Kids today know that evil lurks out there.

Talk with your child about:

1. Getting lost. In rural situations (forests, campgrounds, fishing lakes), teach kids to stop as soon as they think they're lost. Wait. Hug a tree. Don't panic. Yell now and then. Let Mom and Dad come to them. In town, such as in a mall or store, review how to identify salespersons and uniformed public safety officers (police, fire, etc.). As in the woods, kids lost in malls should not go wandering.
2. Being accosted by a stranger. Teach kids to run. Observe. Kick and scream if grabbed. Cause a scene, a ruckus, and if the stranger threatens, yell louder. Kids have a strong sense of fair play now. They think if an adult says something it's true—that if the adult makes a promise ("Be quiet or I'll hurt you!") they mean it. They might. But they're so big and strong they don't have to. One of the best forms of protection a father can convey is to help the child understand that a threatening adult is going to do what he or she wants regardless of the child's actions.
3. Being approached by someone known. By talking about it, help the kids know what's acceptable and what's private. Too, teach them to never keep secrets except for happy ones, such as birthday surprises, no matter what the person says.
4. Fire. Practice leaving the house from any room. Have regular fire exit drills. Teach them the safest moves; to stay low, to check doors for heat before opening them. Identify a safe place away from the house where everyone is to gather as soon as they get out, and stress that they shouldn't go back in for any reason. Teach them how to call the fire department from a neighbor's phone.

5. Health emergencies. Every grade schooler should know how to summon help—aid units, fire department, ambulance. Visit the fire house or emergency room and know what goes on there. Get a CPR (cardiopulmonary resuscitation) card yourself and take your grade schoolers along. They might even pick up good pointers from a first aid class.

6. On the road. You and your child take the bike apart and put it back together, so the child can perform minor repairs, such as untangling a fouled chain. Practice reading street signs and maps. At the airport, even a six-year-old can learn to read arrival and departure monitors.

Ask the father hovering protectively over his children if he would ever fight his grade school-aged kid, and he'd exclaim, "Never!" But in a subtle way, some fathers may do just that. Encouragement and competition are poles apart in their effects, yet they arise in similar circumstances. The good father encourages.

Were you to ask Arnold if he competed with his son, he'd bluster, "Me? Compete with Miles? He's a kid, for crying out loud!" Loosely translated, that response would mean, "Of course not." And yet, in a subtle way, Arnold did that throughout Miles's childhood. And Miles subconsciously picked up on it.

—The Great Encourager/Competitor—

Encouragement and competition both start out the same. The child is reaching out into new dimensions, learning new things, suffering new pains, and experiencing new joys. Ideally, his wagon scout walks beside him, guiding and instructing. One form of encouragement is to help children fulfil their need to achieve.

Feeding the Child's Need to Achieve

This need to achieve, and to be recognized for the achievement, is a major milestone in a grade schooler's development. Achievement and winning help the child define who he or she is, what he or she can do, where the limits are. All are important lessons learned now or probably not at all. Personal achievement is, to use the technical term, a step in individuation.

You'll recall dad is the main font of socialization and individuation. Dad can advance the need to achieve a great deal by encouraging with words and actions.

"That's a great birdhouse you made."

"Great play in left field, kid!" with a side-to-side hug.

"You're coming along all right with your trumpet lessons."

"I watched you tooling around the corner on your bike. You can really handle that thing."

"Thanks for being polite to your sister when she was behaving badly toward you. I appreciate that."

"I appreciate you."

Occasionally the achievements are weighty; usually they are not. No matter. The child must receive recognition for something. The child need not display athletic prowess, or musical genius, or diplomatic savvy. The child need only be affirmed for efforts and for whatever degree of accomplishment is earned.

Arnold snorted. "So what should I have done when Miles screwed up? Lie to him? Praise incompetence? That kid can turn a simple job into a Pentagon nightmare."

The answer to that: constructive criticism. What are the differences between constructive and nonconstructive?

Constructive criticism praises a job and tactfully suggests ways to make a good thing better. Nonconstructive—which is a polite way of saying destructive—criticism cuts the job down. Constructive criticism identifies first the achievement and second whatever the problem is. Constructive criticism then gently suggests a possible solution to the problem. Nonconstructive criticism blurts out, "You did it wrong." Translation: **You failed again.**

Constructive criticism is actually a part of encouragement

because it validates that the child has achieved. With constructive criticism, Dad makes the point that he recognizes the child's efforts.

Carl mowed the lawn as, ahead of him, Janey and Cathy picked up sticks and chased the garter snakes. Carl then raked those areas of the lawn where the mower left thick rows of clippings. He asked Janey to gather the raked piles of clippings and dump them in the compost bin while he made lunch.

She did so, but a ring of loose grass clumps marked where each of the piles had been. It was, by adult measure, a sloppy job. Carl praised the several aspects of her work. No sticks left when he went through, and no chopped snakes. Good job there. She dumped quite a big heap into the compost pile; look at all that grass she moved! "Let's see if we can add even more to the heap." Eagerly, Janey went through again, cleaning up the rings of clumps to dump still more grass into the bin. Only then did Carl praise the neat, clean yard.

He had recognized her achievements, and then had called upon her emergent sense of competition to improve her work. When the yard was properly clean, he praised that performance too.

A few simple twists of meaning, a few words placed in a different sequence, make all the difference to children. They hear literally. They do not hear pride if it's not spoken. They do not hear praise if it's not bestowed. When delivering praise and criticism, never for a minute believe that your child understands your true feelings. You have to express them. Nicely.

If that is so, why don't kids hear unspoken sentiments of praise and admiration? Because of that competitiveness. Too, kids are naturally self-deprecating. They are constantly thinking the worst of themselves, in part because their little-kid reality does not match the larger-than-life nonreality of adults and fictional heroes. It isn't hard to undermine a child's sense of worth and achievement.

Undercutting the Child's Sense of Achievement

Destructive criticism? "What you did is not good enough." With that voiced message comes the unspoken message, "You can't do it as well as I can." Competitive.

"You're never going to amount to anything. You're lazy." The nonverbal meaning: "You'll never be as good as I am. I get to point out that you're lazy because I'm not."

Again, there's that sense of competition. When Dad says that sort of thing he's not meaning to compete with his little kid; neither is he realizing how the messages are being absorbed. The child is preoccupied with competitiveness anyway. He or she will hear everything said in that light.

As he was growing, Miles never managed to be a complete success in his father's eyes, no matter what he did. The paint job on his airplane model was sloppy; a decal crooked. No matter that he was eight when he built it. His father never failed to point out the flaws. For Miles's own good, of course. You can't do better if you don't hear that you need to do better, right?

"You're not as good as your sister."

"Why can't you be more like your brother?"

More competition. Damaging competition.

Much about competition is good at this age. In fact, certain competition is necessary and excellent. Comparisons of the above sort are not.

"Words are so very powerful!" claims Frank Minirth. "We find time and again that the father is the most accurate prophet of what the children are going to be. When he says, 'You're never going to make it. You're a bumbler; you always mess up' and that kind of thing, sure enough, that usually comes true."

Even the father saying those things doesn't want to give his child that heritage any more than you do.

Conversely, when Dad inspires a "can do" spirit through his words and actions, that comes true as well.

Encouraging Through Deeds

Kids hear words, but just as effectively, they hear actions. Fathers encourage their new children of the world by their presence, their interest, and their involvement in their children's lives. Actions are like those motivational and self-improvement tapes you sometimes hear about, with subliminal messages laced in here and there. In theory, the mind picks up the messages even though the eyes and ears do not. Similarly, the minds of neither father nor child realize what Dad says with his actions, but the messages register all the same.

• Share Hobbies

To an adult, hobbies are recreation. Fluff stuff. To a child, hobbies are work just as important and consuming as school or anything else.

Dad can encourage his child profoundly by taking part in the child's hobbies. Sharing in that way is actually very important at this age, this being the age of achievement. Building a model, collecting baseball cards, running Matchbox cars, shooting off rockets—what is your kid into?

To Carl's chagrin, Janey is into ballet. Carl in a tutu? Not in a million years. But he encourages in other ways. While she practices at the barre, he notices and praises. Daddy's rock-solid hand holds hers, helping her balance as she masters tours and arabesques. His attendance at recitals hasn't been perfect, but he tries.

Carl's involvement, even at the most casual level, builds Janey's self-esteem incredibly. His participation says, "You are special. God made you. I like you and the way God made you, and I like being with you as we pursue this hobby." If Carl is particularly astute, he will voice all that verbally as well, and not just once. Janey will profit immeasurably by hearing the spoken message as well as the actions.

While we're talking here about grade school, children of any age benefit from Dad's participation, although as children grow and relate more and more to the world outside the family, Dad's part even in hobbies diminishes.

Things to Think About

When I was a kid I was interested in these hobbies and sports (not just the usual; model building, softball, collecting; but the not-so-usual such as running a trapline in the woods behind the property, volunteering at the arboretum . . .):

1. _____
2. _____
3. _____

These interests shaped my adulthood in these ways (yes or no):

_____ I am in a line of work related to one or more childhood interests.

_____ I now pursue a hobby or hobbies related to those of my childhood.

_____ I married a spouse whose interests reflect my own childhood pursuits.

_____ I find myself encouraging my child to pursue sports or hobbies that were prominent in my own childhood.

_____ Other _____
_____

My own child has these interests that I know of:

1. _____
2. _____
3. _____

I can encourage those interests in these specific ways (actual participation; observation such as at recitals, games; verbal and financial encouragement):

1. _____
2. _____
3. _____

• **Share Activities**

Says Brian Newman, "I can't overemphasize the value of men being involved in kids' activities at this age. I don't mean just hobby interests but the broader activities: Sunday school, Scouting, sport coaching. It's not so much what the father does as a Scout leader or whatever, but that he participates as a father. And you don't have to be the area president, or be the best there is, or make everyone go 'gee whiz' about how good you are. Be there. Help. That's the important part."

Paul Warren agrees heartily. "But there's a caveat. I meet a lot of dads who participate in Scout troops, for instance, who are driving their kids crazy. Accomplish, accomplish, accomplish. Their involvement is actually 'for the fathers themselves; they are trying to reap benefits. Involvement is important; your kid making Eagle Scout is not."

Involvement, both men emphasize, means Dad's presence. At the soccer game, at the school play, Dad is there.

—Deeds of Trust—

After several weeks of being both Mom and Dad to his girls, Carl Jefferson received the help of a neighbor, Jean Maxwell. Jean's girls were in the fourth and sixth grades. Jean took Carl's girls in during those times when he was out of town. What a godsend! Now Carl could get out on his business trips again. Carl was back to selling mud, and he loved it, not that he didn't love being full-time Daddy.

He thought the arrangement was great. But the moment he returned from his first out-of-town trip, waved good-bye to the Maxwells, and loaded the girls into the car, Janey exploded. "Daddy, don't make us stay there! Mrs. Maxwell isn't fair!"

"Make sure your seatbelt's snug. Why isn't she?" Carl pulled out onto the beltway.

"Her kids get to stay up 'til ten, and I hafta be in bed at nine. And she made Cathy go to bed at eight! Clear in bed! No story or anything!"

"Cathy's supposed to be in bed then, and you need your sleep."

"But her kids get to stay up."

"They're older."

"It's not fair! She says we're like her own kids to her. So she should treat us alike."

It's no fair! The theme song of the grade schooler. Children in grade school suddenly develop an intense sense of fair play. They can tell if one kid gets thirty seconds more attention than another, and they don't need a stopwatch to see it. They know if one kid is served seven lima beans and the other child only has to eat six. "Johnny down the street gets to watch scary movies and I don't. It's no fair!"

This sense of fairness constantly rankles kids more than it reassures them. To quote that misanthropic little philosopher Calvin of the *Calvin and Hobbes* cartoons, "I know the world isn't fair, but why isn't it ever unfair in my favor?"

In a way, this yearning for exquisite balance and equity among peers is an extension of the hunger for competition. Through competition, children prove themselves and develop their identity. Fairness, they believe, provides a level playing field (actually, what they really hope for is a field tilted a little bit their way).

Janey was bent out of shape that the Maxwell children had another hour in the evening, despite the fact that they were two and four years older than she. How should Carl handle the fair play issue, knowing that children cannot compete fairly on a level playing field? Their skills and needs vary too much.

With his deeds and with words, Carl, the wagon guide to the world, can teach his children that life, though not fair, ought to be just. Justice actually provides a more level playing field for competition than does fairness, for justice takes the child's age and abilities into account.

It is just that the older children be allowed to stay up later, even as it is just that tiny Cathy should go to bed before second-grader Janey. Like Calvin, kids rarely notice when fair play or justice swings in their favor. They note only the injustices and slights—and bring them to your attention instantly.

Carl, as Dad, has one other essential lesson to teach in the matter of what is fair and just. That lesson is: **You can trust me, your father, to act in your best interest.**

Carl will build trust in his girls in several ways. For Janey, he will explain why he's acting unfairly. For both girls, he will snuggle them in his lap, read to them, hold them, carry them on his shoulder, feed them, listen to them. All these seemingly random actions say "I love you. I am trustworthy." Those actions, more than anything else Carl can do, will build his children's trust in him.

As Janey and Cathy get older, he will convey trust by being careful not to go back on his word. Janey will remember instantly if he made a promise he does not keep. Carl, of course, will keep his promises not to build trust but because of his own integrity; they are promises. The lesson is effective, regardless the motive.

Now and later, when Carl issues a distasteful edict:

- "No, you cannot stay all night at So-and-so's; their family's lifestyle is not amenable to ours."
- "No, you cannot ride the Whoop-De-Doo at the amusement park. It's too dangerous for a kid your age. In a couple years, ask again."
- "No. I'm delighted that your best friend at school has a St. Bernard, but our place isn't big enough. He wouldn't get enough exercise."
- "Yes, you do have to eat broccoli because it has a lot of vitamins and it's on sale this time of year. I don't care what the president thinks of broccoli."

Grade schoolers can understand reasons for rules and edicts, even though they may rail bitterly against them. Dad has a valid reason. He has the child's best interests at heart. Those are the inferred messages that build trust.

—The Ultimate Message—

Miles's dad and wagon guide Arnold, in his own life, never learned a crucial lesson that he must teach Miles. It is this: Worth is not based on what you do; it is based on what you are. Until Arnold masters that basic precept, Miles cannot. Swooping eagles, for whom appearance is everything, have a hard, hard time with any worth not based on behavior.

"The stereotypical father having problems with his kids, the father I see so very, very frequently in counsel, is a good man. He's a very good man. And he sees himself as a good father because he works hard and makes money. He considers that his contribution to the family, and he wants the family to look good in return, just as he looks good," says Paul Warren.

"We're not talking about surface appearances here. I mean he wants the family to be good. Toe the mark and present a wholesome face before the world. He won't rest easy until he realizes 'Worth is who I am, a child of God.' He can't teach his kid that until he's secure with it himself."

—A Child of God—

Janey Jefferson draws pictures of God (which puts her in the same league with Michelangelo, who drew God in the wet plaster of the Sistine Chapel). Michelangelo put loose robes on God; Janey always draws a hat on His divine head. In her mind, the hat places him a cut above everyone else. After all, police officers, state troopers, Smokey Bear, fire fighters, pizza chefs, cowboys, and other prominent people all wear hats.

During her grade school years, Janey's perception of God will change rapidly. The God of the sixth grader is light years beyond the God of the first or second grader. Her daddy will shape those changes by modeling the heavenly Father, and by one-on-one spiritual instruction. Let us next look at how Daddy can guide his children spiritually.

SEVEN

The Spiritual Child

"I can't believe I'm doing this. I'm thirty-nine years old. And I'm playing in a sandbox." Jack Brubaker planted another palm tree beside the oasis and stepped back to survey the results.

His seventeen-year-old daughter Marla moved in beside him. "That's really a work of art, Dad. I must admit we're brilliant."

And she was right. It was indeed a work of art.

Last winter, using a full sheet of plywood, Jack had built a four- by eight-foot sandbox in the basement. It sat on eight sturdy legs, two feet off the floor. Jack had filled it with finely sifted bricklayer's sand. And all the while he was creating this play box, his seven-year-old, Peter, was crowing, "Wow, Dad! This is great!" Jack had scored all sorts of points with Peter.

The younger of the four, Peter and Lynna, ten, played in the sand, literally, for days until the new wore off, tracking the fine grit all over the house. Jack scored few if any points with his wife.

And then one day, as Jack and the kids were reading aloud in Joshua 2, Lynna said, "I don't understand. How could Rahab live in the wall? She had a house with a roof. And a window."

Jack hadn't the foggiest idea, so he asked John and Marla to look it up in the church library. One thing led to another, and the kids decided to build a scene. They'd have sheep and shepherds, people, wells, an oasis, a walled city—or at least the corner of one, maybe camels and donkeys if they could swing it, and they would lay it all out in that huge sandbox.

Jack could handle sheet metal fabrication, any sort of ductwork, any lovely sandbox you might want, but he was not too sure about a Bible scene. So he delegated. Marla, with considerable latent artistic talent, supervised. All four kids made people from those old style one-piece wooden clothespins, dressing them in scraps of fabric, striped and plain. The clothespins' rounded "feet" stuck down in the sand so that the people stood nicely.

They traced camels, donkeys, and sheep from coloring books and transferred the outlines to one-inch stock. Jack, or John under Jack's supervision, cut them out with his bandsaw. The kids painted the wooden animals and arranged them in the scene. "Keep those sheep coming, Dad. We need lots more sheep."

John and Marla collaborated on a cardboard, three-dimensional city wall across one corner, with Rahab's house built right in there. They even hung the red cord in the window.

A mirror, its edges buried irregularly in the sand, became the oasis pool. Rocks became rocks. Palm trees were fringed paper boughs stuck in lengths of plastic tubing. They curved gracefully, thanks to the natural bend in the rolled tubing.

It took little Peter an inordinately long time to fashion a simple shepherd's crook out of a piece of 18-gauge wire, and then it wasn't a very convincing-looking crook. Jack yearned to grab it out of Peter's hand and just do it. He had to hold his own hands behind his back, literally, forcing himself to let Peter handle the job unaided.

Were you to ask Jack about this project he would have shrugged, perhaps a bit embarrassed, and admitted it was kind of fun even for him. He probably would not realize that with that super project, he was teaching his children a variety of splendid lessons about life and about themselves. Not only that, he was giving his children a megadose of personal confidence and esteem. And most of all, he was teaching them about God.

All that in a sandbox? As a matter of fact, you can do all that with activities and projects much simpler than the one Jack got sucked into. A small research project with the kids; an afternoon of "Let's pretend we're shepherds in Bible times" as you loll about in the grass of the city park; a cut-and-paste project you found in the Bible bookstore (great places to go exploring for things to do; check their Sunday school and activities sections). Jack, though, ended up with a monster. Let's look in detail at what he did, for the principles apply just as well to less ambitious activities.

—Know Thy Kid—

Jack's first stroke of genius was to encourage this hands-on activity and to join in. His presence and participation announced, "This is an important topic. Dad is investing time and himself in it." Kids, of course, never think terms like *invest*, but they understand the principle at a nonverbal level.

Small children, remember, have to learn by doing. Their hands are as important as their brains to the learning experience. The younger kids had that opportunity with this project. Older children get more cerebral, but they still benefit from making, creating, fashioning; in fact, so did Jack. In the best way possible, all four children learned. How, and what, did they learn?

Age Appropriate Lessons

Very few grade schoolers are going to wax eloquent on the differences between Baptists and Episcopalians. Pre-schoolers are forgivably a little fuzzy on the deeper precepts of atonement. Junior high kids think Jonah and the whale is baby stuff. What tenets can kids be expected to absorb, and when can they be expected to absorb them? The partial list on pages 119–121 will perhaps give you a general idea of what goes on in kids' minds and hearts as they grow, and what you can reasonably expect them to pick up.

Age appropriateness is not just a matter of how much depth the child can absorb. It also depends on how the child thinks. For example, imagination weighs equally with reality in the preschooler's thinking. Indeed, the child processes reality by means of imagination and pretense. Miracles to a preschooler are not miracles. They are the expected products of magical thinking. So while you may discuss feeding five thousand with a few loaves and fishes, it doesn't seem out of the ordinary to a small child. Jesus wanted, He prayed, it happened. What's the big deal?

The fact that children of these various ages are capable of absorbing these levels of religious instruction does not, of course, mean they are interested or that they want to be. The wise father, however, will not work too far beyond his child's capabilities to really understand spiritual matters.

Jack's kids each handled age-appropriate tasks. The younger children made things within their province. The older children researched more elaborate detail and strove for realism. Jack's fourteen- and seventeen-year-olds took scriptural phrasing word by word and picked it apart. The seven-year-old was content to build trees, shepherds, and crooks. Marla could paint wooden sheep the same as little Peter, but Peter was not quite up to finding exactly how Rahab's house related to the wall. Each child, you see, was operating at his or her level of interest. Each was truly learning the lesson of the age.

Frankly, Jack Brubaker didn't think of any of this. He was more or less at sea during the whole project, without a glimmer as to what might be age appropriate or useful for instruction. What he did that made this all come together was simply to encourage the kids as a participant. He also listened and observed, the two essential activities for the father who understands his kids.

By the end of the project, John's pal Maxy was up to his elbows in sand, shaping dunes. Other kids, too, dropped

AGE APPROPRIATE SPIRITUAL LESSONS

PRESCHOOLER

TRUTHS

God is good. He loves the child. So does Jesus, God's Son.

God is always and everywhere present (Jonah, sailing to the ends of the earth, could not travel beyond Him).

The child can address God in song and prayer, and He will hear anytime, anywhere.

Jesus was once a baby, once a little child. Jesus died and returned from death. Jesus, like God, is now everywhere.

The Bible is God's message to His people.

Angels exist beyond the dimension of men. We can't see them. They are either good or evil. Evil angels we call devils, chief of whom is Satan. Good angels know God face to face.

MEMORIZATION

Short verses and portions of verses. We suggest the New King James or Good News versions for simplicity of language. Most (not all!) small children are brilliant memorizers. Besides John 3:16, which every human being should have on the tip of their tongues, how about: Psalm 118:24, Philippians 3:1 and 4:4, 2 Timothy 3:16–17, 2 Peter 5:7—bright passages of hope and joy.

READING

Try *The Toddler's Bible*, designed for children ages 1 to 3. Read them dramatic Bible stories, picture books such as Gilbert Beers's charming works, *The Big Book of All-Time Favorite Bible Stories* and *My Bedtime Anytime Storybook*.

EARLY GRADE SCHOOL

TRUTHS

God is all knowing and all powerful, yet very personal and intimate.

God loves every person, hates all sin.

Read stories and participate in discussion about God's miracles.

Jesus, the Son, wants to be savior to all. Some will refuse.

The child who accepts will eventually be with Jesus in heaven.

EARLY GRADE SCHOOL, *cont.*

TRUTHS, *cont.*

The Bible should be read as well as memorized. Satan is the tempter. Our own nature tempts us. Forgiveness is taught through modeling.

MEMORIZATION

Full verses and even passages with emphasis on comprehension. Suggestions: Psalms 23 and 118:22–24, Matthew 11:28 and 18:3, John 4:24 and 8:34, Luke 15:10.

READING

Picture Bible and age-appropriate children's books.

LATE GRADE SCHOOL

TRUTHS

The preceding, plus:

God is very personal and also universal. He deals with all nations through history, not just us here and now.

As child's horizons expand, begin exposure to mission stories and efforts.

Jesus served by taking the cloak of mortality.

Jesus provides the model and leader for His own to follow.

Divinity exists as the Trinity.

The Bible is fully trustworthy as fact and truth.

God wants everyone, including the child, to serve Him from day to day.

God, however, allows everyone, including the child, free choice regarding obedience. Without the opportunity for disobedience there would be no true obedience.

The wages of sin is death.

The Holy Spirit is a guide and teacher.

Forgiveness is both modeled and taught.

The child can put Bible teaching into practice by making wise choices.

The meanings of terminology and phrases used in liturgy become clearer.

The child learns basics of Church history, biographies of leaders of the faith, and the differences between major religious bodies.

LATE GRADE SCHOOL, *cont.*

MEMORIZATION   Verses organized to a theme or topic, such as John's whole bread of life passage, portions of the Sermon on the Mount, the beatitudes, the praise psalms.

READING   Bible translations in modern English, C. S. Lewis's Narnia Chronicles, mission stories such as Betty Hockett's, perhaps J. R. R. Tolkien.

ADOLESCENT

TRUTHS   The preceding, with essentially adult theology, including:
Deeper meanings, applications in the familiar old stories.
The adolescent can understand:
The full nature and attributes of the godhead
The full nature and attributes of Satan and evil
The Adamic nature
Personal responsibility
The virgin birth
Full meaning of eternal reward, eternal punishment
Baptisms, spiritual gifts
The -isms (Calvinism, predestination, etc.)
Denominational differences
Detailed church history, geography
Service opportunities; here's the big kids' version of hands-on learning.

MEMORIZATION   Anything and everything. In addition to memorizing, familiarizing self with all books of Scripture.

READING   Extensive reading in the New King James and other translations; nonfiction: Swindoll, Schaeffer; wholesome adult-level fiction (Hilda Stahl's work for adults, Kay Stewart's *Chariots of Dawn*); biography and writings of church leaders; adult level mission-oriented books such as *Peace Child*, *Through Gates of Splendor*.

by and became enchanted, kids of all ages. They helped,
visited, oohed and aahed. Was Jack pleased and proud?

Does Smokey Bear stomp out forest fires?

Universal Lessons

Through their project, Jack Brubaker's kids discerned
that the people and places of Scripture were real, tangible,
and not nearly so exotic as they might seem at first blush.
This is an important precept all students of Scripture must
keep in mind. Sure, the people of Scripture dressed funny.
Sure, they did things such as drove sheep and pressed
olives that most people today have never done. But through
that project they took on three-dimensional form. They existed not in the mind but in a concrete, physical world. In
other words, the kids were personalizing the abstract lessons of Scripture.

Dad as the introducer of the big, wide world plays a
crucial part in this. Are people cardboard or multidimensional? As Dad, representing All Men, is multidimensional,
so he teaches by example. And with this three-dimensional
project, with clothespin people that can be arranged and
rearranged through space, the lesson reached home symbolically as well.

The concept that Bible characters were fully human is
something Dad ought to remember himself. It's easy to
forget, when you've been hearing about Moses since you
were three, that he had warts and virtues in all the dimensions people today do.

Too, the Brubaker kids learned factual things. They found
out how Rahab could live in a wall, the knowledge impressed
in them by eye, ear, and hand. They learned about lifestyles
and the importance of water. As the project took shape,
Jack and the kids used devotional times to read about walled
cities, oases, sheep-keeping, and other related topics.

But the most telling lessons they received had nothing
to do with facts and background. By participating, Jack expressed nonverbally, not just "This Bible stuff is important"

but also "I trust the truth and fidelity of Scripture. See how I accept its literal wording. God said it is so. It is so." Particularly to the very young, Daddy is a god of sorts. Daddy just placed his sanction on the existence of the true God and upon the Bible. Those lessons are very, very powerful, no matter how Dad conveys them.

Nonspiritual Lessons

In the real nitty-gritty world, the spiritual and the secular cannot be neatly separated out and compartmentalized. We all know that. With the project he more or less stumbled into, Jack crossed the line between the purely spiritual and the purely secular time and time again.

For example, he modeled persistence and encouraged it in the kids. They all stuck with the project for the two weeks that it took. They didn't struggle with it; he didn't browbeat them. But he stayed with it, and that in itself encouraged them.

By letting Peter do his work himself without interference, he gave his smallest child a huge boost in self-esteem. This was Peter's work. Daddy did not take it away to do it better. A powerful message. Equally powerful would have been the message, "You're messing it up; you can't do it well," had Jack wrested that simple shepherd's crook away from Peter. Little things so often make big impressions. Little things teach.

—Finding Ways to Teach—

"I'm a trucker, not a teacher," Elgin Mayer always said. So he turned his children's spiritual education over to the wife and the Sunday school. After all, that's what they're for. They're geared for it.

"I don't have a creative bone in my body," Charles Mayer claimed. "How can I teach spiritual principles to tiny kids?" He was all ready to beg off as had his father before him, but Meghan quashed that idea.

"You're the father. Scripture is clear; you're the family's

spiritual leader. Either get creative or get help, but get cracking."

Fortunately, Charles had more options than he realized at first.

Seize the Moment

"Scripture urges men to teach their kids 'when you lie down, and when you rise up.' Throughout the day." Brian Newman spreads another of those boyish grins across his face. "I like that. Look for little times to teach spiritual things. Times when the kids are receptive, not just when a clock says it's time."

Brian himself offers an example of ways to seize the moment, whatever the moment may be. One was as he tucked in preschooler Rachel after the obligatory bedtime story. She said, "Daddy, why do we close our eyes when we pray?"

Brian replied, "We don't have to. Usually, it's so you can focus your attention on what you're doing and avoid distractions. But you can pray anytime, anywhere. Even jumping up and down."

With those huge brown eyes that melt mere daddies, Rachel asked, "Can we?"

So they did.

Jumping up and down.

While out in the kitchen, Debi wondered why herds of elephants were tramping so close to the house.

Dad should be flexible, keeping in mind that his little one does not have the same concept of God that he as an adult enjoys. The child should not have to address God at Daddy's level but at the child's level. For Brian's daughter Rachel, this prayer made perfect sense: "God is great; God is good. Thank You for the food. Thank You for everything except burglars." And no, her house had not been burglarized. This was a preventive prayer.

Incidentally, Dad, you might want to keep handy a notebook in which to record cute stuff your kids do and say. It will serve two purposes. One is memory. As much as you think you'll never forget that moment, you will. A notebook entry will prevent the loss. Too, it will provide a running record of your child's emotional and spiritual growth, the steps your child takes toward God day-by-day. You might even learn a little something yourself, for kids often come up with delightful profundities.

As Brian and his Rachel were cruising down the freeway one fine day, Rachel herself perceived the three A's of Prayer. *Anytime. Anywhere. About Anything.* "So that's the next thing we worked on," Brian concludes, "the three A's of Prayer. She memorized them. Anything, anywhere, anytime. She didn't have anyone telling her this. She was ripe for the instruction, and it flowed naturally."

Thus does the most effective teaching frequently come at odd and unexpected times. Another avenue for Charles to follow with his son Sean Michael and future children is Scripture memorization. This is computer programming at its best.

Memorize the Word

"I emphasize the importance of Bible memory," says Frank Minirth, "as a basic part of spiritual training."

"Memorizing Bible verses is something Dad can do along with his kid." Brian Newman is learning Scripture together with Rachel as they commit verses to memory. He profits nearly as much as she, and the joint project adds interest for both of them.

"There is a balance, though," he adds. "You must never forget you're working with a child. I encourage Rachel, and I work alongside her, but there are times she simply isn't interested. When she doesn't want to, I never push it. That's not fruitful, especially for a preschooler."

It is a curious fact that the brain uses different areas for processing spoken words and sung words. Memorizing the words to songs, therefore, trips different memory paths. Dad might want to sing songs with his kids (unless, like

Charles Mayer, his voice is the sort that embarrasses frogs to tears). A lot of joyful, comforting Bible passages have been set to music. Ask about such songs in Christian bookstores. The grand old traditional hymns teach many spiritual truths as well. Perhaps Dad and his children might commit all four verses of "Amazing Grace" to memory, for starters.

"There are a couple caveats here," Paul Warren cautions.

"Memorizing Scripture must be a priority for the father if it is to be a priority for the child. The father's true attitude toward Scripture will reveal itself the moment he begins working with his children.

"And I disagree for several reasons with the statement that 'a good father makes his kids memorize Scripture.' When such memorization is an act of obedience toward Dad instead of a seeking after God, the purpose is largely lost.

"I hope every dad will emphasize the living God's word and seeking Him rather than memorizing God's Word simply for the sake of doing it; to chalk up points somehow. Memorization is a means to an end; it is not itself an end. Dad should use it as a means for getting to know God." He hesitates, framing his thoughts. "I guess I'm sensitized to the issue by seeing too many kids forced to memorize, or try to, and they can't."

He settles deeper into his chair. "Every now and then I find kids who can't memorize. It's not a matter of will or obedience. Their brains won't make the connections. They physically are not wired to memorize. You can see where this can cause them a lot of grief. Here are all their Sunday school mates, and their parents, and pretty soon they're thinking, 'There must be something wrong with me. Why can't I do it? Everyone says it's so easy.' There's nothing at all wrong with them; they're just different."

Brains are wired in different ways. Some photograph, some blot up, some analyze. Some memorize facts and surroundings by spatial means and others by verbal means.

Children who have trouble with rote memory usually excel in other areas. If memorization is a strength in your child, by all means use it. If it is not, don't make both of you miserable trying to push it. Your child can get to know God better in more effective ways, such as story telling, discussing pictures, reading, poetry, singing.

How do you know if your kid is one of those for whom memorization is difficult or impossible? Children love to show off by reciting memorized verses. So if your child hesitates, stumbles, and doesn't seem able to get the hang of it, you can feel pretty confident that your child is not a memorizer. God will still speak even if the child never memorizes a word.

Helping children with memorization and reading takes definite time and effort. Charles Mayer looks forward eagerly to the day he and Sean Michael can really get serious about the Bible together. But Charles will be teaching when he isn't even trying.

Don't be Hesitant about Using Props

Brian Newman finally found himself a *pre dieu,* a prayer bench or kneeler. It was gorgeous, an antique. He had it redone and proudly installed it in his home. His toddler, Rachel, studied it awhile, ran to her room, and got her children's prayer book. She slipped her book into the book nook in the prayer bench. That night as she prepared for bed, Brian sat down at bedside to pray with her.

"No, Daddy, you forgot. We have to go kneel on the prayer stand." And so they did.

That *pre dieu,* a solid, visible, tactile thing (and because it was unusual, an intriguing piece) served little Rachel as a catalyst for prayer. A reminder. Brian has since bought a prayer bench for each child as an heirloom of their spiritual heritage.

As adults profit from reminders, so much more do children. Children, being very nonabstract, derive great value from material reminders and props. Look for devices of that sort in your child's life. What reminders can you develop that will focus your child's thoughts? What can seize the child's attention and turn it to things of God?

Seek them in your child's everyday world. Make something. Add a "Pray" sign to an inexpensive stuffed toy or figurine. Instead of placecards at the table, set out prayer reminders. The sky's not the limit, which is the whole idea.

Teaching Indirectly; Shaping Mores and Attitudes

"Once upon a time there was a young man named Buffalo Frank. He married an Indian princess who had two sisters who were also princesses. The man and . . . ."

"Oh, Daddy, we know it's you." Frank Minirth's girls giggle gleefully by the campfire. They are doing one of their favorite things, camping out in Arkansas with their dad, and the night is rich with mystery and fun.

"No, no, no! Buffalo Frank and his beautiful wife lived by a big creek . . . ."

Years later and hundreds of miles away in his office at the clinic, Frank Minirth glows as he tells about sitting around a fire in the humid summer darkness, spinning his yarns of Buffalo Frank, and how his little girls so instantly caught on.

Buffalo Frank has a vital purpose. "I love to tell stories," says Frank, as if it didn't show. "If you don't want to make up stories, read stories to your young children. But always with the moral values you want to impart. Always the kind of person you want your children to be. Kids will pick it up.

"My stories are always about three Indian girls; they're the heroes of the stories." Buffalo Frank, you see, teaches strong moral standards and values, not by preaching (which tends to fall on deaf ears anyway), but by example.

"Sometimes my older children tell me stories."

Never underestimate fiction. When children identify with the fictional protagonist, they unconsciously adopt the character's attitudes, for better or worse. Is this a cynical protagonist? The reader will unconsciously share that cynicism.

Morally upright? The child will blot up that mind-set. Children are learning whenever they read or hear "fluff."

Also, there is no such thing as fluff.

Kids also identify with Dad himself; in an abstract way, even girls do. Kids identify not with his maleness as such but with the spiritual and ethical person that he is.

The Twenty-Four-Hour Message Dad Sends

"It's so sad, the number of people out there who have an unhealthy fear of their father," Frank Minirth says. "It has a very negative impact on their lives, and especially on their attitude toward God. They have a skewed image of God as only a wrathful, angry, hostile God. Their God is a person they want to avoid. And that's not accurate. He loves us."

A young woman we know taught Sunday school in an inner-city mission project. "In the projects," she says, "when you talk to the kids, you never refer to God as father. Because with these inner-city kids, father is likely to bring up thoughts of the man who left me, the man who beats me, who beats my mother. The kids have so many negative images of fathers. So we always refer to God as a best friend. Best friend. The kids know what that is. It's a positive concept. We start there and work into God's other attributes."

Miles's father Arnold was, like it or not, teaching Miles about God. Miles had in fact screwed up royally. His misdeed would stay with him forever. But so would his father's blind reaction to it. The greatest impact is that the father's behavior is shaping the son's future behavior. Miles was being shown how not to be a father. Unfortunately, he was learning to do it that way.

What About You?

"Maybe you out there had a horrible father." Brian Newman addressed a group of fathers at a recent retreat. "That may well affect your relationship with God. It may be wise for you to first think of God as a best friend. Approach Him as best friend. That's not untruth; best friend is one of His key attributes, solidly rooted in Scripture. That may open the door to a deeper relationship between yourself and God, if you can see God as a father secondarily."

1. When I was a kid, I remember my dad as being:

_____ Angry all the time.

_____ Angry rarely.

_____ The swooping eagle we were talking about.

_____ Easy to be with.

_____ Fearsome.

_____ A "marshmallow."

_____ Other _____

2. I see God as being:

_____ Angry and ready to swoop.

_____ Friendly and caring.

_____ Approachable.

_____ Distant.

_____ Other _____

Comparing 1 and 2, you'll probably see similarities. But take this little exercise two steps further. First, consider how much more than your father God must be. What do you wish your own father had been? Easier to get close to? Angrier when you deserved it? Spend a while to transfer that wish list over to your concept of God. He's probably like that, too, you know.

Second, decide how you want your children to see God. As your father shaped your view of God, so shall you shape your children's. Think about how much of that concept you are showing them as their earthly father.

_____ An angry, disciplining God.

_____ A gentle, affectionate God.

_____ A wise, protective guide.

_____ A just judge of behavior.

_____ A good provider.

_____ A loving mentor.
_____ Other _____

When Brian Newman engages in lighthearted and enthusiastic Scripture memorization and includes his preschooler, Rachel, he is teaching her more than Scripture. Rachel indirectly blots up his own confidence in Scripture and his desire to know. "There is such a hunger for God in children," he observes. When Daddy hungers too, it validates the child's interest as nothing else can.

On that subject, Paul Warren sits back and ponders some of the attitudes he finds in his clientele—attitudes that cause more harm than good.

"Dad does well to avoid precepts and theories that limit who God is," he begins. "You get fathers shirking their responsibility to lead and teach their children by saying, 'God is inside all of us'; meaning, 'the kid doesn't need me to find God.' It's untrue, a false hope. 'Hope not in yourself.'

"I also hear the 'angry cop in the sky' description of God. Toe Daddy's mark or God will get you. Fathers may emphasize one side of God only, depending on how it serves Dad's needs. All mercy and no justice, for example, or harsh discipline, no love."

The bottom line Dad must always remember is that children's concepts of God invariably start with the patterns they see in their earthly father.

Dad's kids will blot up his attitudes and assumptions from the very beginning. For that reason, Dad reading God's Word for his own sake, his own good pleasure, is important. For the kids to want to grow spiritually, Dad must model the spirit of growth as a priority. He has to be seen seeking God in His Word. Paul Warren clarifies that. "Seeking God's face rather than His power.

"To teach children the ideal attitude, which is a love for God and God's Word, Dad should be seen enjoying God's Word for what it is—a love letter, a beautiful piece, rather than a hammer to beat kids over the head with. Taking pleasure in God and His Word is the key.

"Here the father takes the lead by believing he can get to know God by studying His Word. He knows he won't get to know God by watching trees. He sure won't get to know God watching TV. He will know the person God by reading His love letter."

Paul Warren hesitates only a moment before airing one of his pet peeves. "That peeve," he says, "is the attitude of some fathers—fathers and mothers both, actually—that somehow 'I can understand and control God.' Mason illustrated that."

Mason, a graduate of a two-year Bible school, went on to take correspondence courses in a variety of theological subjects. Down deep inside, Mason firmly believed that if you just study hard enough in God's Word, you can understand God and thereby, somehow, manipulate Him.

"Don't try to understand God," says Paul Warren, frustrated. "Seek to know God! Here it is again: Relationships come first. Dad must have a relationship with God, not just knowledge about God, if he would lead his kids to God.

"So many good Christian fathers I meet in counsel know the Word of God but they don't know God. This turns kids off immediately. Children of pastors, even, talk about their fathers being so involved in Bible study, but the men don't know their kids. I believe the men already think they can control their kids. Now they want to control God by understanding Him. They are serving the misconception that if you just know every aspect of a thing you can control it. Not with God, you can't."

All this is well and good, but Dad cannot assume his leadership role and fulfil it well so long as he is alone in his efforts. Men need the companionship and support of other men, and they need that support in ways somewhat different from women's needs. They have to recharge their batteries. Dad can't do it in a vacuum.

The Gender Gap

Charles Mayer pulled his sweats on over his volleyball shorts and got his sneakers out of the closet.

His wife, Meghan, watched him and sneered, "This is Tuesday, so it must be Bible study again, right?"

Charles couldn't quite figure out if he were amused or annoyed by Meghan's sarcasm every Tuesday as he headed out the door to play a few games with his buddies. He pointed to the ceiling and intoned soberly, "I am called to serve!" He sent a volleyball air serve over the air net.

"Cute." She turned on her heel and stalked off into the living room. He walked outside and grabbed his ten-speed without giving Meghan her usual kiss good-bye.

"Women underestimate the importance of men to have male time together," says Brian Newman. "The wives say, 'Oh, they're just going to play football, or basketball, or something.' But you see, that's when men talk about what's going on in their lives. That's their forum.

"Men need other men spiritually, to encourage and support them. Men have gotten away from it, though. More and more these days wives are pushing spiritual issues, and children need spiritual guidance, and the men frankly feel somewhat threatened. A woman can't fill that need for spiritual support. That's why men should be supporting men."

When Charles arrived at the grade school gym, sides were already forming up. Eight on one team and seven on the other was close enough to even. Charles stripped his sweats and took an open position at the net.

In the space of ten minutes, Charles and his cronies fell into the rhythm of the game, needled and cajoled each other, found out who was getting divorced, and made a few comments about things best left unmentioned.

Then Hal came in, evening the sides up to eight each. But his wife came too to watch the games from the bleachers, and the conversation—and bonding—froze. It thawed somewhat, eventually—everyone there knew Hal's wife was a good sport—but it wasn't quite the same. The atmosphere completely changed.

In an all-male group outside work or home, men can talk about things they can't discuss anywhere else. They can let down their guard a little and display vulnerability. In an office or work setting, a promotion, possibly even a distant promotion, might be at stake. In the home, their role as protector keeps that guard up, that mask of invulnerability.

Brian explains, "When women are present, men are naturally more reserved. And the more controlled the situation, the more reserved they get. That's just how it is. Men learn better and speak up better when they're to themselves. If you take the women out of it, the men get more involved. Men need to be with men." He shrugs. "Try it and see. You'll be amazed."

Moreover, men's study groups do not take the same direction women's Bible study groups take; neither do they use the same methods of study. Women tend to be more prone to relationship. Whether this is nature or nurture is moot. In group studies, the rule seems to hold. Men do not approach study to the same emotional and relational degree that women do, but they traditionally do better in other areas, such as cold logic and fact-finding. (This dependence on logic hinders rather than helps most men's spiritual growth. Jesus wants you to come to Him like a little child, not like Einstein.)

"In many families," Brian Newman suggests, "the husbands are not as strong in the faith as their wives. A better way to say it is that they're not as strong in the same areas of the faith as their wives are. Interests and strengths differ between men and women. So in this gray area of spiritual training, men can perceive that their wives are more mature in certain ways, and that's threatening. Because here's the wife pushing for her husband to be the spiritual leader the way she wants to be led. Some interesting research shows men want to grow in these areas they're traditionally weak in, but they're scared to go after it.

"That's not sexist, and I repeat that whether it's nature or nurture doesn't matter. It's the way it is. Women find it easier to submit to God's authority. To simply accept. Too, women tend more to right-brain inclusive thinking, and men to left-brain linear thinking. Jesus says 'come as a little child,' because kids fit under authority naturally and comfortably. Then there's Dad, wondering why he's questioning the tenets, always going back to the Bible. It's because he is approaching the faith in a different way, and he too often feels defensive about it."

Paul Warren expands on that theme. "There are two reasons we lose young males in church: One has to do with the way males in the presence of females change their behavior somewhat, especially in controlled settings. You find boys in classes with girls and women, and they're not on the same wavelength. Particularly in the early teens, boys and girls just do not think alike.

"The second reason is that churches don't treat sex as a spiritual thing. And yet, it looms enormous in a boy's life. It seems to him as though everyone ignores it. Besides, here you have, almost always, a woman teacher who says to love Jesus. That's confusing, even repugnant, to a boy who is just learning about his sexuality and still isn't comfortable with it. And sexuality is never addressed in any other context. That's not comfortable either. Kids who aren't comfortable in a setting are not going to cheerfully keep returning to that setting. Hardly anybody would."

Closing the Gender Gap

The gender gap, as men and women struggle together to find their unique niches in God's plan, is fundamentally a relationship gap. Fathers can close it; or at least narrow it to the point where it's jumpable; by taking several steps as spiritual leaders.

• Build Relationships with Men

If dads cannot lead their kids spiritually in a vacuum, the logical first step is to ease the vacuum.

"Men's breakfasts?" Meghan Mayer asked, and the look of doubt was still there.

"We hope it's more than just men's breakfasts," we would reply, "but it's as good a place as any to start." Use that focal point to build a solid system of male relationships. Too often churches, if they do anything at all, offer only episodic events.

The churches who maintain the most spiritually valuable groups for fathers emphasize challenge and accomplishment. They may set up domestic or overseas mission trips in which their men build schools, churches, or homes. One church singles out two dozen men in the spring and sets them up as coaches for a community street hockey league. The teams draw a few church kids and a lot of unchurched kids for games and special "messages" emphasizing biblical principles. Fathers support fathers, and the kids receive eternal benefit.

One southern California church features "contacts for men." The groups meet weekly, anywhere they feel comfortable, from donut shops to firing ranges, at any time of the twenty-four-hour day. A local paper recently featured a group of five men who rise at 4:30 each Thursday morning. They meet by prearrangement at a diner or restaurant for breakfast together. What do they tell each other at breakfast? Everything they can't tell anyone else. "Before I got together with these guys," complained a member, "I didn't even know there were two four-thirties in a day."

If you and a couple other men feel like getting together for any reason, any place, any time, create your own interest group. Pastors who watched men's fellowships, men's breakfasts, men's Bible studies, and men's retreats fizzle and fold discover that these unlabelled interest groups work. They'll work for you.

• Build a Relationship with a Friend

Men one-on-one with men. Today's men rarely think they have to have a best male friend. That's what women do. Men who find a trusted male friend stand amazed at the difference that friendship makes in their lives:

- Dad can confess weaknesses and even sins to a trusted male confidant when he does not feel right about telling his wife.
- Dad can bounce ideas and frustrations and victories and challenges off his friend and know he'll receive support and possibly even sound advice.
- Dad can goof off with this friend knowing the friend, too, is enjoying the companionship.
- With his friend, Dad can loosen up and joke and talk guy talk (no, ladies, it's not lascivious; it's just, well, it's guy talk). Just as he is listened to, Dad can listen, and thereby make a positive difference in his friend's life.
- Dad has someone to turn to when crisis and tragedy strike. Doesn't the wife assume that position? Not if the tragedy or crisis involves the family, as so many do. She's dealing with her own pain. And whereas both husband and wife can share that pain, talk, and cope, the woman can find solace with a female friend, the man with a male friend, beyond what they can offer each other.

Whether or not Dad's support group, as defined, is in place, he can begin immediately to build his most important bond as a father (second only to the bond he builds as husband): The relationship with his children.

• Build Relationships with Kids

The YMCA offers a program called Indian Princess. Men and their daughters, starting when the girls are in kindergarten, participate together. Brian Newman explains. "You and your daughter get 'Indian' names. You attend events with Indian themes, weave baskets, make moccasins, do strange things with feathers . . . ." Different clubs may attend or sponsor gatherings replete with tepees.

Meeting with other fathers and daughters builds important relationship bonds within and between the participants. A merit system similar to that of Scouting, with badges, adds the element of recognition school-aged youngsters need. Indian Guides is the father-son counterpart.

Christian Service Brigade is another father-son program like Scouts, providing a unique emphasis. Boys can work their way to the equivalent of Eagle Scout, Herald of Truth. They earn recognition for undertaking mission projects, reading books, and memorizing Scripture.

"Kudos to those programs," says Paul Warren, "but, why do we have to codify it into a formal program? Organize it? Dad should be doing this anyway."

Jack Brubaker, with the humongous sandbox project, was doing much the same sort of thing with his children. Nobody earned badges or camped out in a tepee. Their project was unlike anything the other groups usually take up. But it was theirs.

The actual activity is of limited importance, you see. The only real, lasting importance derives from the father-child bond.

• Build a Family Spiritual Identity

"In too many churches these days," Brian Newman complains, "we can't go to church as a family. The kids troop off to children's church, and we're disassembled as a family. In the original New Testament church, everyone was in it together. I think kids should be going with parents. Sunday school is different; that's primarily a learning situation. Worship is a group activity, corporate worship. And the whole body, kids and old people and everyone, should be raising their hearts and voices as one."

Drs. Newman, Warren, and Minirth all believe strongly in regular family devotions. A number of resources, monthly periodicals and such, are available for families looking for topical or textual material for devotions. Dad should take the lead, with everyone participating.

A warning here: Family devotion time is not the time to browbeat the kids into behavior compliance. It is a time to get better acquainted with God. And never, ever, ever should Dad be saying, "God told me to tell you to [get a haircut] [clean your room] [shape up]." Not even if Dad is certain God actually did say that.

"Dad has a hard row to hoe here," Paul Warren concludes. "There are several new books out addressing the spiritual lives of children. Unfortunately, they're usually by New Agers. They know the value of teaching kids early on, and Christians are not aggressive enough in it. This fresh sensitivity to spiritual things came out of New Age philosophies. It's sad that it didn't come out of the Christian movement.

"True, you should be aware of criticism by people who claim you're brainwashing your kids. Evaluate yourself; is there a nugget of truth in that? Are you too legalistic? Jamming the Bible down your kids' throats? That kind of approach won't wash. You're abusing religious training when you go to an extreme. The kids aren't learning about God then. They're learning to dislike Him. You must achieve balance between not enough spiritual instruction and overdoing it, if you would see your children truly grow in the faith. And the balance is different in every household. Seek it out diligently."

There, if ever there was one, is a call and a challenge to Dad, to make a difference.

To Think About

When I was growing up, I learned about God:

_____ In church.

_____ From my dad.

_____ From my mom.

_____ From friends and relatives, hit and miss.

_____ From an evangelist during a formal outreach.

_____ From an organized group such as Scouts, Young Life, youth clubs.

_____ On my own.

_____ Other _____

Thinking about how I learned what I know about God, I can see that of the above, these means would be very effective with my children:

_____

_____

_____

I doubt these means would make a significant impact:

_____

_____

_____

As a father, a grandfather, an uncle, I want to reach the children in my life by these means:

_____ Taking them to church.

_____ Talking to them one-on-one.

_____ Directing them to their mom for answers to questions.

_____ Exposing them to the friendships of others who are strong in the faith.

_____ Taking them to a formal evangelistic outreach program.

_____ Enrolling them in organized groups.

_____ Sending them to a Bible school.

_____ On my own.

_____ Other _____

If I were the only one in the world who could make a difference in my children's spiritual lives, I would emphasize this item above all others:

_____

Having thought about all this, I will take these specific steps to encourage my children's spiritual growth, starting now:

1. _____

2. _____

3. _____

—The Sexual Child—

As uncomfortable as a father might feel about leading his child's spiritual development, the discomfort is nothing compared to leading the sexual development. This, too, falls squarely on Dad's shoulders, and for good reason. Once he gets past his own doubts and misgivings, Dad can be a crackerjack guide through these dangerous wilds.

The birds and bees of a generation ago were simple compared to the things kids have to know these days. Let's explore the ways Dad can help.

EIGHT

Dad and His Kids' Sexuality

A t least for the moment, eleven-year-old Billy Morrow enjoyed ultimate status in the eyes of every other kid in his sixth grade class. Billy Morrow's dad, Cal, was being interviewed on TV, and there is absolutely nothing like a live television appearance to earn big points in grade school. Cal Morrow was an outfitter, leading hunting and tourist parties into the wilderness areas of New Mexico. Two weeks ago, he became a hero of sorts, although he claimed he was only doing his job.

The party he was escorting, four men and four women, were hunting in the high country when a freak snowstorm blew in. Cal managed to gather in seven of the eight and send them down the main trail to lower elevation and safety. One of the women he could not locate. He didn't find her until the blizzard was screaming around their ears. He knew the area well enough to remember an abandoned cabin, and the two managed to reach it before the worst of the storm dumped three feet of snow in the high country.

For three days no one knew whether Cal and the woman were alive or dead. Those were the worst three days of Billy Morrow's life. He had already lost his mom in a car accident. Now his dad was missing, possibly dead as well. His dad was on TV then, too. The TV news didn't let anyone forget about those two missing people. Billy's grandma started turning the news off as soon as it came on. "Enough already," she said.

Once the storm abated, search and rescue helicopters found Cal Morrow and Miss Beal safe in that cabin and choppered them out to civilization. A big Chinook helicopter with those dual rotors even got the snowbound horses out! And now, the two were being interviewed on the local afternoon TV newsmagazine.

Billy videotaped the whole program, of course. After the show, his grampa threw a happy evening barbecue when all the aunts and uncles and cousins came swooping in to celebrate both the safe return and the TV adventure. Afterward, in the darkness of late night, Billy hunkered down in front of the television set with the VCR's remote control.

His dad found him there. "Billy, I said 'off to bed' an hour ago. Go on! Scoot."

"Dad, this is important. Sit down here a minute, huh?" Billy was taking a chance. He knew that when Dad gave orders, either to kids or to horses, he expected them to be obeyed right now.

"What?"

Billy fast-forwarded to a part of the interview he had already memorized. "Here. The reporter's asking you and Miss Beal about being intimate. She says it's the question everyone's been dying to ask." Billy looked at his father. "Is she talking about sex?"

"Yeah . . . ."

"And here she's saying neither you nor Miss Beal is married, and you were all snowed in, in that cabin—and then she talks about how romantic that is . . . ."

"Yeah . . . ."

"So what does romantic mean exactly, and what exactly is 'it'?"

—Explaining Sex to Children—

"What exactly is 'it'?" Every parent gets the question sooner or later, and lately it's been sooner. Dad cringes. It's one thing to be a sexually sophisticated adult. But this tyke was in diapers a couple years ago. When precisely should the child be hearing about sexuality, and what on earth ought Dad to say?

When

In a 1939 magazine ad for feminine napkins, a fully grown young woman sits before a counselor's desk looking worried and frightened. A counselor old enough to have shaken hands with Moses sits behind the desk. The caption reads, "These girls must be told," and refers not to sex education itself but to information about menstruation.

That was 1939. These days, thanks to a world gone haywire, the young woman in front of the desk is probably in grade school.

She will probably begin menses a little earlier than girls did two generations ago. But that is not the biggest change. The biggest change is the child's very early exposure to sexual references, sexual dangers, and sexual temptations. These girls—and boys—indeed must be told, and the sooner the better.

"To a point." Paul Warren comes up against this question constantly. When is the right time? "Only to a point. You can get into all that stuff too early, when they're too young and can't understand yet. Most parents, though, wait too long."

Dad is already instructing his child about sexuality, and he will continue doing so, in three ways. He will model the male sexual role, as he has been. He is constantly modeling a man's appropriate attitude toward the female. He will teach directly by answering questions asked. And he will teach indirectly by making comments about the subject as the opportunity arises.

The child will receive the message from modeling throughout life, the vignettes imprinted as memories. Teaching will be almost all subliminal, below the conscious. Dad doesn't set out to teach sexuality when he makes a kind comment about his wife, or an unkind one. He doesn't realize he's teaching when he treats a woman courteously or mumbles and howls when he flattens his thumb with the hammer. The kid doesn't actively think, "So this is how a man behaves." The child is picking it all up below the conscious level.

Verbalized comments and answers, though, will pass from head to head, spoken and heard. The child's maturity and level of understanding will shape how much the child grasps of verbal discussion. The child's sexual development is one of several kinds of maturity that influence your teaching. Cognitive development—how much the child understands intellectually—is also important.

"So many fathers—nearly all of them—sit around waiting for some pronouncement from on high saying, 'Now is the time to tell your kids about sex.' The kid grows up, Mom handles it if it gets handled at all, and the opportunity is gone forever." Paul Warren wags his head sadly. "That is the worst field for sharing there is between fathers and kids, and it's far and away the most important."

—Imparting Deep Values—

The most important reason Dad should be his children's primary sex educator is that only by doing it himself will he know that the information is being delivered in a wholesome moral context. Where does God fit in? And what does He expect? Dad is the arbiter and shaper of his children's high moral standards. They will usually turn out to be much like his own, although they'll take a few exploratory bumps along the way. Standards of morality are the guiding light of sex education, and only the parents can handle it adequately.

Dad also needs to be an instructor regarding the dating game. After all, he's a veteran of the dating wars from his own youth. Paul Warren says, "Fathers sometimes back away from their responsibility in teaching boys about dating. They're always watching out for their daughter. They should be protective of their sons too. Boys need guidance just as much as girls.

"Talk to your sons about dating. What's proper, what's not proper. Everything from manners and etiquette to where they're going. I can't tell you how many horror stories I hear about dates of teens with nothing to do. They end up in disaster. Dad should be emphasizing, 'Have someplace to go and go there. Have something to do and do it.'"

Brian Newman recalls from his own youth the particularly helpful father of a friend. "He and my buddy would just sort of sit around and jaw about dating. I don't mean 'now don't do this and don't do that.' Fun stuff.

"Like, he said," and Brian drops his voice to a gravelly baritone, "'Now, Richard, what you do when you pick up your girl is bring a big bouquet of flowers. You pluck one flower out of the bouquet and hand it to your girl, and you hand the rest of the bouquet to her mom. Works like a champ. The girl's mom was planning to say 'Be back by nine' before you walked in that door. Now she's gonna say, "Come back anytime you like, dear."'"

There is more than a grain of wisdom in that ploy. Usually, it's the mothers who end up setting curfews and time limits. And all too often, the restrictions turn into a fight between Mom and her child. Better that Dad join Mom, that together they can set the limits and standards, and the reasons for them.

As crucially important as Dad is to his children's sexual awareness and education, he (and Mom) can't do it all. There are certain issues kids just won't discuss with their parents. Perhaps this is caused by the inborn taboo of incest. Whatever the source of it, kids don't talk as much as you think they ought, and they don't talk about everything. Kids, particularly older kids, maintain some distance from their parents.

All kids—every one of them, including the ones being taught in their home about the principles of moral sexual behavior—will seek information beyond the home. They will be seeking, in essence, ways to corroborate and support what the parents teach. When the parents fail to teach, the kids seek to fill a vacuum the parents never filled.

The most common external sources are pornography and street lore. A high percentage of what most boys learn they learn from porn. Girls learn from romance novels, the soaps, the talk shows. You can see that such sources can leave gaps in education.

An important external source of information that Dad can help his children find is a significant other adult. Dad needs to encourage the child's contact with a trusted adult, and facilitate it. A church youth leader, some teachers—it's a small and select list of candidates from which one or a few will be carefully chosen.

This is hard for Dad and Mom to do. It's so easy to become jealous and resentful of that other adult. Dad's going to have to put some heavy brakes on his own pride and self-esteem and let that other adult take over some of his child's education.

Paul Warren was involved in a weekend retreat for teens for several years. It was essentially a sex information weekend for high school and junior high kids. The retreat served several purposes, one of which was to bring trusted, knowledgeable adults into contact with the kids who needed their input.

"It was church-sponsored," he explains. "Friday night and all day Saturday. The girls were separate from the boys—in fact, different weekends for kids in early teens. We had a large number of healthy significant other adults from the church as well as a medical professional and a youth leader.

"An important element was a meeting with the parents first. We showed them what material would be presented. And at that meeting the parents learned who the adults were and got to know them.

"Another unique and important element was the letter. We asked the parents to write a letter to their kids. We would take the letters with us and pass them out to the kids during the weekend. A big part of the letter was basically to welcome their teens into adulthood, affirm how much they love them and were proud of them. We handed those letters out following group meetings at about the two-thirds mark.

The kids had to be separate to read them." His voice softens. "It was a very moving time."

At these retreats there was a lot of food, a lot of games, and strenuous activities. Interspersed, and in the quiet dark of evenings, kids and adults together talked about the mechanics of sex, maleness, femaleness, respect for your body, the value of restraint, and the dangers. The adults spoke with honesty; so did the kids.

"Question and answer sessions," he muses. "Once we got the questions started, they came in truckloads. Some were quite sophisticated and some weren't. There was everything from 'How do twins happen?' to "Can you get pregnant from a Coke bottle?'" Most of the questions, though, indicated the kids had a pretty clear understanding of the physical aspects of sex and were very interested in the emotional bonds and moral aspects.

Because sex education pivots around a healthy relationship with the parents, these retreats caused problems for a few of the youngsters. "Sex abuse," Paul Warren explains. "For some kids the session made life more difficult, because it brought sex abuse to the surface; it planted the seeds of awareness that it really is abuse."

Paul Warren believes the father should encourage his child's attendance at something of that sort to the point of insistence. Because the father needs it even more than the kid does.

"You see," he explains, "a major reason for the weekend is to draw our stereotypical parent, especially the father, out of the traditional role into the new position of shaping his child's sexuality.

"Father should be able to write to his daughter about her beauty and femaleness, to a son about Dad's pride in his growing maleness. The children benefit immensely, but Dad even more. The father may not be ready to accept that his kids are maturing, but it's there. It will march right past him ready or not. Not only will he miss out on the joy, he'll miss the opportunity to shape his child. It's one of the great responsibilities of being Dad.

"His kids will miss out some in their sex education because their dad wasn't part of it. And they'll ever and always have gaps in their ability to be comfortable with sex." Dr. Warren grimaces. "I see an incredible vacuum in kids, especially boys, between what they need and what they get from Dad."

What

"The flowering moments of the mind drop half their petals in our speech," said Oliver Wendell Holmes. Boy, don't they! Part of the problem is simply not knowing what to say.

The chart below summarizes approximately what sexual knowledge a child is capable of assimilating and when. Assimilation is keyed to the child's development, just as spiritual concepts were, and cannot really be rushed. Be advised that the fact that the child bandies certain sexually significant words about does not necessarily mean that the child understands what they are. Kids can pick up a lot of salacious language on the school bus and still be totally ignorant.

Children's Development

Age	Achievement	Dad's Role
Birth to 3	Identity apart from parents.	Model attitude he wants child to have toward females; model maleness.
3 to 5	Oedipal phenomenon and observation. Clarify sexual roles, identities.	Above, plus refrain from competing for affection.

Children's Development, *cont.*

Age	Achievement	Dad's Role
Early grades	"Hates" opposite sex; completing grasp of maleness and femaleness.	Answer questions as simply as possible. No detail. Don't volunteer.
Late grades	Beginning to look around (won't admit it). Starting to pick up innuendo in media. Noticing changes in body.	Time to be honest when confronted with pointed questions. Child should learn about disease, pregnancy.
Junior high	Aware of sex. Girls and boys sublimate sexual energy with grandiose daydreaming, violent activity.	Dad explains birds and bees, dangers; shares some of sexual feelings of this age and his teens. Answer questions fully.
High school	Girls intrigued by romantic thoughts and dreams. Boys feel physical desires. Sexes mutually attracted with desire to experiment.	Dad models chastity, fidelity. Enables other adults to provide kids with information, support. No prying; keep communication open, empathize.

We offer a few caveats here. Media events such as the recent disclosures of HIV infection by Magic Johnson, the child's personal experience of being threatened or accosted, or an incident in the family or neighborhood could force some volunteering of information. Withholding may be worse than explaining when children are frightened, traumatized, or confronted by a major mystery. The schedule can develop kinks.

Cal Morrow hit just such a kink. His son Billy, at age eleven, was pushing the issue. Billy wanted to know what "it" was and what romance is all about. Cal was sorely tempted to just brush the kid off for a few more years. The temptation is common.

Paul Warren is just as tempted. "I talk about sex with kids all the time," he says. "Now here's my son, eight years old, and I'm not sure I want Matt to know this. I had to step up my existing plan by several years because kids are talking about it in grade school. They know about AIDS, the street lore about how you get it. You'd be surprised how many know a little bit about prostitutes. As a father, I find the whole thing really difficult.

"Dad must give health information in grade school because the issue's been forced now by the Magic Johnson implication."

Cal didn't succumb to temptation either. Billy had just come through a troubling, trying experience—the possible loss of his dad, his only remaining parent. In fact, Billy's not knowing for three days was probably worse than Cal being holed up in a cabin with a boring woman. Probably.

And these weren't casual questions asked in passing. Billy was intent to know. He was ripe for the information. With extreme reluctance, Cal put his own reticence aside.

Cal scooped Billy into his lap, took over the remote, and turned the VCR off. "Okay, kid," he commenced. "I'll give you the whole bale of hay, instead of one piece of straw at a time."

Billy snuggled in against him. "What's sex?"

"You know how a man is shaped. His male parts. A woman is, uh, shaped, uh . . . ." This was going to be harder than he thought. "Okay, you plug the toaster in, right? The plug is the male end and the socket is the female. Shaped like the plug only outside in. In fact, plumbers refer to male couplings and female couplings."

"Sure." Billy seemed not the least nonplussed. "Same thing with cable connections on a computer. Male connections and female connections. The pins."

"Right." Cal would not have thought of computers. "The word *intercourse*, or *sex*, or *copulation*, means the man and woman join their anatomy just the way a toaster plugs in." He found himself trying to keep it as faceless and technical as possible.

"So when someone says something about going to bed with someone, they don't mean just sleeping in the same bed like me and Garth at Grandma's. They're talking about sex. Intercourse."

"Almost always."

Silence.

Cal fervently wished Billy were falling asleep. He knew better. Splack this kid's mind up against a new idea and it stuck like Velcro™.

At length Billy spoke. "Okay. Girls are built to do it. But how can two guys . . . ? Kids talk about homosexuals. Or two girls. Jake in Mrs. Eaton's class says two girls can do it. I mean, they just aren't built that way."

"Two girls? The word's *lesbian*. That's . . . ."

"Oh. So that's what that means."

"Yeah. And how two women get together is beyond me. I haven't the foggiest. Two guys, they use what's available. Mouth or anus."

That opened the door on oral and anal sex, a door Cal would fervently have wished remained closed. But it was wide open now, so he used it. He was giving Billy the whole bale, and the kid did seem to understand the theory, which is all Cal wanted.

Billy was young, but not too young. He could comprehend. Were he not really getting any of the details, Cal would have been wise to postpone the talk a year or two.

By the age of fourteen or so, then, today's kid should know about these things specifically, and Dad is by far the best source of information on them:

- Exactly what the physical act of love is. They should know the terminology, as Billy learned. Use the words *penis* and *vagina*. You're not spreading lascivious gossip, you're imparting information. This is the appropriate time for correct terminology.
- What oral and anal sex are. Unfortunately, the child is going to be exposed to the terms and a lot of innuendo, no matter how sheltering you try to be. Best that it come from you.
- Precisely how genital herpes, HIV (the virus that causes AIDS), syphilis, gonorrhea, and other diseases are transmitted, their symptoms, and what those diseases do to the human body.

"This almost certainly means Dad is going to have to do some reading," Dr. Minirth advises. "Especially regarding HIV and sexually transmitted diseases. There's a lot of misinformation out there among the adults too. And this is so important: When he doesn't know the answer, he must be able to say, 'I'll get back to you on that,' and then do it. Not a back gate to get out of discussing it at all. No, no! But not Mr. Know-It-All, either, perpetuating false information."

- The several effects and purposes of God-given sex; that is, that it was ordained for marriage. It bonds a couple as nothing else can and is a primary uniting factor in a lasting marriage—a very good thing. You don't want to be negative; just factual.

The stereotypical dad, if he contributes to his children's sex education at all, tends to give only information about the bad part. What's immoral. What's wrong. What's dangerous. What's going to get you in trouble. It's a sort of corollary to the swooping eagle, wherein Dad sees himself only as the corrections officer.

Today's dad, wisely, will step beyond that stereotype. Certainly he will issue the standard warnings and describe the dire consequences, but sexuality is healthy. It's a God-given gift, a part of the child from birth on. It's necessary. It's enjoyable in the marriage bond. Kids have to hear these positive things too, and Dad is the one to deliver that very upbeat message.

"Dad?" Billy's voice sounded distant. Either he was absorbed in the topic or getting sleepy. "Did you?"

"Did I what?"

"You and Miss Beal. Did you?"

Cal thought about all the different ways he could respond. He could moralize, or lie, or tell the truth, or evade the question. Or, he could work in one more lesson a son ought to know. "I'm not going to say."

"Aw, come on, Dad!"

"No, I'm not. It's the business of three people and only three. Me, the lady, and my Lord. Nobody else. Not even you."

"That's what you told the lady on TV."

"It's important, Billy. God knows what you're thinking and everything you do. Sooner or later you have to answer to Him. So He's involved.

"The girl is certainly involved. You're going to hear a lot of guy talk in the rest rooms and lockers. Guys boasting about who all they've laid, and the latest girl they went all the way with. If you're wise, you won't discuss any of it. Not a word. Especially since almost everything you'll hear is lies. Guys don't tell the truth, but they damage a lot of girls' reputations."

"Really?"

"Trust me on that."

The little head bobbed against Cal's shoulder, nodding. The voice purred knowingly, "I bet you didn't."

Over an hour had passed. Usually, Billy's attention span was like a butterfly tasting daisies. Flit, flit, flit. Cal assumed the discussion was about over.

Fat chance. "Dad? What's romance?"

And Cal had to admit, "I don't know. I don't get into romance too much, but women do. Girls love it. The interviewer was a woman, you noticed. I don't think a man would have brought it up that way." He snorted. "Terribly romantic, huh?"

Two people snowbound. But the interviewer didn't split wood for hours a day to force-feed a wood stove built from a fifty-five-gallon drum, trying to jack temperatures to above freezing in that abandoned cabin. She didn't try to build meals out of outdated, frozen cans of soup and beans they happened to find. She didn't have to melt snow for drinking water. She didn't spend a whole day trying to keep the path to the privy cleared enough to use. She didn't go without a toothbrush for seventy-two hours.

Cal thought about it awhile. "I guess two people alone, no chance they'll be interrupted, the only two people in the world, you know? That could be romantic. Women seem to like soft light, gentle music . . . ."

"What's 'soft light' mean?"

"It means, not much of it. Candles. That kind of thing. We used a kerosene lamp in the cabin. That'd be soft light."

They talked about embracing and holding hands, about things you can learn about romance from pictures in magazine ads.

"One way to find out what a girl would like that's romantic is just ask her," Cal suggested. "'What do you want to do? Where do you think would be a romantic place to go?'"

And as a part of him paid attention to that conversation, another part of him felt the sensation of his son curled up in his lap, the way Billy used to when he was five. And Cal revelled in the closeness, the weight and warmth of that little body snuggled in against him. He listened to the soprano voice, knowing the day would soon arrive when the voice would turn tenor, or maybe even baritone like his own, and there would be no more snuggling.

Talking to Sons and Daughters

Cal was treading on uncertain ground as he talked about a topic he had little interest in—romance. Were Billy a daughter, he would have had to get into a lot more depth, for boys and girls view sexuality so differently.

As Cal thought about it, he concluded that romance is far more than soft lights and music and two people alone. It's mutual devotion. Emotional intimacy and caring. Doing extra little things for each other. Hugging. Holding hands.

"In fact," he continued, "romance and sex aren't the same thing at all."

"Huh?" Billy didn't sound like he wanted to be bothered.

"Sex and romance. Each one makes the other seem nicer, better. But you can have one without the other." Yes, that's what he would have told a daughter. **Seek romance. Romance is a girl's delight. But sex is reserved for the marriage bed.**

Like Cal, today's dad will also recognize the profound difference between girls and boys as they mature sexually, and he will respond to it. Dad knows that girls are much more romantic and relational in their sexuality than are boys. They dream of knights on white horses, guys who call and hold them in their arms. They're not so much touching-oriented as they are embracing-oriented. And Dad knows from his own growing-up days that boys are innately physical, tangible, and visually oriented. Put bluntly, guys love to look and touch. To them, romance is not a big deal.

As Billy gets older, Cal can help him come to terms with his sexuality in three uniquely male ways.

1. Citing his own experience as a teen, Cal can acknowledge his son's hormonal urges. That acknowledgement is a powerful release. It verifies in Billy's mind that he's not some freak with weird, dark desires. He's normal. Only Cal can do that verification well by virtue of his role as All Males.
2. He can encourage Billy (without harping on it!) to maintain appropriate moral standards.

    "I know how it is, and I know how hard it is to keep your hands off a girl when you're alone with her. But a good man does what's right, not what his body yells for."

3. He can provide suggestions and guidelines regarding dating. Guys, especially early teens, are scared to death of dating—of this whole boy-girl business. Much as they want to be around girls, and talk to them, and relate to them, they intensely fear messing up. Being laughed at is about the worst nightmare a young teen can dream up. Dad can suggest places to go, things to do, even things to talk about.

Dad would be wise to coach his son on appropriate manners on dates. "You don't sit in the car and honk the horn. You go to the door and escort her to the car. Don't tell me it's old-fashioned. You want to impress her and her folks? That's the way."

"My dad was really old-fashioned," a friend named Tony told us. "He insisted that if we, his sons, loved a woman enough to marry her, we could ask her father for her hand. Man, I was floored. That went out with horses and buggies! So my brother drove clear over to Midland to his girl's parents' house before he proposed to her. Asked her dad. He said her dad was floored too.

"Then when I got serious with Cathy, I figured, okay, if Dad wants me to, I'll do it. Boy, was I nervous! But when I asked to marry his daughter, Cathy's dad wept. Tears! He gave us his blessing. It's really the way to start a marriage out!"

Whether Dad is old-fashioned or up-to-the-minute, his guidance is invaluable. His guidance is invaluable to his daughters just as much, but because he has not experienced what she is experiencing, his guidance will take other turns.

He will certainly advise her on dating etiquette. But there's much more. As we build a greater body of information about how children develop psychologically and sexually, we are finding that fathers have more of an impact on girls' attitudes about femaleness, sexuality, and themselves than mothers do. What do you do to give your daughter the best possible boost in those directions?

• **Be a Good Model.**

You would think this goes without saying. We say it because fathers don't think about the model they are providing. If you respond affirmatively to these statements, you're perfect:

_____ I never speak disparagingly of women in general (revealing an attitude of disdain, fear, or anger).

_____ I never speak disparagingly about my wife.

_____ I never speak disparagingly of my daughter(s), implying things such as "You're a loser," "You're not lovable," "You're not desirable," "You leave much to be desired."

_____ I never speak disparagingly about my own sex, putting neither men nor myself down.

_____ My daughter has visited my place of work.

_____ I have presented my daughter (of any age) to coworkers and friends.

_____ My daughter and I do things together once every two weeks or (preferably) more often (watching TV, etc., doesn't count).

_____ I know my daughter's birthday and age.

_____ I carry at least one picture of my daughter.

_____ I've been to my daughter's school and met her teacher.

_____ I know at least three of my daughter's friends by name.

_____ I can list at least three of my daughter's favorite things (foods, colors, activities, movies, people, and such).

_____ I have expressed fatherly affection for her today by (a hug, saying so, affirming her, praise . . .)

_____

_____ At this moment, my daughter's career choice is

_____

_____ If she were to fulfil my dream for her, her career would be as a _____

These questions do two things. For one, they reflect how well you are conveying respect for the uniqueness of the sexes and for your daughter specifically. They reflect how much esteem in which you hold your child.

[Know her self-esteem will mirror your feelings about her exactly.

If you don't appreciate her much, she won't like herself. If you hold her in high regard, she'll feel great about herself. That's the way it is, Dad. Always.

The questions also represent the nuts and bolts of how you go about developing a strong relationship with your daughter. Over and over, we and other writers in the field all say, "Get involved with your daughters/kids." You have to know your child well to be able to answer these questions easily. If you can't answer them knowledgeably and confidently, ask her for the answers. Talk about the subjects these questions represent. Go do some of the activities she says she likes (she's out to please you, so be careful she's not listing activities she thinks you like; get her preferences).

If it's something that you think will bore you (such as sitting in the mall), talk to her while you're both doing it and find out why she likes it. Look for elements of it, whatever it is, that appeal to you. Who knows? Maybe the mall is displaying classic Corvairs this weekend or something.

The bottom line of your investment in your children, the involvement, means talking, listening, and doing. These three things will do more for your daughter than all the lecturing and disciplining and browbeating in the world.

"Yes," you insist, "but sex ed from sitting in the mall? Going to the ball game?"

"Sure," we affirm. Consider yourself a laboratory of teaching about sexuality, on parade at all times. She's learning what maleness is all about from you. And when a male (that's you) takes an interest in her and her interests, that male (you!) conveys a powerful, powerful message: "You are desirable!" (This desirability need not be sexual, not even as she bounces through her teens. Desirability extends far beyond mere sexual connotations.) She absorbs the message, "I am important because this male takes interest in me, and he is All Males." "Daddy doesn't just say he loves me. He is showing me he loves me! Therefore I am lovable!"

The exclamation points are intentional. These are strong messages in a daughter's heart. She doesn't think about them consciously, remember, and were you to ask her, she wouldn't be able to articulate them. They're there, working their magic to build her up, all the same.

The Importance of Being Dad

"I don't want to be an alarmist here, but neither do I want to whitewash the problems that can occur when Dad disavows his responsibilities." Paul Warren speaks from the perspective of a man whose job it is to deal with the problems and the miseries of kids who can't handle early adolescence. "When fathers don't appropriately teach their daughters about sex and sexuality, and especially fail to develop a good father-daughter relationship with their girls— when that doesn't happen—you can get a girl who seeks physical sexual relationships with guys at a very early age."

Consider the case of a man we'll call Grant. Grant had his own issues to deal with, and frankly, he didn't deal with them well. A rageaholic who could boil over in angry diatribes for little or no reason at all, he spent his life storming at his wife and kids.

He shaped and disciplined his daughter Penny by giving her rules, harsh limits, and lectures, all in anger. His only relationship with her was as the stern disciplinarian and overseer. No embracing, no holding, no snuggling, no smiles.

When his wife finally threatened to leave, Grant entered therapy. He made changes, excellent, healthy changes. Call them giant steps as he came face to face with the issues of his past. His healthy new beginning saved his marriage but not his daughter. She had passed the window of opportunity, puberty, by the time he got his act together.

Penny at the age of fourteen had known, literally, dozens of lovers. Starved for male attention, she tried to alleviate her hunger by physically seducing males all around her. One guy after another. There was never an emotional basis for her romantic involvements; in fact, they were never all that romantic. And none of them met her need.

She's older now. Penny never did understand that a physical relationship can never meet her emotional need. She has no background of healthy male attention, which would best be provided by a father-daughter relationship. Now she's afraid of emotional involvement with men, and she can't talk herself out of that fear. It runs deeper than words can reach.

Grant today is working hard to build a relationship with his baby, Penny's sister, who's just entering sixth grade. The younger girl has not yet begun to blossom, and Grant's own recovery is progressing well. The future looks good, at last.

"As your child grows," says Brian Newman, "you must read and talk to others who know. As this process of getting the children through their teens gets more and more complex, today's fathers need support. With tiny kids, you could bluff your way through. Not now."

Says Paul Warren, "Dad doesn't sit down just one time with a talk about birds and bees and that's it, either. He should be planning over a period of time—have a plan for giving his child healthy, specific information on sexuality."

Your average dad, worried by now that he might actually have to carry through with this, will probably think, "Peachy, just peachy. I want my kids to stay clean, but I'm supposed to give them a how-to course on intercourse. Glamorize it. No way!"

Not at all. You can avoid much of the enticing nature by keeping the discussion of physical functions clinical and sort of building "it pays to wait" into discussions of emotional impact. And you can keep it clinical by neither glamorizing nor disparaging the sexual union.

Things to Think About

Paul Warren suggests having a sex-ed plan in mind, and then adjusting it as needed. Let's put together a working plan.

If your children are young, you need such a plan. If your children are already well into their teens or even beyond, you may feel it's too late. Not at all. You might skip some of the preliminaries, but there is still wisdom you can offer. Too, you may well be called upon as the significant other adult in a child's life, the person that child turns to beyond his or her own dad and mom. A plan can be a very handy thing to have then too.

- **First, review your own experience.**

  I would characterize my own father as being:

  _____ Moody.

  _____ Bright and open.

  _____ Comfortable with his own sexuality.

  _____ Uncomfortable with his masculinity.

  _____ A man you can hug.

  _____ Able to talk about sexual feelings.

  _____ Unable to discuss sexual feelings.

  I first became aware of the facts of life around the age of _____.

  I learned them from:

  _____ Dad

  _____ Mom

  _____ A significant other adult

_____ Friends
_____ Books or magazines
_____ Movies and videos
_____ Trial and error
_____ Other _____

• **What do you derive from that experience?**

Relearning the facts of life:

_____ It worked for me; it can work for my kid.
_____ I wouldn't recommend it for anybody.
_____ Other _____

I learned:

_____ Pretty good stuff.
_____ A lot of misinformation.
_____ Other _____

Relearning about masculinity from Dad I felt:

_____ Good.
_____ Inadequate.
_____ Rotten and stupid.
_____ Other _____
_____ This is the kind of man I want my kids to know as a father.
_____ This is not the kind of fathering I want my kids to know.

To conform more to the man I want to be, I should make the following adjustments in myself and my relations toward my children: _____
_____

• **Now, decide what you want for your children.**

Based on my own experience, I would like my kids to know:

By the age of _____ about experimentation and activities to avoid;

By the age of _____ about the actual act itself;

By the age of _____ about romance, what turns people on;

By the age of _____ about pregnancy and available birth control methods, with discussion about whether or not to consider them;

By the age of _____ about diseases and their common modes of transmission;

By the age of _____ about the celebrations and positive aspects of sexuality in human beings;

By the age of _____ about God's intent for the man-woman relationship as I see it.

That's just wishing. To be practical, based on what I read in the papers and hear from neighbors, my kids ought to know:

By the age of _____ about experimentation and activities to avoid;

By the age of _____ about the actual act itself;

By the age of _____ about romance, what turns people on;

By the age of _____ about pregnancy and available birth control methods, with discussion about whether or not to consider them;

By the age of _____ about diseases and their common modes of transmission;

By the age of _____ about the celebrations and positive aspects of sexuality in human beings.

If the opportunity does not present itself spontaneously, or dictate its own time (as when Cal seized the occasion to talk to Billy, and Paul Warren decided to move his plan forward), I will create this opportunity:

_____ An extended activity such as a weekend fishing trip.

_____ A dinner out, a drive in the country, other special occasion.

_____ A quiet evening at home.

_____ Other _____

Develop a plan of when and where and how for each of your children individually. Where will you keep that information to access it as you need it?

Cal Morrow thought of all the things he was—a lay reader and deacon in his church, a good trail guide, an excellent wrangler, a pretty fair camp cook, a softball outfielder, an amateur auto mechanic, a farrier at times, a gunsmith and reloader, an occasional cartoonist, and a father. And of all those various things, nothing—not even his work for Jesus Christ in the church—was more rewarding, more satisfying, than being Dad.

Had Cal thought more about it, he might have realized that being Dad was his most important work for Jesus Christ.

—Here Come de Teens!—

Jack Brubaker, the guy who copped a real winner with that sandbox thing, not to mention the family devotional times he maintained on a regular basis, still had problems. He felt out of control much of the time, as his two older kids in particular bounced off the walls. It seemed they were bouncing right out of his life. How do you be a father to kids who consider themselves past fathering? The teen years are fraught with change and adjustment worth a careful look.

NINE

The Headlong Plunge
into Early Adolescence

Arnold talked about his Miles. "The teen years. I hate 'em. Miles was manageable up until he turned twelve, and whoomph!"

"All elbows and appetite?" Dr. Warren nodded.

Arnold chuckled. "That, too. Clumsy as an ox on ice skates." It was the first time since Paul Warren met him that Arnold had ever smiled. The smile faded quickly. "It was as if he woke up one morning with a different kid inside him."

"He did."

Arnold frowned.

"As they enter puberty, children change so utterly that they are essentially new. What they become depends in large part upon what they were, and upon the relationships that shaped them to this point. But that makes the changes in them no less profound."

Great. Just as you're finally getting a handle on your grade schooler, the kid turns from Jekyll to Hyde? Let's take a closer look.

—The Changes—

Most parents are aware of the physical changes children experience as they enter puberty around age twelve or so. Girls "blossom." Guys "sprout." Secondary sexual characteristics such as girls' breasts and boys' beards, hair on legs and armpits, shape shifts, and shape changes in the genitalia can emerge rather slowly or pop out overnight.

And they get hungry! A girl developing from child to woman will eat half again what she normally does. But an active boy spurting into manhood will put away over 4,000 calories a day. For comparison, a normal day of meals—breakfast, lunch, dinner, and maybe dessert—provides about 1,800 to 2,000 calories.

When Dad complains, "That kid eats twice what I do!" he's right on the ticket.

Despite the huge fuel intake, the emergent adolescent's energy is channeled primarily into changing physically. The child seems lazy, sleeping more, loafing more, seemingly incapable of sustained effort, either operating at fever pitch or zonking out. It's not laziness *per se;* the child is simply burning all those calories unseen.

But those are just design alterations in the exterior package. The real child, the inner child, changes even more.

If Dad thinks he is unnerved by the overnight changes in his child, imagine how the child must feel. All the feelings, the fun stuff, the simplicity, the yearnings of yesterday just flew over the verandah rail. Pastimes that used to provide hours of satisfaction and delight seem boring. Emotional highs and lows the child used to roll with suddenly become insufferable. Random incidents—a pimple, a pop quiz—become crises.

Quite literally, words fail the child. The changes come on so rapidly the child cannot understand them, let alone articulate them. To the outsider listening to this child's speech, the kid has a mouth full of rubber bands and a room temperature IQ.

As they enter this growth spurt, kids find themselves unable to say what they mean.

The cry, "I hate you!", were it translated into its true meaning, would become, "I'm scared and you're not able to help."

"I don't want you to go to my game again, Dad!" most likely does not mean don't come to a game again but rather, "You embarrassed me, Dad."

Too often, Dad takes the surface words (which is only logical; that's what the kid said, right? and Dad is supposed to listen to his kid) and ignores the real meaning of this inarticulate age. It's frustrating for parent and child both. How can you tell what's really going on inside? You can't. You guess.

For example, as his daughter Dorie entered her mid-teens, a friend we'll call Carl found himself fighting with her more and more often. He would relax the rules a little now and then, as appropriate for a child growing up, but it was never enough to please her. She wanted more, always more. She wanted the moon.

Carl, a down-to-earth kind of guy who subcontracted as a plumber, didn't couch much nonsense. After a particularly nasty shouting match one evening, Carl exploded with, "All right! If you're such a hot ticket that you don't need the rules, you can just move out!"

To his consternation, she did. She stormed out. At eleven she finally phoned her mom, telling her not to call the cops. She wasn't lost or kidnapped. She had checked into a hotel downtown.

Carl also could use a few lessons in saying what you mean. But in the larger view, he missed the whole point. He took Dorie's anger personally. Her frustration was not so much at him, or even at his rules, but at her frightening new desire to be separate from the family she had grown up in. She lashed out blindly, and Carl, as the maker of the rules, got caught.

"Dad," we counsel fathers, "don't take it personally. Your child may or may not mean anything in the neighborhood of what is actually said. Developing responsibility for the words spoken, in fact, is a chore kids must master, and it takes them some time. It's one of the primary things we work on, communication in both parent and child, when families enter our counsel."

Changes just as pervasive occur as the child matures from early teens into midteens.

"There are adults in this world, so somebody's teen somewhere is outgrowing all this nonsense. There's hope, I suppose." Arnold stretched out in the armchair in Paul Warren's office and wearily studied the tops of his shoes. "You think Miles will survive this?" He looked up. "I guess the real question is, 'Will I?'"

Fortunately for all mankind, fathers and their children usually survive the trials of adolescence without actually murdering or mutilating each other. The kids make one more quantum leap rather late in their teens, from midteen to near-adult. Although individual growth schedules vary widely—indeed, extremely widely—as a general rule, early adolescence commences somewhere around age twelve or thirteen, during the fifth to seventh grade. Middle adolescence occurs, usually, somewhere around ages fourteen to sixteen, grades eight to ten. Finally (and blessedly, from the parents' viewpoint), kids from age seventeen on, juniors or seniors, ripen into creditable young adults. Yes, Arnold, there is hope.

We will examine the mid- to late-teens in Chapter Ten. Here in Nine, let us focus on that first big plunge, early adolescence.

Paul Warren has dealt with hundreds of troubled teens, kids from "nice" families who are having problems getting through these drastic changes of adolescence. "All teens want a relationship with their father," he affirms. "All. Every one."

Arnold snorted. "Well, you just met your first one who doesn't, then. Miles, he's close to his mom. Too close. But the only time he's interested in me is when he feels like fighting."

Paul Warren completed the point he was going to make. "And very rarely have I ever met teens who feel their fathers are open to it, girls or boys."

"To 'it,' you mean a friendship kind of relationship?"

Dr. Warren nodded.

"And you're looking straight at me."

"The issue seems to be more acute with fathers than with mothers."

Hostile Dependency

Think for a moment what's going on here. The burgeoning child/adult has one leg firmly planted in a childhood of little or no responsibility, and the other leg in adulthood, craving the full responsibility accrued to an adult.

Dad, in this situation, thinks he's going nuts. He also plays a crucial role. This is his cue to step in firmly, keeping in mind the child/adult's dual status of the moment, and make clear statements of expectations and of empathy.

He does this primarily by holding on to his relationship with his child, whatever stage the relationship is in, and improving it. The kids won't give him any help with the task. Kids in early adolescence feel the urge to break away from the family, and yet they are afraid of leaving the nurturing nest. There's an enormous tug-of-war going on inside.

It's the same point in time, remember, when they're discovering their perfect, godlike parents are fallible after all. They therefore often appear resistant to any involvement with their hopelessly inadequate mom and dad. They shun being with their parents as they desperately hunger for the contact.

Dad can help now, even if on the surface they resist his help. He can help by being with them. By empathizing (understanding the feelings from personal experience) or at least listening (understanding that the kids' feelings are not baseless), he can help his children figure out their emotional ups-and-downs.

By remembering his own feelings, Dad can cut through to clear, honest expectations. He's been there, regardless how dim the memories. These will form a solid guideline for directing the child's behavior, a beacon through the murky fog. "I expect this of you. You are capable of that. Let's let this ride a couple years. You're ready for that." Dad, of course, tailors expectations to the individual child.

This means changes in the way Dad works. Because he's not dealing with a little kid, this is a whole new ballgame; he needs whole new ways to handle his child.

—Dad's New Fathering Strategies—

As Dad could do certain things with and for his preschooler that were uniquely his province, so the dad of an adolescent takes on certain special roles. Ideally, he becomes the child's protector in a new and different dimension. And by building the relationship to a new level of communication, he can guide his child through the harrowing years of change. His wagon scout days are far from over yet.

The New Guide and Protector

"Protect? What's to protect?" Jack Brubaker, one of the world's brilliant air conditioning specialists, couldn't begin to get a line on where his seventeen-year-old Marla and fourteen-year-old John were coming from. "The kids are out 'til all hours. Arlene, my wife, might slap a curfew on them, and then they'll call from fifty miles away two minutes before they're scheduled to turn into a pumpkin. . . . I can't tag along after them and keep them out of trouble, Marla especially. It's hopeless."

Actually, Jack is on the right road.

A dad has to realize that his children are bound to grow away, and he cannot control every aspect of their lives and choices forever. Hopeless, no. Unrealistic, yes. Too, they mature at their own breakneck rate, ready-or-not. Dad doesn't have the luxury of guiding that maturation at a leisurely pace of his own choosing. He is under the tight constraints of keeping up with the rapid changes and perhaps, Lord willing, even anticipating them.

As the tables show, just at the time kids need more leeway, they tend to lose their balance and sense of moderation. Whatever wisdom they may have gathered as children all sails right out the window.

"I hear that." Jack Brubaker paused and leaned on the fender of his pickup, its dipstick still in his hand. "I can't understand Marla. We'll be getting along great and the next minute she's really freaked out. Like for instance, her nose. Now she's had her nose her whole life, right? Seventeen years, no gripes. One morning she wakes up and all of a sudden it's too long. Out of nowhere she's giving me this big spiel about how she can earn the money for a nose job, and it won't cost me a cent. I thought she was so sensible and then she comes up with something like that. It's scary." He rubbed the dipstick tip between his fingers. "Kind of dark. Guess I'll change it."

Brian Newman grinned. "So what shape nose is she getting?"

Jack's eyes narrowed. "A flat one, if she doesn't start thinking past the end of it." He wandered off to the garage for his filter wrench.

The Discipline V

Because, like Marla, kids this age skip about at giddy extremes, and get what might charitably be called unusual ideas, Dad has a hard time loosening up the reins. And yet, this is just the age at which he must.

To illustrate, Brian Newman stretches his arms up and out in a "V" shape that reaches toward the ceiling. "The child grows in the manner of a V. At birth, the narrow end, the child's world, doesn't extend beyond the door. As the baby becomes a toddler, that world expands. Grade school, another big expansion. And now in junior high and high school the child's world is getting as big as an adult's. As the child's horizons spread out in this expanding V, so must the discipline and guidance broaden."

Paul Warren nods. "Discipline now is much different from just controlling the child's behavior. By now, the child's conscience should be pretty well internalized. The kid knows right and wrong. Discipline is no longer teaching right and wrong so much as letting the child's boundaries widen out while the child has the safety of the home to fall back on."

Think of it as a wind-up clock. In fact, for this age, we might appropriately think of a cuckoo clock. Gravity, acting on the clock weights, provides the power to run both the hands and the little wooden cuckoo bird. You wind the weights upward and gravity draws them downward. The weights would plunge immediately to the floor as the hands spun crazily and the cuckoo hooted frenetically were it not for the escapement. The escapement, a trip-lever and a toothed wheel, lets the potential power out a tiny bit at a time. The hands turn at a measured rate determined by the pendulum; the bird sings its predictable songs.

Dad is the escapement on his teens' breakneck energy and their need to taste life. He puts the brakes on with a measured, disciplined, guiding hand. He lets the power out steadily, more and more, as time goes by.

In essence, that means the child must be allowed to experiment with life more. It is time for the child to be exposed to life as it is. Most important, the child must have the opportunity to try new things and quite possibly to fail in the attempts. This is the V at its widest. The reins are loosened and the child, still in the safety of home and parental influence, begins to taste life as it is.

Paul Warren cites a case early in his work, one of too many he has seen, in which the parents never widened the V beyond a certain narrow point. Their children, growing up, never watched *Bewitched* reruns because of the witch aspect. They were not allowed to watch shows that depicted divorced families. Sex and violence in any form were strictly proscribed. The kids went nowhere unchaperoned, did nothing unaccompanied (usually by the parents).

These were excellent rules for an impressionable child. They protected the young child in exactly the ways Frank Minirth so consistently recommends. Avoid exposing the children to traumatic memories and desensitizing images. But these particular parents maintained that tight control right through their children's high school years. Friends, pursuits, classes, choices—everything was monitored. Their V never widened out the least bit.

Proudly, they sent their oldest daughter off to a prestigious school, confident they had just raised the purest, most principled child in the country. Within a semester she was sunk deep in drugs and alcohol and experimenting with lesbianism. "What happened to our daughter?" they wailed, and considered suing the school.

What happened was that until the day they released her to go forth into the wide world of academe, they afforded their daughter no opportunity to make decisions for herself. She understood right and wrong well enough, but she had never had to choose between right and wrong. She knew the theory down pat, but she had no practice.

It's an inaccurate picture, but think of children having choice muscles just as they have physical muscles. Those choice muscles must be exercised and trained if they are to perform well in the competition of life. When children practice making decisions, then suffer the consequences or enjoy the fruits, they are exercising their choice muscles. By choosing while still encompassed in the safety of their home and nurtured by Dad's guidance, they are building up the strength to make truly hard choices.

That exercise should begin in earnest as the teens begin in earnest.

The Limits of the V

Jack Brubaker rolled his eyes. "Oh, sure! I can just see giving John the leeway to act on all his goofy choices. This is the kid who nearly drowned when he and Maxy built a waterbed out of plastic produce bags they filled from the hose. Or Marla, either. No. Huh uh. *Ix nay*. Forget it." He thought about it a moment. "There's gotta be some sort of rule."

There is indeed.

Paul Warren suggests, "My guideline is: Things that are unacceptable are illegal, immoral, permanent, or destructive behaviors. Everything that's reversible, not illegal, and not immoral is acceptable. That takes in a lot. Marla's nose job, for instance, would be permanent. Irreversible. A hairstyle is not.

"In fact, of the two external sources of friction I come up against most in parent-child relationships, one is hairstyle and the other is music, and they usually crop up in the early teens."

There is a reason for hairstyle and all the other serious shifts in stability.

The Great Experiment

Just about the time kids thought they pretty well knew themselves, those monstrous changes came and they are strangers again to their own thoughts and feelings. Their abilities have changed dramatically too. They are stronger, wiser, more capable. Their coordination, nothing to write songs about as they first embark upon puberty, sharpens until they can become amazingly skilled at sports, music, dance, fine art, shopwork . . . it's a heady source of pleasure to know you're getting better and better at things.

So the kids test these new limits by trying on different experimental lifestyles. They change their clothes and hair, and perhaps their mannerisms, to create a new look. It's all external, and they can thereby try out the lifestyle without actually investing much. Punk? Formal? Casual? Is this me? Do I like this? How about if I change to such-and-so?

This experimentation is not conscious, in that the kids don't fully realize they're doing it. From Dad's viewpoint, they are shifting with the wind, blown this way and that by every idle breeze. Can't those kids make up their minds?

"The swooping eagle again," Paul Warren points out. "The eagle is more concerned about hairstyle or clothing choice than about the kid. There's an obvious reason. Rock music, hairstyle, clothing are surface. That's all the deeper he knows his kid. So all of a sudden here's a daughter with her hair bleached, a son with a ponytail, Dad's going to have to straighten that out. In he swoops. It just won't work."

"Hair grows back in," Paul Warren philosophizes. "Clothes go out of date. It's not permanent. Don't make that your battleground.

"The other rule we suggest is, no situation they can't handle. Kids think they're invulnerable and that tragedy can't strike them personally, but we, sadly, know better. So we maintain a corral of safety for them within the world of perils."

Letting kids stay out late or prowl unsavory places is allowing them into situations they don't have experience enough to handle. Sexual acting out is not only a situation kids can't manage, it's permanent—permanent loss of virginity, permanent misery if sexually transmitted diseases appear, permanent parenthood if a pregnancy results.

Paul Warren continues, "'Nothing permanent' and 'nothing they can't handle' are the rails, the boundaries. But inside that corral, let the child be free to err. By that I mean that separation and individuation require a time where they're free to make mistakes within a protective framework."

When Marla was fourteen, an acquaintance at school asked to borrow her camera and she quickly loaned it out. Jack had warned her about trusting people she didn't know well, but it was her choice. She never saw the girl again, or her camera. Marla learned a costly and very important lesson. She came away from the experience wiser by far. Had Jack forbidden her to loan her own property, the lesson would have been lost.

Freedom to err.

When a shave-one-side-of-the-head fad swept through his middle school, John immediately took part. The night he got home from the barber and looked in his mirror he also learned a costly and valuable lesson. Here, alone in his room, he evaluated his new appearance and felt like a guy wearing a tuxedo to play volleyball on the beach. Fad or not, he looked absolutely asinine. It took seven weeks to grow it in to a style he could live with. His dad didn't have to say a word.

Freedom to err.

Growth Changes in Early Adolescence

Grade Schooler	Early Adolescent
Talks constantly. If no words seem appropriate, makes noise.	Seems to have forgotten the mother tongue.
Parents and home are center of existence. Friends, while very important, are peripheral.	Peer group (not individuals) becomes primary. Parents, while very important, are peripheral.
Parents' moral and spiritual values are accepted without question. Parents considered perfect. Identity derives primarily from parents.	Child begins to see imperfection in parents, to question parents' values. Tends to see self as all good or all bad. Extreme.
Easily interested in games, play, activities, going places, doing things. Expects to travel and do things as family unit.	Easily bored, finds games and play childish. Self-centered. Fearlessness and self-assurance is a facade; the child is frightened of the changes within. Resists family activities.
The child has become fairly comfortable with emotions.	Intensity of emotions, love and hate especially, unexpectedly sharpens.

—Dad Builds a Relationship—

"Rock music. You ever really listen to that stuff? It's obscene. Putrid." Jack Brubaker wagged his head.

"I hate that stuff. I won't have it. Miles is not going to

listen to that garbage and that's that." In the next breath, Arnold admitted that Miles knew every group, every performer, every song. It was not rote memorization from printed material.

Contemporary music. Here's another target the swooping eagle cannot resist. He will find some way to stop his child from listening to it, or bust.

And he's absolutely right about the music. Certain forms of contemporary music not only fail to classify as art by any stretch of the definition, the message therein is inappropriate for any listener of any age. Certain performers in some forms of contemporary music promote just plain hatred— class hatred, racial hatred, hatred of authority—messages neither adults nor children need to hear. The sexual messages of some music demean and trivialize women, men, genuine love, and the physical act itself.

"And so, old Dad comes down hard," Paul Warren says, "as if music were the problem. When it gets to that point, music is not the issue. Relationship is. Dad will find he has to yield his power enough to allow his kid the responsibility to make choices. It's hard. Dad has to learn that there are precious few things he can control anymore. So his strategy must change."

Control

What can Dad still control?

He can control his response to his children's behaviors. The swooping eagle, particularly to older kids, doesn't earn much respect anymore. The eagle still frightens them. The eagle can still enforce his way while the kids are in his sight and in his grasp. The moment they're out of the yard, the most powerful eagle in the neighborhood is powerless. The kids know it. The eagle himself is sometimes a little slow to catch on.

He can control what goes on in his house. "I have specific reasons for disliking that kind of music, and they are (_____), (_____), and (_____). I will not permit it in my house. If you listen to it elsewhere, that's your business. But you won't bring it into my home here."

Do you see the difference? When Dad issues an unenforceable edict, he knows, and his children know, that he can't do much about it. More importantly, when Dad forbids the music by flat edict, he is not giving his children the opportunity to be accountable to themselves. But he can exercise dominion over his home. Both he and his child recognize that authority.

Dad observes that when his kids listen to certain music, their language and behavior worsen. When he cites that observation, he's no longer just ranting an opinion; he has data to back it up. Dad hears language he knows comes from objectionable sources. He can make his case and declare the objectionable sources off limits in his home.

An even better response is, "Here's what I don't like about your music: (_____), (_____), and (_____). I'm interested; what do you see in it?"

Now he's engaging the kids in a personal give-and-take relationship. Kids respond to that, provided it's done sincerely. There must be rules and limits. By far the best way to establish rules is agree about them by working with each other. Dad doesn't like that stuff in the house? He doesn't like its effect on his kids? Let's work something out.

Engaging the kids in the process recognizes their maturity; kids respond to that too. Babies hear "no, no." Little kids get rules, whether there's a reason voiced or not. Adolescents want to know why, and a good solid reason why goes far in helping them accept rules and limits. "By this age," Dr. Warren concludes, "rules must be formed with father-like logic, if they're going to be observed at all. Too, don't fight attitude. Their attitude is unstable at this age. Deal with behavior."

Modeling; the Right to Be Heard

By now, kids are pretty keen observers of adult behavior. They still bow to power and authority, but they consider neither adults in general nor parents in particular as being godlike or all-powerful. Dad must observe reasonable limits for his own interests and entertainment, leading by example. If he is to be a scout, a guide, he must earn the respect and right to lead. Just being a grown-up is no longer enough.

Says Paul Warren, "I can't tell you the number of fathers who go on and on about the music their kids are listening to. And then the kid says, 'Dad doesn't have anything to say. He's got porn records stashed all over.'"

To maintain high moral standards is, of course, in the parents' best interests in many ways. And to present absolutely the best example to their growing, observant children, parents should be obedient to God for the love of God, and through a true desire to please Him. Moral standards, or any other aspects of a parent's lifestyle, should never become a tool to show off parents' power and control or to wield control over their children.

"I recall an interesting case from a while back," Paul Warren relates. "A mother brought her boys in. They were thirteen and fourteen when they first came in. She was desperately afraid they were both sexually active. The father was involved in the family, but not consistently so. He was a swooping eagle, but he wasn't quite sure what he should be swooping at."

Although in counsel they never used these exact words, Mom and Dad's initial reaction toward their sons could probably be phrased as, "How dare you even think about sex! Don't you know you might embarrass us?"

They shifted from concern about appearances—what the neighbors might think of their boys and them—to concern about how the boys' best interests could be served. That shift right there is a quantum shift. Appearances are not significant when balanced against children's health and welfare.

Dad also shifted from an eagle who swept down to make pronouncements to a father who sat down with the kids and talked about it. He came to realize he could not control his two boys, no matter how he tried—and that it was against their best interests therefore for him to try what he could not do anyway.

His new approach worked. "Because we can't control your every moment, we can't make these decisions for you. Only you can determine your behavior. But here's the reason we say 'no': Sexual activity before marriage is wrong for you."

He listed not emotional issues based on his own discomfort or fear of neighbors' wagging tongues, but practical ones. **To protect your emotional happiness; to protect your health (much as you hate to believe it, you are not immune to sexually transmitted diseases), to protect the girls (they're not immune to pregnancy or emotional turmoil, either).** Here again, you see, was the father's logic behind the rules and the reasons for them, an approach of limited use to youngsters but very effective for older kids.

At our urging he undertook a task he had until then assumed he could avoid: the birds-and-bees lecture. Dads are usually so nervous about that aspect of fathering, especially if their children are daughters, they tend to foist the job off on Mom, the school, a casually placed book . . . anything but face to face. This dad steeled himself and took first the fourteen-year-old, and later the younger one, to the stock car races, out for pizza, and then a quiet man-to-man in the city park.

Also to his immense credit, he did not pry into their degree of sexual activity thus far. He didn't preach, and he tried not to sound like an eagle dive-bombing his nervous kids.

The mom and dad had already, throughout their life together, been executing the other crucial step that makes discipline work. They were providing a good example with their lifestyle. Everything from sexuality, to paying taxes, to handling anger toward a neighbor, weighed in the composite picture of the way adults should handle themselves. The birds-and-bees discussion was not the only dose; it was the culmination of the covert teaching that had been going on for years.

Communication

During the Second World War, Navajo signal corpsmen earned fame and honor by handling communications in their native language. They simply conversed. And because the Navajo tongue is so complex, and so foreign to the rest of the world's languages, it worked as an arcane, naturally occurring code no enemy could crack. Today, you can purchase language texts such as *French Made Easy, Spanish Made Easy, Portuguese Made Easy.* But in that series there is no title, *Navajo Made Easy.* Only *Navajo Made Easier.*

Communication with teens is a lot like Navajo. It seems to be a code impossible to crack. Words you think mean the same thing mean different things. Words for different things are actually the same thing. Add to that the problems of articulation kids suffer around this time. It cannot be made easy. It can only be made a little easier. Actually connecting with his kids is one of the most difficult tasks Dad can undertake.

"There are some proven methods that will help," Drs. Warren and Newman agree. When they work with kids, teens especially, they employ these techniques that fathers will find useful as well.

Empathize First

- "I felt like that before."
- "I understand what it's like."
- "That never happened to me quite that way, but I can imagine it's devastating."
- "Boys are like that. Trust me; I used to be one."
- "I hear you. I remember when you were little. That kind of thing used to bug you then, too.

Listen

Listening intently serves all sorts of functions other than just alerting you to what's said. When you listen carefully, you are conveying self-esteem to your child. By your attentiveness you are saying, "This is important," which is saying, "You are important." Too, when you listen carefully, the kid in return starts listening.

Once you hear what they're saying, you can work on what they're actually trying to say. What is the child's body language saying? Frightened? Ashamed? Excited? Angry? Is the body language at cross purposes with the spoken words? What meanings beneath the spoken words are the gestures and attitudes revealing?

Give the Two Permissions

Permission to talk. Permission to not talk. We emphasize these in counsel. The children have permission to speak what's on their mind. They may say whatever they wish. They also have permission to not speak. If they don't want to approach a subject (even the subject that is ostensibly the topic of conversation at the moment), they need not.

This blanket permission to talk without prejudice or to not talk is extremely freeing. No longer under pressure to cover themselves, or to come up with what the children think Dad wants to hear, they loosen up. They may not get onto the topic right away, but within twenty minutes they'll be pouring their hearts out, provided that Dad is being open and attentive himself.

If he preaches, they never do open up. Which leads us to:

Think "Communication," not "Coercion"

"Communication is give and take. Preaching is give.

"In the case of many fathers," says Paul Warren, "the few times they talk with their teens, it's conflict. The eagle swoops again, but there's no real relationship. When Dad is chewing his kid out, or preaching, or trying to coerce some behavior, he's not communicating. The flow of ideas is from Dad to kid, but not from kid to Dad. So Dad's not getting very far for all his preaching.

"I've found that most of those fathers opt for generational chauvinism. 'It was tougher when I was your age, and you're not making it, so there's something wrong with you.'

That kind of thing. It's blatantly false, but since Dad isn't involved enough to know what's going on in his kid's life, it sounds good to him."

Hold Everyone Accountable

Say what you mean. Mean what you say. Hold Dad and kid alike responsible for what is said. This may mean a few false starts, a lot of rephrasing. It may mean cooling off awhile before discussing a topic that has one or both communicants hot under the collar.

To hold each other accountable, the classic ploy is: when A says something, B repeats what he or she thinks A said. B gives an answer. A rephrases what he or she thinks B said. A responds. Sounds clumsy, but it works surprisingly well.

Son: Tell ya, Dad, I think ( ).
Dad: So you think ( ). Well, I can't—
Son (interrupts): No, not exactly. What I mean is [rephrase].
Dad: Oh. I can go along with that, in part. I think ( ).
Son: ( ), huh?
Dad: I didn't say that. I—
Son: Yes you did, Dad. You said ( ).
Dad: Okay, but what I meant was . . . .

Navajo made easier.

You see how the ideas can move back and forth between two people without being warped by misstatement? That's communication.

Don't Read Minds

Dad doesn't expect the kids to read his mind, and he doesn't try to read theirs. Easily said. Hard to do. On the surface this runs counter to our earlier observation that kids this age have trouble saying what they really mean—the example that "I hate you" probably does not mean "I hate you." Actually, it's the solution to the problem of inarticulation.

By making clear from the outset that he is going to take statements as they are given and will do his best to explain what he really means, Dad signals that he is not able to read his child's mind. Dad in turn will take particular care that he will not say one thing and mean another. Unlike our friend Carl, he will not yell at Dorie to move out if she doesn't like the rules. If he does say it, he will amend it. Two statements will hold all parties in good stead here:

"I didn't mean that. What I mean is . . . ."

"Do you really mean what you just said?"

Communicate Things in Common

"I have a stock question I use in my office," Paul Warren says. "I ask the father and the kid, 'What do you two have in common? I heard all kinds of things you don't agree with—that you don't have in common. What's the other side of the picture?'

"As it turns out, they usually have quite a lot in common. And the fathers and teens who get along least are the fathers and teens who are temperamentally the same. When they realize that, when they can see that a lot of friction is personality stuff, they find it easier to see past it. They can talk to each other beyond the surface irritations."

What About You?

Answer these questions for yourself and ask your teen to answer them also. Then compare answers. How similar are you?

_____ I like everything to be just so. When I balance a checkbook or add up money, it has to be to the penny.

_____ So-so is sufficient. If my checkbook balances to within ten bucks, that's good enough for me.

_____ I won't live in a pigpen. The place has to be in order.

_____ I prefer that lived-in look.

_____ I get mad quickly.

_____ My anger comes slowly and boils a long time.

_____ Simple things make me happy.

_____ I wish I had more money to spend.

_____ I can think of two or three things I fear or worry about.

_____ Nothing scares me.

_____ If other people don't pick up the ball and go, I will.

_____ I prefer to follow, not lead.

Use this exercise to spur in-depth conversation between you and your child.

Talk About Things Kids Want to Talk About

Kathy was talking about her father, and she was weeping. "Daddy doesn't know how much I want to be with him and talk to him about things I like. Just talk. About basketball and hockey . . . I like sports as much as he does. Stuff like that. The only thing Daddy will spend time with me on is going to movies, and that's not spending time with me. We just sit in the same room watching a movie. We never even talk about the movie afterward."

Kids have a wide variety of interests, and they are not necessarily stereotypical. Fathers relate a little better to sons, being ex-boys themselves, and may feel uncomfortable with a girl they perceive as being interested only in boys.

Teens are interested in serious things. When Dad was growing up, the future looked rosy. Most parents assumed their kids would enjoy a higher standard of living than they themselves had. That assumption is no longer viable. Kids today face a rocky, uncertain future, and they know it.

Get It Started

In all this communication, and the fumbling attempts at communication, Dad is going to have to initiate contact. His teen-aged kids want that contact desperately. They need it. They thrive on it. But they almost certainly will not initiate it.

So move out. Take the first step, the second.

How? How about taking your daughter out on a date? Take your son out on a date. Goofy as it sounds, Dr. Warren claims, every teen girl and boy want a date with Father. Not a prom-and-flowers date, of course. Go out to the miniature golf course. The riding stable. Fishing. Up to the lake to rent a rowboat or paddle-boat. To the mall to people-watch. A picnic.

Because kids feel reticent and uncertain about open communication with Dad, especially a Dad that up 'til now was an eagle, they can't just sit down and open up. If you choose some activity of mutual interest or general mindless fun, you can, in essence, break the ice. The kids have the opportunity to make conversation peripheral, without pressure to talk. They'll talk. The words will flow. The release of pressure does it.

Midteen Changes

Early Adolescent	Midteen Adolescent
Seems to have forgotten the mother tongue.	Rediscovering the mother tongue. Dry wit.
Peer group (not individuals) becomes primary. Parents, while very important, are peripheral.	Identifies with peers as individuals. Autonomy (independence from parents) begins.
Child begins to see imperfection in parents, to question parents' values. Tends to see self as all good or all bad. Extreme.	Experiments to define personal boundaries, identity. Parents are seen as boring, stupid, old-fashioned, totally imperfect. Child not only questions but may reject the values of these imperfect parents.
Easily bored, finds games and play childish. Self-centered. Fearlessness and self-assurance is a facade; the child is frightened of the changes within.	Wants to have it all; feels invulnerable, exempt from natural laws—"It can't happen to me." Experiments with lifestyles, experiences, thrives on extreme highs and lows.

As growing teens forcibly pry themselves apart from their family, the final steps into the Big World, some friction is bound to occur. Dad is likely to feel it a lot because he is the one in a family, usually, who feels the need to control. And a kid leaving the nest is leaving control. As teens embark on their journey of individuation, each step on the way presents a cue to Dad to alter the family structure.

The Step from Family to Peers

In their early adolescence, kids shift their view of themselves from "family member" to "peer group member." The cue to Dad: the kids take on the same manners, fashions, fads, attributes, and surface appearances that all their friends do. By costume and mannerisms they identify themselves with their peers, not their parents. This is the signal for Dad and Mom to relax their expectations that their child's life will continue revolving around home. Home has become a staging area and a refuge. It's a place to stash belongings, to be when there's nowhere else to be, to be accepted. When Dad sees the necessity of this step and tailors his discipline and rules to fit, the child's whole painful adjustment is made much easier for all.

Dad should be alert to signs that the family relationships are slipping too far askew. Paul Warren likens the family to a triangle. Ideally, it's an equilateral triangle with all three sides the same relative length. It symbolizes a normal, healthy family. Mom and Dad are well-united. The kids are well-loved.

If the leg between Mom and Dad is shortened for some reason, the legs from Mom to kid or Dad to kid might lengthen. That's a symbolic way of saying that if the marriage encounters trouble, one or the other of the parents may attach themselves to a child to an unwholesome degree. As leader of the pack, Dad should be watching for it.

For instance, Brian Newman tells of a client who was deeply enmeshed with his ten-year-old daughter. "Engage this man in a conversation and pretty soon you notice he never talks about his wife. His words and thoughts are all about his daughter. Always he and his kid.

"That's a good way to tell if you're getting overly involved—*enmeshed* is the psychological term—with a kid instead of your spouse. Whom do you talk about all the time? Whom do you think about all the time? Where is your primary interest focused?"

So what's so wrong with being involved? Dad is supposed to be close to his kid. Enmeshment invites the parent to engage the child as a counselor ("What am I going to do about your mom, Son?"), interpreter ("I don't know. What do you think Mom would say about this?"), or communicator ("Look. You go tell your mom I'm not moving out of this chair until the game is over." "What am I trying to say? Help me here.") spouse.

Spouse. Yes. The enmeshed parent becomes so emotionally wedded to the child that the same kind of emotional bond develops as would develop in marriage. This is abuse, pure and simple. We call it emotional incest, and its result is that the child is no longer free to be a child. The child must act as surrogate adult, a role he or she is simply not equipped for. Tossing your kid into a deep pool when the child cannot swim would be abusive. So is tossing the child into situations he or she has not been trained to handle.

Taken to extreme, an emotionally abusive enmeshment situation can lead to actual sexual abuse. But even when it falls far short of that extreme, enmeshment causes damage.

There is another sort of imbalance we watch for when counseling families. It's hard to describe because people, hearing the description, take our meaning wrongly. Stereotypically, Dad provides a skills-enabling love (the how-to, the doing, the complete-the-project stuff). Mom provides the nurturing love (cuddle, snuggle, feed, pamper, nurse).

Dad's unique approach to love balances Mom's unique approach. Mom's love with no balance, or counterweight, could become smothering to a child. Dad's love, with no balance from Mom, would deprive the child of the closeness every kid requires. Ideally, each kind of love balances the other well, providing the child with the best of both worlds. The child feels neither neglected nor smothered.

To Think About

Your approach to this age group as a father, and to an extent your degree of comfort with your kids, depend upon your own adolescence. You are influenced by your memories and experiences. Think back to those daring days of yesteryear.

During my junior high years, my main peer group was

_____ A sports team, Scout troop, or club.

_____ A clique or gang I hung around with.

_____ Just a bunch of guys.

_____ The other band members.

_____ Other _____

_____ I didn't have one.

My main interests in seventh and eighth grade were

_____ Sports.

_____ Cars, skateboards, bikes and such.

_____ Music or drama; something artsy.

_____ Books, TV, indoor stuff.

You could say regarding these interests that I

_____ Excelled.

_____ Was so-so but liked it.

_____ Was pushed to excel by my parents or other adults.

_____ Was a dud.

My major frustration at this age was:

_____ Slow to get my size.

_____ Too big; I stuck out.

_____ The group I wanted wouldn't admit me.

_____ Parents' rules were too restrictive, or

_____ Not restrictive enough.

Now picture an early teen, yours or someone else's, answering the above questions. Go through them again, one by one. How would he or she respond? How do your child's experiences mirror yours?

My experience with my own early adolescence helps me be a better, more understanding father in these ways:

_____ Better empathy for the pains and trials of this age.
_____ Better understanding of the temptations.
_____ Better feeling for the temporary peer group identi-
       fication.
_____ Better tolerance for the quirks of this age's mind-
       set.
_____ Other _____

Picture yourself in a conducive situation, talking with a teen-ager (your own, if possible). You are talking about all the items you just enumerated above. What advice, hopes, dreams, fears for the adolescent would you express, based on what you learned growing up? Now *that's* communication!

TEN

Dad and His Older Teen

During his off season, Cal Morrow works on cutting horses. A cutting horse and its rider function together to remove, or cut out, one particular cow or calf from a herd of cattle. Cattle of any age strongly resist being separated from their herd. Savvy creatures, they will dodge and bolt in all directions to get back to the safety of the herd. To keep the cow from rejoining its kind, the horse will spontaneously charge, duck aside, feint, and pivot to block the animal's movements and haze it to wherever else it is supposed to go—to a holding pen, for branding or medication, into a truck. Either a horse takes naturally to the specialized skill of cutting cattle or it never will. If it does, training consists basically of getting the horse, once it is well broken to saddle, to think along the same lines as its rider.

Breaking comes first. As soon as the horse responds well and instantly to its rider's cues and requests, the real fun begins. Cal rides his trainee out into a loose bunch of cows, chooses an obvious one, and uses the horse to separate it out. At first, he has to direct every movement of his trainee. As the horse's skills develop, Cal does less and less. Eventually the horse requires no direction at all. Once it zeroes in on its cow, it will not be distracted by any other cattle or horses. And it does the cutting virtually unassisted.

"You can just about tell the moment when your horse figures out what's expected—gets into the thrill of the chase, you might say," says Cal. "From then on, it's just a matter of fine tuning. When a horse is ready, all you have to do is think about which cow you want, and your horse will cut it for you slick as a warm knife through butter.

"There's a sort of maturity a cutting horse develops," Cal concludes. "A steadiness. They get sensible, you might say. A frittery colt or filly isn't mature; a good cutting horse is. I can't explain it, but I know it when I see it."

Teen-agers are pretty much the same.

Frittery colt or filly about describes changeable, bouncing-off-the-walls early teens. They need solid direction. They must learn to keep their eye on the goal. Eventually, they'll pursue their goal virtually unassisted. Maturity has settled the frittery youngster.

That final growth spurt produces these changes, as described in the following comparison table:

From Teen to Near-Adult

Midteen Adolescent	The Late Teens
Rediscovering the mother tongue; dry wit.	Miraculously acquires ability to genuinely converse.
Identifies with peers as individuals. Autonomy (independence from parents) begins.	Completes autonomy while keeping attachments to significant adults, peers.
Experiments to define personal boundaries, identity. Parents are seen as boring, stupid, old-fashioned, totally imperfect. Child not only questions but may reject the values of these imperfect parents.	Developing capacity for intimacy. Building own values system that is probably much like parents'. Parents not quite as insane as first believed. Personal boundaries, identity stabilizing.

From Teen to Near-Adult, *cont.*

Midteen Adolescent	The Late Teens
Wants to have it all; feels invulnerable, exempt from natural laws—"It can't happen to me." Experiments with lifestyles, experiences, thrives on extreme highs and lows.	Begins to see beyond the moment, plans for future. Can examine career choices with mature eye, develop career goals. Invulnerability still present, but highs and lows less extreme. Idealistic.

—The New Person Inside Your Teen—

Clark Kent steps inside a phone booth and emerges . . .

. . . minus a quarter.

. . . as Superman!

Superman can escape anything. He is so unique, the statistics that apply to other human beings do not apply to him. He's invulnerable. He's exempt from the petty difficulties of life such as disease, debt, and disappointment. If disaster strikes, Superman will not only escape unscathed, he will clothe himself in glory, a hero. Superman can do anything. Solve the national debt? No problem! Cure poverty? Couple weeks. Superman is perfect and holds the highest ideals.

Sixteen-year-olds, boy or girl, Superpeople—every one of them. Psychologists, of course, have a word for it. The teens of this age consider themselves overadequate.

Dad is in the perfect position to understand that and to empathize. Dad was Superman once, before life hit him square between the eyes and he wised up. He can temper Superperson's idealism with realism—gently, gently, so as not to destroy it.

Dad is still his kids' window on the world, as he has always been, but now he is a window on a greater world, a more complex, nonmaterial world of finance, danger, law, and untrustworthy people. The child is face-to-face with the real one now.

Middle teens act as if they are avoiding their parents. They keep different hours, do different things. Sometimes it seems they try deliberately to annoy. In spite of that kind of behavior, we've learned, every teen wants a strong relationship with Dad, and on a new and somewhat different basis.

The teen wants to feel, "Dad is with me on this. Since he is with me, he'll clamp down with good rules. Not just rules. Good rules." We call it an affiliative relationship. It's still father-child, but now it's thinking, empathetic father-child.

Dad, remembering what it was like to be young, understands a teen's needs, at least somewhat, and makes the right moves and rules. That's what the teen yearns for.

Dad's Specific Gifts for Superperson

Jack Brubaker, as opposed to his wife, was what people call an early riser. So was his seventeen-year-old Marla. Let the other family members sleep in. Jack and Marla were out and about, cheerfully accomplishing a day's work before those clowns were out of bed. Today, though, Marla sat under a dark cloud. Jack hated eating breakfast with a grump.

"What's the matter?"

"Nothing."

"What used to be the matter?"

"Nothing."

Superpeople don't always communicate eagerly.

Jack dumped a spoonful of brown sugar on her half-eaten oatmeal.

She glared at him.

"You need something to sweeten you up. What's happening?"

"Nothing." Her voice faltered. She knew from experience that he wasn't going to let her off. "I got a C on that history test. I'm probably going to get a B for the semester now."

"What's wrong with a B?"

"Daaa-deee!"

"I know you had your heart set on a straight-A year, but you're doing great. You're not sloughing off."

"If I had studied more—"

Jack interrupted, "You wouldn't have been able to finish the project for youth group, and it was an important piece of work."

"Yes, but—"

"You're balancing your life well, and I'm proud of you, Sugar. You're doing great."

"But a C, Daddy!"

• Helping Superperson Average Out

One of the things Dad can do for his teen is to help his child be average. By that we don't mean that a C level in school is to be encouraged if the child is capable of B or A. Rather we mean to convince the child, by encouragement and repetition, that everyone has strengths and weaknesses and nobody can be the best at everything. And that includes idealistic, energetic teens. The strengths and the weaknesses balance out to a whole person.

"Dad's crucial lesson is this," says Paul Warren. "It's okay to not be best at everything. It is important, for the kid's self-esteem, to do as well as you can at what you undertake. And, this does not necessarily mean doing something well. The bottom-line message is always, no one can do everything. Idealistic, overadequate kids can't grasp that at first."

You would think that doing the best he or she can would be sufficient for the Superperson. Not so. Their idealism demands that they excel. That's where Dad's support and encouragement, given when the opportunity arises, can be so very helpful.

This is not easy for Dad. The stereotypical father is so task-oriented and completion-oriented, he falls right into the overadequate teen's own mind-set. "You've got to be your best! Be excellent, get that scholarship, get those grades, get that trophy! You've got a lot of work to do."

Jack Brubaker was really into the work-and-achieve pro- gram because of his own success with his business. He had built his reputation and his clientele on hard work. Favorable word-of-mouth got him an awful lot of business. He wanted to engrain this same success ethic in his kids.

It never would occur to Jack, the traditional dad, to simply say, "Hey, kick back enough to enjoy being [fifteen] [six- teen] [seventeen] while you can." And yet, that is the very advice the teen must hear at this age, lest those important developmental years slip away.

This is the age when kids complete their separation from the family, learn to socialize well with the opposite sex, begin to learn how to achieve real intimacy. These lessons can only be learned by developing relationships, losing them, letting them stagnate, helping them grow.

Dad gets awfully impatient with his midteen who can talk about nothing but the opposite sex, who takes too much interest in who is dating whom, who broke up with whom, why so-and-so can't stand so-and-so. However, all that non- sense serves an important function. The preschooler pro- cessed the outside world by going through motions during pretending and play, rather than by thinking and verbalizing. In much the same way, the teen is processing roles, person- alities, relationships, and other social concepts. Nonver- bally. By manipulation, exploration—yes, and pretense. When other goals prevent that processing, the teen will have more difficulty later in adjusting to close personal relationships.

Dad's hunger for achievement can also get in the way of another all-important human quality, identity. The teen whose identity hinges on achievements and laurels won is going to be in big trouble when, later in life, the achieve- ments come less frequently and the laurels, perhaps, not at all. It's that same old thing again, as Dr. Warren phrases it: "Worth must be based not on what I do but on what I am; a child of God."

At this particular age, though, with the idealism and over-adequacy, worth-based-on-achievement takes a particularly heavy toll. The child is already oriented toward achievement.

"Many, many who were Miss Everybody in high school or Mr. Big Man," says Paul Warren, "are really struggling at the ten-year reunion. Their feelings of self-worth have always depended upon being the big frog in the pond. They're as big as they ever were, but the pond suddenly got so much larger."

• Taking on a New Protector's Role

Jack Brubaker can no longer keep a protective wing over his seventeen-year-old Marla when she's out and about, or even over fourteen-year-old John, for that matter. But, just as his discipline helped his children internalize conscience, so his guidance can help them internalize protection. Moreover, as they step out into the world, their protection must be extremely sophisticated. Holding their hand as they cross the street won't cut it anymore. All manner of sharks are out there, waiting to prey upon the naive, the unwary.

We can assume that Dad has already drilled into his kids how to respond to strangers, what to do in case of fire or other emergency, the importance of remaining alert and cautious. Those lessons of childhood have by now been internalized.

Consider these new lessons, things every child should know by the time he or she leaves high school. Very few of them are lessons taught in school. Even those that are are not as well absorbed in the school setting as they are when Dad delivers them. Dad taking an interactive role with his kid can teach anything, and it will stick a lot better.

Could you discuss these topics with a teen-ager, should the subject come up?

_____ How do swindlers operate? What are some of the common scams, the gimmicks that always seem to find unwary victims?

_____ When a telemarketer calls, how do you respond?

_____ A guy calls and says you just won a major prize. Did you?

When you're making a major purchase; a house, a car, a stereo:

_____ What do you look for in the warranty?

_____ What about those maintenance contracts?

_____ How do you calculate loan interest?

_____ Why get everything in writing?

When you move into a new apartment:

_____ How do you read the electric and gas meters?

_____ Why bother?

_____ Do you understand damage deposits? Advance rents? Rental contracts?

_____ How do unscrupulous landlords gouge tenants, and how do you protect yourself?

What about banking practices?

_____ What's the wisest use of various banking services?

_____ Any tricks to balancing accounts?

_____ What are points in the mortgage trade?

_____ What about overdraft protection?

_____ How do you protect your credit cards from misuse?

_____ When should you use them and when abstain?

_____ What are some of the common automotive repair scams?

_____ Where's the best place to get tires, parts, services?

When interviewing for a job:

_____ What would Dad look for if he were the interviewer?

_____ What kind of dress and attitude will win points?

_____ How do you calculate the hidden costs of a job, such as transportation, wardrobe, safety equipment?

_____ The cops are holding you. What are your rights?

_____ What's a misdemeanor as opposed to a felony? A rolling violation? A tort claim? A class action?

The more the child knows about this stuff in the beginning, the wiser will be his or her decisions, the less often the child will be victimized by the unscrupulous. In short, kids today desperately need this information, and Dad can derive immense satisfaction from providing it.

Dad can also take immense satisfaction in seeing his kids through their rites of passage from childhood to adulthood. But first he has to ferret out those rites.

—Rites of Passage—

It was Sol Neiman's son's bar mitzvah, and Brian Newman and Paul Warren were among the Christian friends Sol had invited.

They stood around afterwards, sipping sparkling cider and nibbling world-class kosher corned beef. Not unexpectedly, the conversation turned to rites of passage in various cultures.

"I really appreciate the concept of *mensch*," Paul Warren said. "The Jewish ideal of the well-rounded man who's tough and tender. Wise. Upright."

Brian nodded. "That's the new father we talk about. He's the traditional macho combined with the man who has enough sensitivity to understand."

"'So be a mensch!'" A man named Fred shifted into a vaguely Yiddish accent. "I cannot tell you how many times I heard that growing up. From Mama. From Papa. The bar mitzvah is the official rite of passage, but we were taught what a mensch is from the cradle up."

"Circumcision, then, is the rite that brings the boy baby into the family of Judaism, right?" Brian asked.

"Physically sets us apart," Fred added, "but it's symbolic. Lots of Gentiles practice circumcision. And then there's some tribe, I think in New Guinea or someplace like that, who circumcise their thirteen- or fourteen-year-old boys with a hot stone."

Brian Newman whistled, his eyes the size of compact discs.

"It's true, though," Paul Warren mused. "There is no rite of passage in the church as a whole for kids entering adolescence. Some denominations have confirmation, for instance, but not universally. So they create a youth group because they don't know what else to do with you."

"There needs to be an event run by fathers as a rite of passage. Something recognized by everyone, like a bar mitzvah. In the family and also in the spiritual family, the church," said Brian.

"There is one rite of passage for girls," suggested Fred, the father of five sons. "Period time."

Today I Am a Woman; Today I Am a Man

Fathers in our culture are not much involved when their daughters' menstrual cycles begin. Mom takes over, and rightly so. She handles the instruction, the exploration of drug store shelves to survey the attendant products, whatever celebration there is.

"There should be," Paul Warren suggests, "a celebration involving Dad too. Handled delicately, of course. But a celebration of some sort. How about: 'I'm proud you're a woman; let's go out to dinner.' Maybe flowers, a small gift, something to mark this occasion. Dad has to initiate it. The girl won't. They both may be a bit self-conscious. They certainly won't be announcing the occasion to the world. That's all right. It's a moment of intimacy between father and daughter. And that means the world to her."

The driver's license marks a milestone in a girl's life, and an important one, but it's not quite the rite of passage that it is for a boy. But then, girls frequently are feted at Sweet Sixteen birthday parties. Boys hardly ever are, eschewing any thought that they're sweet.

Paul Warren speaks, and sadness clouds his voice. "In

some subcultures among kids, jail is the rite of passage.
You're not a man until you've spent a night in the municipal
slammer."

The New Rite of Passage

The driver's license. In a culture nearly devoid of celebrations to mark a person's advance from child to adult, here's
our one true-blue rite of passage. "There is a powerful,
powerful symbolic meaning here," Drs. Warren, Newman,
and Minirth all agree. By definition, rites of passage confer
new, important responsibilities, new adult functions.

"'Driver's license' means 'responsible,'" says Brian
Newman. "You're taking responsibility for a lethal weapon
in a confusing, complex situation—that is, modern traffic.
You don't have many chances anymore to putt-putt along
one-lane country roads, the way drivers did at the turn of
the century. With freeways and gridlock you have to be in
the right place exactly. And it's awfully easy to kill somebody."

Says Paul Warren, "In counsel we use the driver's license
as a litmus test on kids. Kids who don't sign up for instruction, won't try the test, are afraid of the future. Almost
always it's boys, and usually they're in a relationship tangle
with Mom. They're struggling with growing up. It's almost
indicative that the kid has dependency issues to work out."

We mentioned previously that Dad's love delicately balances Mom's. Here's where Dad can help the child move
forward.

"What we do in counsel," says Paul Warren, "is set the
father down together with the child—usually the son, as I
said—and work out a plan of action toward getting that
driver's license. On this date, we'll go get the permit. We'll
sign up for driver's ed on that date. You see, I use the
driver's license to nudge the kid into independence. It's not
necessary for the child to drive. Just get the license. That's
how strong the symbolism is."

So universally recognized is the driver's license as the
final rite of passage into adulthood, the symbolism works in

both directions. The child may eagerly obtain it as a sign that he or she is now a responsible adult. Conversely, by obtaining it, like it or not, the child intuitively recognizes that he or she has taken the big step into responsible adulthood. That in itself helps resolve the relationship difficulty.

Dad is usually up to his ears in the process of getting his kid licensed. Too often it is not a positive thing.

"The traditional father," Brian Newman claims, "sets down all these rules. He fumes about the insurance. He fusses about safety and whether the kid can take the car out past ten P.M. All that kind of thing. You can't blame him. He's financially responsible for a kid who hasn't demonstrated a whole lot of responsibility so far in life. He can just see all those twenty-dollar bills flying out the window on little silver wings."

Paul Warren nods sagely. His own Matthew is going to be applying for a permit in too few years hence. "With the traditional father, there's no celebration of growth or affirmation. I hope the new father can step beyond that. Of course have the rules. Share your fear and trepidation. But also celebrate.

"The new father can convey to his kid, through words and actions both, 'I rejoice in this big step you're taking into adulthood. I look forward to giving you this responsibility, and I'm proud to be part of it. I'm proud of you!'"

In short, the new father embodies the traditional father and then moves two steps beyond.

So who's to celebrate when the kid messes up? Jack Brubaker was not pleased when Marla came home with a speeding ticket less than six months after she got her license. To his credit, he avoided being an eagle and played the situation very well.

She had to take the afternoon off from school to appear in traffic court. Jack went along. But he waited out in the hall when she went in before the judge. She got the ticket, he figured; she was on her own. Afterwards she could have returned to class for the final hour-and-a-half of the day.

Instead, Jack bought her a giant cola and sat with her for an hour out in the city park. They talked about squirrels and traffic court and the ticket and the guy who asked her out next Saturday night and whether John, the fourteen-year-old, was doing okay in freshman English. Jack described the two tickets he received in his past. They laughed over them.

Relationship.

The judge let her off easy and didn't put the ticket on her record, provided she kept her record clean. She has never received another.

—The New Face of Dad—

Jack would never have guessed, but when he described his own traffic tickets to Marla—one for speeding and one for driving in a city-owned irrigation ditch chasing escaped ponies—he was giving Marla a very important message. Actually, two of them. One, don't chase your neighbor's livestock home through irrigation channels unless you're on a horse; and two, Dad is not perfect.

Dad is not perfect. By now the kid realizes that, pretty much. It's been a major disillusionment, learning that fact, because the kid's whole childhood was based on growing up under perfect guides and mentors. It's a major disillusionment for Dad, too, realizing that his kids see him as he is.

Paul Warren sees it all the time. "The child of twelve or thirteen tells Dad he's not perfect, it doesn't hurt much. But when older teens, the seventeen-, eighteen-, and nineteen-year-olds say it, Dad has a much greater struggle hearing it.

"I'm not sure of reasons for that. Part of it, I suppose, is that younger kids have less credibility. Mostly, I think it's a control thing. It relates to the fact that most fathers think they can still control their young adolescents. But the older adolescents are beyond control. To hear from them that you're imperfect and make lots of mistakes is very difficult."

There's the other side of the coin; Dad has to come to grips with the fact that as a father he did indeed make mistakes, and dads don't often do that. A lot of selective memory is involved here. Dad genuinely does not remember his own bad choices, making it exceedingly difficult to admit them. Dad probably had bought into the myth of the perfect parent just as much as did the grade-schooler.

Even if he didn't make all that many bad choices, he was surely tempted to. What the father should be seeking out is a sense of empathy, of understanding for his flawed teen. And that empathy is founded in his own flaws.

Frank Minirth would add to that, "The most powerful position a father can be in when it comes to answering kids' questions is to not have all the answers. The most powerful response can be 'I don't know the answer to that.'"

Two implications are made here. Dad admits that he doesn't know everything, and that is an adjunct of the "Okay, I admit I'm not perfect" statement. The other implication is, Dad doesn't hold all the power.

"I can think of a case," says Paul Warren, "about a sixteen-year-old girl. The kid and her dad were at complete loggerheads. The girl was asking for more privileges—for a later curfew, some other things. Her dad's response was, 'Absolutely not. I can't think of any reason your curfew should be extended.' Then the girl would respond in anger. And it went on and on like that. Mom made a few efforts to adjudicate and patch it up, but she couldn't get anywhere.

"The girl saw her father as being the man who thought he had all the answers all the time and she had none. And therefore no power, no chance to negotiate. Then on this one particular occasion, she asked for something and her dad said, 'I don't know the answer now. I'll talk to your mom about it.'"

Paul Warren snaps his fingers. "Overnight, the girl's attitude changed. Her rebelliousness faded, because Dad presented himself as not having all the power, all the answers."

You, Dad, have very firm and clear beliefs about certain

things. About others, your opinions are not so clear. Admit that. The act of admission nudges this blossoming adult into abandoning the natural tug-of-war about power and privilege. Near-adults need some power and some privilege, and Dad dare not hog them. When Dad admits he doesn't have all the ready answers and all the power, he forces his teens to spend energy on growing and seeking personal identity, and not on a fruitless fight for a little power. Spending all their years in a power play, a tug-of-war with their parents, draws kids away from the process of growing up. It is another form of dependency, and an unhealthy one.

One other powerful statement Dad can communicate is apology. Here is where the father comes to grips with his errors of omission and commission, acknowledges them, and comes to terms with them.

1. I don't have all the answers.
2. From time to time I've blown it.
3. I'm sorry. I apologize.

It is the standard confession worshippers in the Christian church make, in most denominations at every service. Dad confesses before God. When he takes the extra step of confessing thusly to his children, he releases them from the myth of the perfect father and provides them a measure of peace and power.

It turns out to be necessary for Dad's growth as well. He can let his kids go a little easier now; whether they need a perfect mentor or not, Dad is no longer it. Dad can now place his children squarely in the hands of their heavenly Father and step back to second-in-charge. Only by removing himself as God, can he give them to God.

It's a slow process for fathers of adolescents. It peaks only after the children reach, say, sixteen or so. By then, the child is taking on another responsibility of adulthood, that of earning money. And therein lies a whole new area where Dad can make a difference. Let's look at the ways

Dad specifically shapes his kid's development as a financially independent adult.

—Dad's Kid Goes to Work—

A toddler wanted a particular toy, not realizing that were she to actually receive it, she'd probably have more fun playing with the box it came in.

Her mom asked, "Where do you think Daddy would get the money for a toy that expensive?"

The toddler shrugged. "He put he hand in he pockey."

Where else does money come from? Daddy's pocket.

By grade school, kids are receiving an allowance. Some of the allowance may depend upon chores done around the house, but it's an allowance. Payment for being a kid. The first big lesson in controlling money.

Since allowances never go as far as they ought (and if given by a stereotypical eagle sort of father, always delivered with the generationally chauvinistic line, "Five bucks? I got fifty cents when I was a kid and thought it was a lot."), the child dabbles in private enterprise. Lemonade stand. Shoveling sidewalks in winter. Raking leaves. Baby-sitting.

"A lot of opportunities like that are gone with history," a friend named Bill muses. "I remember when Ringling Brothers circus still arrived on the train, when I was a kid. This one time some friends and I were watching them set up in the big fairgrounds field. A burly guy came over and said, 'You kids can have free tickets if you'll work for a couple hours.' We followed him like rats after the Pied Piper."

Bill grins, his face full of memories. "What an afternoon! They erected the main tent, the big top, and we kids pulled on ropes and tugged on canvas. I remember standing there holding on to a rope like the guy told me to do, and I got bumped in the back. Shoved me three feet. I turned around, and this elephant was going by, wearing a huge, heavy harness. It was pulling on one of the ropes that hauls the tent up to the top of its main pole. They had trucks and elephants and everything there, putting up that tent.

"Then we helped set up the bleachers. It was hard for kids as small as we were. Really a grunt. We were filthy, dusty, dirty, and we loved every minute of it. Worked our tails off." He pauses. "Good tickets too, right down in front."

And a sense of achievement and satisfaction that still glows bright, forty years later.

Dad the Hard-Nosed Teacher

As part of his role as introducer to the world, Dad more than Mom must insist that his kids have actual work experience before leaving home. Every child needs the opportunity to earn money and also to be responsible for it. Dad all along has been involved in teaching money management. This is a big part of those lessons.

When the child starts bringing home that paycheck, it is appropriate that Dad should lead in suggesting what percentage of the money ought to go where. He is right to say, for example, "Put X percent into a college fund or savings." That percentage should probably range between ten as a minimum to twenty-five as a maximum. The rest should be discretionary. That means, the parents don't make decisions about it. The only lines parents need draw are at blowing all of it and saving none, or at spending even one cent on illegal or immoral things.

Paul Warren has just emerged from the excruciating annual infliction of income taxes, and he's understandably a little sensitive about money issues. "I usually don't cite people I don't know personally, but this is the friend of a friend. I don't remember the boy's name, but he's a teenager, apparently fairly responsible, kind of a problem kid at school. He's not bad, he just does poorly in school, but he really loves his part-time job. His parents have rules that he gives so much to the church and puts so much in savings. Good. That's good.

"But then they take his discretionary as well. He's just furious. Money's tight in his family, and his father's afraid he'll waste it on something. Well, it's true. He might. In fact he definitely would. And he should. Worse than his anger, which is bad enough, is that he's not getting any experience handling money. He can't make mistakes—in essence, waste it—and the way you learn to handle money is by making mistakes."

Only a part of learning to handle money well is the discovery that you have spent unwisely. Another is the experience of spending it, needing some more, begging for a loan, and hearing, "Sorry, son. Sorry, daughter. It's not in your best interest to loan you more. You must learn how far a dollar will go."

That was Dad the Teacher speaking. The lesson sinks in well.

Dad the Employer?

"'Brubaker and Sons.' Has a nice ring to it. I've always kind of wished and expected that my boys would go into the business with me and carry it on." Jack Brubaker waves a hand. "Hey, it's for their own good. It's a very good trade. Steady work. Sometimes it's only medium and sometimes it's really busy, but it's never real slow. They can make a nice living."

Jack expresses the desire most fathers have, not only that their children will do well, but that their children will continue the name in Dad's general line of work. It's not all for the kids' benefit, of course, and Jack would probably be among the first to admit that. It's for Dad's satisfaction and pride too.

"Regardless whether the son or daughter eventually enters Dad's line of work," Paul Warren counsels, "the kid probably shouldn't start there."

The child not enter the family business? What could be wrong with that? As Brian Newman states it, "It's not really good for kids to work in the family business. Especially late teens working for Dad as boss. They may come back to the business later, and that's fine. But as they're starting out, they need to be under some other person as boss."

As a part of a teen's separation from the family, he or she should have the experience of being under the authority of another adult. "How do I meet the expectations and requirements of this person who bears no relationship to me save as the signer of my paycheck?"

Jack Brubaker smirked. "Sure opened Marla's eyes! When she was sixteen, she found a job as a clerk at a resort up on the lake. 'Resort' is using the term loosely—one of those raggedy little mom-and-pop operations. Rent out dented tin canoes. Take money for overpriced pop and snacks. She stayed at a dorm during the week and came home weekends.

"She would bend my ear for hours, complaining about her supervisor, who was the missus. Mrs. Eller kept trying to fix her up with the unmarried Eller son. Mrs. Eller expected her to keep the place cleaned up and work the cash register at the same time. Mrs. Eller talked too much. Mrs. Eller wanted this, and then she'd change her mind and want that. Drove Marla nuts.

"Marla was right, to some extent. Mrs. Eller is kind of indecisive. But Marla stuck it out, the whole summer. I'm really proud of her."

Marla showed no signs of interest in entering her father's air conditioning and sheet metal fabrication business. John at fourteen was not quite ready to make career choices. And the two little ones are both too young to be thinking about that. Did Jack have any hope at all for "Brubaker and Sons—or Daughters"?

Time will tell. His Marla has taken giant strides in becoming an adult by learning to meet the expectations of others. She will take further strides as she samples the different kinds of work experience waiting for her out in the world. She will be able to come home and unload her frustrations on Daddy, perhaps even to receive gentle, wise counsel in return.

Whether or not she takes over the family business, Marla will do just fine.

—The Final Affirmation—

About all any father can do by the time his child reaches late adolescence is to affirm. All kids growing up seek their father's affirmation. All.

Paul Warren wags his head. "And the stereotypical swooping eagle is still in there swooping. He'll keep trying, but he's not effective now."

Brian Newman chimes in. "Here returns that developmental V we talked about. If Dad hasn't widened it, giving his kids the latitude to make mistakes and go forward, his kid hasn't been learning critical lessons, hasn't been separating well from the family."

Paul Warren nods agreement. "By this age, if Dad still has the clamps down tight, the kid is not thinking. Either the kid is following Dad's orders or rebelling against Dad's orders. Either way, the kid is not his own person."

The choice muscles we mentioned earlier, which do not exist, of course, have not been strengthened. And by the late teens they are about to be called upon to support a new adult. It's awfully late to start exercising them. Some strength will be permanently lost.

"Eighty percent of fathering is done before fifteen," Frank Minirth says. "Maybe more than eighty. And yet, in our culture, fathers only become aware of what they didn't get done when their children reach fifteen or so. Then's when they try to do it." He shakes his head. "The teaching, training, nurturing are done by then. You're not the teacher/trainer/nurturer anymore."

What every child yearns for, whether following Dad's orders, rebelling against them, or thinking on his or her own, is for Dad's affirmation. And affirmation is a hard, hard act for the traditional, stereotypical father to drum up. Such a dad rages. He overprotects.

"I can give you an example," says Brian Newman. "A dozen examples. For instance, you have a girl interested in boys and social things, bombs out at school. She's not doing her homework. The father hears about her grades from Mom. He rages, blows, says 'I'm gonna ground you for the rest of your life! Now you're gonna do this and that!' Then off he goes to the school to a conference with her teachers and tries to beg off for his girl. I see it a hundred different ways."

Paul Warren counsels, "If Mom and Dad are going to the teacher, they should bring the teen-ager with them. Otherwise they're not getting at a solution. The child needs to be involved in the process.

"Another lack of affirmation comes as Dad swoops in when his kids make bad choices, but he never comes in to identify good choices. Fathers especially need to see and know good choices, and reward those choices with sincere approval.

"It's more observing than lecturing. He watches. Then he can say, 'That was a bad choice, but these were good choices.'

"I remember a case—let's call her Gloria. She went to a friend's house for a slumber party. The girls got pretty giddy and decided to sneak out in the middle of the night. They didn't really do anything, just walked around. The host parents found out and they were furious. Gloria's parents dragged her home, and her dad was absolutely raging.

"They brought her in to me because they were afraid she was going wrong. So I asked her what good decisions she made. She couldn't think of any. Not one. Her father never once identified any good decisions, although he swooped on bad ones instantly. Actually she made a lot of good ones. Good grades. Good choices of friends."

Most teens make mostly good choices. Even those kids making rotten choices do not make exclusively rotten choices. Dad will do much for his kid as he seeks out and affirms the good choices of life. Being Dad should not be a burden, a duty, an onus without relief or fun. In fact, done well, being Dad is exhilarating. Positive.

Dad also expresses his interest. Says Paul Warren, "Father needs to meet the guy dating his daughter. Girls want their dad to care enough to have some rules in place and to know the guy. Furthermore, every teen girl wants the father of the boy she's dating also to have rules—rules about dating and about respect for girls.

"Dad should be making sure, too, that the boy respects the parents of the girl. That the boy respects the parents' wishes. If Dad sets a curfew and the boy tells the daughter, 'Ah, that's not important . . .'; that's the kind of disrespect I mean.

"Most of all, Dad must eventually come to recognize that his kids are rapidly approaching being an equal adult with him. That child is no longer just his child. There's precious little written about parents moving on to see their kids as fellow adults."

Traditionally, Dad says good-bye to his daughter as she marries. There is much symbolism involved in Daddy giving his daughter away, and both father and daughter pick up that symbolism intuitively. The very phrase, "giving his daughter away in marriage," says it all. Through that act, Dad affirms her choice of mate, and he bestows his blessing on the union. It's a vivid and emotional experience.

Dad doesn't give his son away. And not every girl marries under the protection of her father. In those circumstances, Dad may find himself called upon to get creative. Talk to himself. Explain the kids are grown. Set up a situation in which he officially releases them. Watch for an opportunity to symbolically release them.

A father we'll call Bill was not able to give his daughter away. She married while at graduate school, two states distant. Bill met her husband a couple times when he visited her at school in her state. The summer she and her husband accepted their master's degrees, they drove to Bill's for a two-week visit.

As they left to return to their own home and their life, the daughter dissolved in tears. She thought she was being silly; she'd left home before plenty of times, and nary a tear shed. But this time, you see, was different. She was not gaily waltzing away to begin a new phase of life. This time her husband was claiming her. He was driving the car. It was a very moving moment for Bill too.

At last, in essence, he was giving his daughter away.

Things to Think About

When the actor/director Alan Alda spoke at his daughter's college commencement, he closed in this vein: "Good-bye, my daughter. Hello, my friend."

Sooner or later, Dad, you will also cross that bar. Here are some things to think about that might make the crossing easier.

- **Appreciate Your Kids Now**

  For each of your children, identify three good choices that child has made in the last week or so (You'll want to answer the following for the other children on a separate sheet of paper):

  1. _____
  2. _____
  3. _____

  Have you mentioned them to your child(ren)? Praise and recognition are powerful tools. An affirmation you could give your child of whatever age right now would be (a simple "I like you" for a small child; a heartfelt "good choices there!" for an older one; positive strokes):

  _____
  _____

  For each child, identify at least three positive attributes that child possesses that will help him or her succeed in the adult world.

  1. _____
  2. _____
  3. _____

Did you play a part in the development of those positive qualities?

Think about the skills your child(ren) (of whatever age) possesses.

_____ In organized sports.

_____ In art and music.

_____ Outdoor activities such as swimming, biking.

_____ Indoor activities—model building, Nintendo®, reading.

_____ Adult skills such as driving, handling a bank account.

_____ Job-related skills and mechanics; anything from mowing lawns to computer repair.

_____ Domestic skills; cooking, housekeeping, sewing, gardening.

_____ Other _____

What part did you play as a skills-enabler as the child developed those abilities?

_____ Teach?

_____ Encourage?

_____ Help the child practice and become proficient?

_____ Finance the child's lessons and participation?

_____ Transport the child?

_____ Outfit the child with equipment, uniform?

_____ Other _____

You, no less than your children, could use some affirmation. How about a round of applause for Dad's part? You deserve it.

• Releasing Your Kids—Releasing Yourself

You have completed the bulk of the book to this point and have a good idea now how far today's father has stepped beyond the traditional role. Identify at least three roles in which you've done pretty well as a father up to now. Those roles might be as provider, protector, nur-

turer, caretaker, companion, teacher, mentor, disciplinarian . . . .

1. _____
2. _____
3. _____

Consider each of those roles. You are going to have to
let go of them one by one. For example, your role as
provider will pass once your children are out of school
and on their own. For every child in turn, picture in your
mind at what age you will likely let go of each of these
roles (they probably won't all happen simultaneously).
Forewarned is forearmed.

_____ Provider
_____ Protector
_____ Nurturer
_____ Companion
_____ Teacher
_____ Disciplinarian
_____ Other, unique to your situation

One role is not included here: mentor. You'll never outlive
that one. Do any other roles above qualify as never-
quite-done?

—Boys and Girls Together—

A lot of confusion about the new roles of men and women,
in the work place and in society, means that Dad has to
rethink his fathering role if he is going to prepare his children
adequately. Let's look at that next.

ELEVEN

Boys and Girls Together

When Annie was just a tiny tot, she loved to sit on the little wooden stool in the hall and read her picture books. When she was older she learned that her great-grandfather had built that sturdy stool in his woodshop class, a course every high-school lad took in her grandfather's day. Annie's dad pursued woodworking as a hobby, so she grew up knowing what a chisel could do. Her dad made amazing dovetail joints.

Imagine Annie's delight when she learned that in her high-school woodshop students made stools very much like that one great-grandfather had built. The class was open to students of either gender. She signed right up . . . . And was rudely disappointed.

First they planed boards. Annie planed hers to the millimeter. It was a good job, but the instructor didn't seem to notice. They learned the different kinds of saws, and how to use a drill. The instructor showed the boys where to drill and they drilled. He showed Annie where to drill and then drilled the holes for her. He ended up cutting her pieces of wood for her, uninvited. The boys were shown how to assemble the pieces. The instructor "helped" Annie by putting her stool together for her. Annie was allowed to sand. Sanding is boring.

Annie was being treated like a girl.

And it infuriated her.

—The Gender Difference—

To men's consternation, a lot of innocent actions and attitudes infuriate today's new woman. Dad has to deal with this in the workplace and in the home and in casual situations. And he has to prepare his kids to deal successfully with a strange new world.

"Women seem to think they should be treated the same as men. You're a jerk if you don't," Jack Brubaker complained. "I have a teenaged girl and a younger teenaged boy. It's just plain frustrating, trying to treat them the same. I don't think I should have to. I mean—a boy's a boy. A girl's a girl. What's a father going to do?"

So much heat, and so little light, has been cast on gender roles in the last few years, Jack is understandably confused and put out. Now he has four kids to raise in this atmosphere. How does he help them prepare for heaven-knows-what attitudes to come? Roles have changed radically in the last few years; what will the next few years bring?

"I counsel adults primarily," says Brian Newman. "Men come in. They let their hair down and really unload. And many, many times, one of their major worries that surfaces is, 'I'm scared. I want my daughters to be feminine and my boys to be masculine and I don't know how to achieve that. What if . . .' and then their voice trails off."

Paul Warren hears the same fear voiced, over and over. "A father does not affirm his child's gender identity by reinforcing the old stereotypes. They don't work in today's society; he'd be doing his children a terrible disservice. Another disservice would be to try to equalize maleness and femaleness in a spirit of competition. You see that a lot. The competitive spirit says, 'If boys get this, girls should get that.' 'Girls are as good as boys at fill-in-the-blank,' whether they really are or not. These are individuals, and individual kids may or may not be competitive in whatever the fill-in-the-blank happens to be.

"A father affirms his child's gender by respecting and celebrating the differences of maleness and femaleness. When Dad does that, the child will sort out the reality of gender differences and find his or her niche appropriately. The child will be flexible enough to shift with changing social standards and practices. I can't emphasize it too much. I repeat it: Dad teaches best by enjoying his own gender and respecting both genders."

Dad's role, summarized, might be charted as follows:

Things Fathers Have a Special Opportunity to Teach

Girls	Boys
There is strength in true gentleness.	There is gentleness in genuine strength.
Healthy submissiveness in relationships is servanthood, not passivity, dependency, or codependency.	True strength in relationships is not dominance and control, but servanthood.
An appreciation for beauty, for aesthetics, and for feelings is enhanced by the use of clear and logical thinking.	Logical and analytic thinking is most effective when it is balanced by an appreciation for feelings, beauty, and aesthetics.

The traditional male image in our culture downplays aesthetics and beauty. (Other cultures celebrate the full nature of men. For example, a standard Navajo blessing/greeting is "Walk in beauty.") Dad can give his boys back some of that which was lost. Dominance and control—that is, power— figure large in our culture. The traditional male considers it his gender prerogative to crack the whip. Dad can lead his children beyond that into the true, Christlike servanthood.

His sons and daughters will not learn servanthood by being treated like servants but by observing servants in action. Yep; that's Dad. How does Dad the Servant model a Christlike attitude in the everyday? Here are a few of many possible suggestions:

• He puts his own activities aside temporarily in order to help his kids. An example: Daughter is building a birdhouse and needs some help drilling the hole. Son is taking the training wheels off his bike. Dad puts the newspaper down until after the needs of Daughter and Son have been met.

- He helps his wife in her tasks, including the menial and the "woman's work." He's not too proud to scrub a toilet any more than Jesus considered Himself above footwashing.

- He places his family's interests above his own. He chooses to take the family down to the reservoir for a picnic instead of going golfing. He buys the mini-van that the family needs and continues to wait for that motorcycle he's always wanted. He'd like to skip Sunday school and take on a men's study for the unchurched down at the fire hall. But he can't do both and as worthy as the study project is, he knows his family needs his participation in Sunday school, so he keeps going to Sunday school.

Burdensome responsibilities? You will be amazed how freeing they are. The father who ungrudgingly takes on a servant role teaches his boys deep, deep lessons about what a real man is. His girls learn thereby not to be a man but to recognize a good one when they meet him. His girls will assume their own female qualities.

Encourage and Affirm

Dad's role of encourager and affirmer will never go out of fashion. Words of affirmation and encouragement from Dad will make a profound and positive difference in his kids' lives. That is also true when Dad is encouraging and affirming of his children's gender.

Paul Warren says, "With my son, it can be as simple as talking about 'It's great to be male.' Dad must carefully avoid putting down female. The "great to be male' must not be construed as ending in "aren't you glad you're not female?'

" 'That's the way men are' tells a child there are differences. And there certainly are differences. Men and women differ in unseen, immaterial ways just as they differ in physical ways."

Dad can affirm his son's maleness by encouraging him to identify with his maleness. *That's the way men and boys do it* (whatever *it* is) affirms masculinity. It may well be that is also the way women and girls do it. That's beside the point. The point is, *This is how males do it and we are males.*

Dad can encourage his girl in her femaleness in two ways. In a passive way, he can avoid encouraging her to identify with him directly, as he might with a son. Hear the subtle difference in meaning between "Do it like I'm doing it" and "Do it this way." "Be strong, like I am" and "Be strong." A daughter will pick up on the subtlety, at least at an unconscious level.

He does not expect her to approach things the way he does, to do things the way he does, to see life as he sees it. And he never ever criticizes her if her viewpoint departs from his.

Dad can actively encourage his daughter in her femaleness by respecting the innate differences and *valuing those differences*. "I like the way you described that; I would have described it differently." "I like the way you think." "Girls are so graceful when they swim." (Boys may well be just as graceful, but Dad is talking to a girl; whether boys are or not is beside the point here.)

The basics of affirmation and encouragement—praise for a job well attempted; the principle of "I like you because you are you"; the Gaithers' beautiful concept expressed in the song, "You are special; you are the only one of your kind"—don't change with gender.

Boys and girls together need these immensely important messages from Dad. And they need to hear from him that their gender is all right.

Teach and Skills-Enable

In her woodshop class, Annie found what might be called the Traditional attitude in her instructor. She was there to learn a skill not usually associated with girls. He was there to teach boys a skill associated with boys. He rightly assumed she was as capable as a boy. Capability was never an issue. It simply never occurred to him that she should be allowed to make the same mistakes and imperfections a boy would make. He helped her build a stool worthy of an experienced woodworker (himself), better than one a beginner would put together. The unspoken traditional precept: Girls are protected and cared for. They are protected from harm and they are protected from errors.

Role expectations—what a woman's work is as opposed to what a man's skills should be, and whether the woman is the protector or the protectee—have been deeply ingrained in fathers for generations. Now here are women, pushing hard to dis-ingrain them.

A friend of ours, a research director for a conservation organization, celebrated her half-century birthday several years ago. She says, "In college in the fifties, the few girls in biology became biology teachers or laboratory researchers in bacteriology and genetics; one became a scientific illustrator. All did indoors stuff: lab and classroom.

"But me, I liked the field courses: herpetology, out catching snakes and toads; mammalogy with your traplines, mutilating white-footed mice; plant ecology, running transects all over the peapatch. I was the only female in every field course I took except ornithology. So early one morning in general entomology, we were out netting dragonflies and the professor took me aside and said in all earnestness, 'Now, Miss Jones. You'll do a lot better if you stop chasing the young men and let them come to you.'

"It floored me. He assumed the only reason a girl would be taking field courses was to find a husband." She pauses. "Of course, that was back in the fifties. These days, most men's attitudes have progressed well into the early sixties."

Miss Jones is being unduly critical. (Miss Jones, incidentally, married an historian. He teaches Latin American history and current events—all indoors stuff. At the moment, he's in the library and she's in the ancient forests of Idaho, running traplines and transects.) A world of possibilities has opened for Dad's daughters that was closed to his sisters.

And women aren't the only ones enjoying this new world. Men have awakened to bright new possibilities. "I always felt this attraction for medicine," a friend named Roger told us. "And I envied girls. They got to take nursing. In a couple years they had their certificate or a degree and they were on their way. I frankly didn't have the grades to get into medical school or the resources to see it through. It was out of the question for me. And becoming a Physician's Assistant takes just about as much. So I trained as a paramedic and worked for ambulance companies a few years, but mopping up emergencies wasn't really my favorite thing. What I really enjoyed was kids.

"Then one day I came across a male nurse in an emergency room. You know, until that moment it never occurred to me that maybe I could take nursing. I was forty-two years old!"

Today Roger works as a nurse in the pediatric ward of a major hospital, and he loves it. Twice he has turned down promotions that would take him off the front lines and put him behind a desk. Increasingly, stories like his are becoming common.

The present generation of new fathers is, again, the one on the bubble. These fathers are being called upon to abandon the old sexual stereotypes. Their sons will have it easier as they enter fatherhood tomorrow, for Dad can show the way today. He can best prepare his daughters for that new world by giving them the same life skills he teaches his sons. Just as importantly, he must also give his sons the life skills his daughters traditionally receive.

Enabling as we use it here means "encouragement to keep growing." Were Dad to couch it as a sentence, he might say "I'm going to help you learn how to conquer the world and cope with the world." Girls and boys together, therefore, need to master much the same life skills, for girls are going to cope in the open marketplace on the same footing as their brothers.

"The father," says Frank Minirth, whose own daughters are beginning enthusiastically to step out into the world, "needs to avoid his tendency just to protect his girls."

Dr. Warren agrees. "The stereotypical father focuses only on protecting his delicate little doll and doesn't give her the skills she needs. I catch myself doing that with my own niece—not just protecting her, but subtly encouraging her to be that little girl who needs protection. I find myself with an attitude of, 'I'll take care of that mean old bully for you.' Too, a stereotypical father talking to his son might say something like, "How come you can't do this? Come on! Let's do it!' You just don't find yourself doing that with a little girl."

What skills are necessary to teach your children these days? To get through life these days, a girl needs training and competence in:

_____ Automotive maintenance and elementary mechanics

_____ Small engine and appliance maintenance, minor repair

_____ Tool use and household repairs, including plumbing

_____ Elementary carpentry, painting, fix-up

_____ Cooking and housekeeping

_____ Childcare and basics of child development

_____ At least enough sewing to alter and repair garments

_____ Personal finance and investment

_____ Personal safety skills and training to use them

In contrast, what do boys need in order to cope well? Exactly that same list. Exactly. Every item on it.

These days, men and women tend to marry later. Both will probably work. Both will probably live alone at least part of their lives. Therefore, both need the skills to move with ease through the annoyances and routines of everyday living, both with and without small children.

The wise father trains his child to respect the marriage bond and to treat it as a lifetime commitment. The wise father will also prepare his child to function alone, through death or disablement, at any moment.

"Fathers give their boys the macho thing," says Brian Newman, "but not gentleness. Dad has to be careful not to just model the usual enabling skills for his boy—finishing the basement as a family room, fixing the lawn mower, pruning the apple tree—but also to model nurturing. Taking care of babies. Cooking things that aren't just barbecued. In true strength there is always gentleness. That's what Jesus meant by *meekness*. 'For I am meek and lowly.' Meek is not wishy-washy. It's power under control."

Paul Warren nods. "*A truly gentle knight.* I like that phrase. Knights were warriors, you know. Brutal, ready to swing that lance and battle axe. And that was the highest compliment you could pay a knight. That he was gentle."

Jack Brubaker would cast a highly critical eye on all this. "So you're saying, then, that I raise the girls and boys up to be unisex clones. Neither fish nor fowl."

Actually, no. You can teach boys and girls the same life skills, and encourage them both with praise and affirmation, but they will still emerge at the adult end of your influence as wholly male men and wholly female women.

—The Gender Completion—

"The goal," says Paul Warren, "is to make each child a fuller person—able to taste more of life and to savor it better.

People today are no longer locked into narrow role expectations, and that's exciting."

"It's not simply a matter of today's stereotypical feminist rebelling." Brian Newman expands on the topic. "Men are resisting the old stereotype too. Too many men have missed out on a lot of satisfaction and happiness by dumping the child-rearing onto their wives. They want that satisfaction that comes from being an involved father. So we give our sons and daughters similar training. Let them all partake fully of life."

"I'm thinking of an analogy with a paint store," Paul Warren muses. "To make this color, you add a little of this, and for that color, a little of that. The stock can on the shelf is plain by comparison. The old roles were plain stock. Dad is adding attractive, exciting new color for his kids."

Can you treat girls and boys alike? Not really, try as you would. Thanks to our past, it doesn't come naturally. But as their primary skills-enabler, you can teach both of them the same coping skills. And as their primary protector, you can give them equal opportunity to err and to grow. Send them out into life together, with a hearty heigh-ho and here we go!

"Above all," says Paul Warren, "fathers affirm gender identity by teaching and modeling honesty and openness in relationships, rather than promoting stereotypes. Honest relationships. With them, children can move into the roles and wholeness God intended for them."

Brian Newman concludes, "We don't want to treat kids differently from each other, so much. What we want is to treat them differently from the past.

Things to Think About

Think about the following questions for each of your children, individually. They're each very different—even twins. We've left blanks for you to write about the first child. You may want to write about the others on a separate sheet of paper.

Identify three attributes your child has that are traditionally considered positive or favorable for that sex (speed
in a boy, lovely eyes in a girl . . .):

1. _____
2. _____
3. _____

Now identify three attributes that child enjoys that would
be praised in the opposite sex (strength in a girl, a gentle
voice in a boy . . .):

1. _____
2. _____
3. _____

What specific words of praise or affirmation can you give
that child which reflect the attributes above?

1. _____
2. _____
3. _____

During this next week, find opportunity to speak them.

What new skill has that child attempted or mastered in
the last month? _____
_____

Did you participate in the learning process? _____

How can you participate in the next month as your child
improves or masters that skill?_____
_____

What words of encouragement will you offer regarding
that skill?_____
_____

Think about a friend or other person who is working in
what you would consider a nontraditional job (a female
police officer, a male secretary or clerk). How would you
help a son prepare to fill that job?_____
_____

A daughter?_____

_____

For each child in your immediate and extended family (that includes nieces, nephews, and all), identify at least one attribute or achievement that impresses you. Now plan for each child a statement of praise or affirmation that does not mention that attribute or achievement.

And of course you are going to speak that praise, aren't you?

TWELVE

Solo Dad

You're a movie or television producer with major clout. You are going to create a film or TV series that will garner lots of enthusiasm and make you lots of money. You're not out for art here, necessarily, but for popularity. A formula that works, over and over.

If you want to tilt the odds strongly in your favor, you'll build your project around a single father struggling to manage cute kids.

Dozens of shows and films based upon that theme have proven highly successful. Apparently there is something poignant and charming about this handsome guy (they're always handsome, with sex appeal) beleaguered by fatherhood. Three men versus a photogenic baby. Bachelor father. Bachelor uncle saddled with kids. Total stranger saddled with kids. Apple Dumpling gang.

The reality, almost always, is far more rending than *Kramer vs. Kramer*. Whether he is widowed, divorced, or never married, the single father inexplicably finds himself fighting intense, bitter emotions and attitudes he never knew existed. And all that comes on top of trying to be a halfway decent dad—or feeling guilt because he is not.

There is no way to turn the single-father experience into the bluebirds and bright endings of TV sitcoms and movies, but there are ways to minimize the negative impact. The single father makes the best of his world by first dealing with his own special problems and then helping his children through theirs.

"Physician, heal thyself." And then, "Heal thy children."

—Dad Deals With His Issues—

Robert May always considered himself a pretty good husband and father. He provided well for his family, he went to church, he didn't drink or smoke, he didn't fool around. He usually worked swing shift at a manufacturing plant, or sometimes night shift. They moved him around a lot because he could handle just about any job at his end of the factory. A forty-hour work week, a couple hours of television, regular meals. Rob May was reasonably content.

Then his wife left him. And took the kids.

Shocked and bewildered—he hadn't the vaguest idea why she'd take it into her head suddenly to do that—he didn't fight hard enough, fast enough for his rights and wants. Suddenly she had it all—the house, the child support, the kids—and he got to visit and take them somewhere every other weekend.

Robert May found himself in a lackluster little apartment watching TV on a twenty-two-inch set. And he still didn't know why.

Robert May is an extreme example, but a common one. Statistically speaking, the kids go to Mom. Their standard of living will drop significantly, and their father's will rise. Within two years, still statistically speaking, Dad will have severed all, or nearly all, contact with them.

Not only do those statistics damage the children significantly, they lay a burden on Dad he may not even know he is carrying. That burden will weigh him down to the point that he cannot be an adequate father. He cannot make a good second marriage or renew the first, and, statistically speaking again, that burden will tip him over into some sort of addictive behavior.

The burden is his load of guilt, grief, and anger. Until he deals with that burden, he cannot help either himself or his children.

Dad's Anger

"Don't get mad, get even" is vacuous advice because you get mad anyway. You cannot escape it. You cannot even control it to any large extent. Even the widower experiences intense anger. Anger is an emotion of the heart, not the head. The heart feels angry. The head comes along secondarily and picks a target to be angry at. Most people fail to realize that's the way it works, and they spend all their effort on the target, not the anger itself. The target must be forgiven. But underlying sources must be acknowledged too.

Most people fail to realize that nearly all anger is rooted in fear. One of the big reasons a man backs out of his kids' lives is fear. He didn't feel man enough to stay with his kids. Now he's afraid his kids hate him. To avoid getting hit in the face with their hatred, he stays away.

The widower experiences anger just as much as does the ex-husband. He is angry at his wife for doing this to him, for leaving him behind. Rarely will he acknowledge that anger. He is probably angry at God for allowing it to happen—perhaps, heaven forbid, even for orchestrating it. He is angry at life, at fate, at himself. The widower must work on his anger just as must the divorced father.

Both men will deal with it in two ways: One, they must acknowledge the anger exists, and two, they can then apply the guilt and grief steps below to their anger.

Rob May was one of those people who doesn't get visibly angry. He didn't yell and throw things. He didn't even act sour, at least not much. He let the anger simmer inside and didn't really accept that it was there. It evidenced itself by the fact that his mind kept turning to what his wife had done to him. It expressed itself as a heavy depression. It hindered him from concentrating on his work or even on TV. It did not truly emerge until he was well into the grieving process.

Things to Think About

I can think of these actions I've taken in the past, or am taking now, that reveal my anger (unexplained fury, short temper, depression, impatience with others, hatred . . .)

1. _____

2. _____

3. _____

If you are divorced or widowed, consider these possible sources of anger in your life. We're not talking about your part now, if any, but your wife's. And yes, widowers do find themselves angry with their spouses. It's not a source of shame. It's a natural heart's response. That doesn't mean, though, that you have to live with it.

_____ My wife didn't care enough about the union to work something out.

_____ She took my kids.

_____ She left me with the kids and I can't handle parenting well alone.

_____ Her vices (drinking, drugs, perfectionism) wedged us apart.

_____ She has never asked forgiveness for her part in the mess.

_____ She is (was) insensitive to my needs and wants.

_____ Women are supposed to be nurturing, but she sure didn't nurture me.

_____ She let her individual life get in the way of our life as a couple by insisting on [career, travel, _____].

_____ Other sources of anger _____

_____

Dad's Guilt

No matter how his singleness occurred, Dad feels guilty. If it was his choice to leave a marriage—perhaps for another woman, career aspirations, or even boredom—the guilt nags. Perhaps he felt trapped, unable to handle the responsibility. If so, he feels guilty about being inadequate for a role every other adult male seems to take in stride.

If the dissolution was not his choice, there must have

been something he could have done to prevent this break-up. Had he given a little more, had he asserted himself or backed off, had he . . . . He lost the power to control his life and his family somehow, and somehow it was his fault.

A widower's guilt is of a different kind, but it still makes itself felt. The man may feel he did not provide enough, or didn't come through better, or could have done something to prevent the death of his spouse. In his widowhood, he feels guilty for not parenting the (presumably superior) way his wife would have, for not spending enough time with the kids, for falling short in this matter or that.

No matter what the reason, the guilt will be there to some degree. Dad may well talk himself out of seeing it, with "I did my best." "It's all her fault." "I'm innocent." Such statements, even if they are true, mask guilt feelings.

The first key, then, for single fathers is:

• **Recognize the Guilt Feelings**

"Hard to do. It's so hard." Frank Minirth speaks from the experience of a professional who sees hundreds of such cases. "Denial kicks in. You see, it's even harder for a man to admit he has guilt feelings than to admit he's guilty. The macho stereotype: 'I'm tougher than feelings. Feelings don't affect me.'"

To get past denial, try this: Picture the things that have happened in your life, the events or attitudes, as happening to someone else. Would they conceivably generate some guilt feelings in that other person? You are that other person.

Notice we didn't say, "recognize the guilt." We're urging you to recognize the feelings. Whether the guilt is justified or not is not at issue here. The feelings are.

• **Evaluate Yourself**

To do this well, you really ought to sit down with a trusted friend, bounce the ideas off him or her, and listen to what he or she has to say. We mean really listen. You need some-one who can see from the outside, someone who can take a less subjective viewpoint than yours. A sounding board. A mentor.

If you thought recognizing guilt feelings was tough, wait until you get into this. It's hard. Painful. And very necessary.

Don't dwell on what your wife did or did not do. You are looking only at you. Admit the mistakes you made, and only the mistakes you yourself made. What actions that you took— or failed to take—have hurt others, especially your children?

What does your mentor have to say about it? Listen carefully.

• Acknowledge Your Part

Having identified actions and events where guilt is justified, we recommend doing as the church does: confess them, provide restitution if possible (that's not always possible), ask forgiveness, grieve the loss, and move beyond them. If you are a member of a church where confession and forgiveness play a major part in public and private worship, by all means use that avenue. Also, confess and ask forgiveness from the persons involved in your life, the persons you affected.

Not just surface forgiveness. Genuine, real forgiveness does not require forgetting afterwards. It is an act done for the benefit of the forgiver more than the forgivee. And it is an act done to a person because of a transgression (or perceived transgression), not the person's transgression itself. If forgiveness is a problem for you, seek other sources, such as the book *Passages of Marriage*, where forgiveness is dealt with at length.

If those persons refuse to forgive you, that is their privilege. The ball, so to speak, is now in their court. You must ask. And it is the sincere asking that is most important to you.

So is grieving.

In Rob May's case, he identified himself as an unwitting victim of a woman's caprice. He did find a mentor, and that's good. His confidante was a forty-year-old divorced woman who worked near him on an assembly line. However, we strongly recommend you find a male to help you.

She provided Rob with valuable insight. She got him talking about the complaints his wife had made ("harped on," as he put it) during the last six months of the marriage. His inaccessibility. His self-absorption. His lack of attention to his wife and kids. The lousy working hours that he made no effort to improve.

He saw many ways in which his wife could have done more, or could have gotten him to improve his participation. But that did not diminish his own role. Whether or not his wife's complaints were justified, he had made no effort to respond to her. He came eventually to the conclusion that many of her complaints were indeed justified, and that he had fallen far short of being the functioning father and partner in the marriage that he should have been.

Things to Think About

The mother of my child(ren) has accused me of:

1. _____
2. _____
3. _____

She is probably at least partially right about:

1. _____
2. _____
3. _____

I acknowledge that these and other issues could make me feel guilty.

After reading this chapter, I am taking these specific steps to deal with guilt issues:

1. _____
2. _____
3. _____

I am enlisting as a mentor and listener, this person:

_____

From those realizations came Rob May's acknowledgement of guilt, and from that the next step, grief.

Dad's Grief

The single father has much to grieve. There is the whole issue of loss. The family is shattered. The kids are hurting. You are hurting. If your situation includes divorce, your ex-wife is just as broken.

Grief issues differ somewhat in different situations. The divorced father who chose to leave must grieve his choice, no matter how happy he thinks he is now. If the wife chose, Dad must grieve not only for the lost marriage but for the lost control of his own life—for a very painful and personal defeat, especially if his wife left for another man. Inadequacy always looms large, and this is a very big inadequacy issue.

The widower is expected to grieve more than the divorced man. Widowers, however, don't always. There's that machismo thing again. The widower may have to give himself permission to grieve and then insist to himself that he follow through.

Grief is not over in one episode of sadness. It progresses in stages. It is critically important that the single father, whatever his circumstance, understand the grieving process and use it. The steps of grief are these:

• **Denial**

It didn't really happen that way.

It's not my fault.

It's not as bad as it looks.

The kids are better off now.

I'm not hurting; I'm happy. See the smile on my face?

That's all denial. Denial is the necessary first step of the process, the pregnant pause before the hard part. It allows your heart to adjust to the reality you will be grieving. It can last a few moments or many years. The danger is getting stuck in it. Staying with denial derails the rest of the grieving process.

• Anger

This step is really easy! You can get angry at your wife, your kids, your boss, yourself . . . the sky's the limit. Here's the full realization of what you must grieve, and you're furious. Good! Just find a safe, nondestructive way to vent it. It's the necessary, logical next step, and it's all right.

• Depression

Depression has been defined as "anger turned inward." Imagine the energy you expend being angry at something. All that same energy buries itself inside you, eating at you. You don't sleep well, or you sleep too much. You feel lousy, morbid; maybe you simply feel "blah." Life isn't pretty, but then, neither is anything else. Depression.

In the true grieving process, the period of depression will be temporary. If it persists, you should seek help from a trusted counselor or other professional.

• Bargaining

Have I got a deal for you! If you just agree to dot all your I's from now on, and cross all your T's, I'll restore your marriage. If you'll just do such-and-so, I'll heal your kids.

That's bargaining. Everyone goes through it, but bargains made, if made at all, never work. When your mind-set shifts to making bargains with God, your ex-wife, or yourself, rejoice. You've reached this stage. You're nearly there.

• Sadness and Resolution

"I've been sad ever since I became single," you may complain. "So what's new?" This is a different sadness. This is the sadness that comes of realizing that the denial, the anger, the depression, the bargaining won't work. This is the true grief. This is the end of the rope.

It is also the beginning of renewal. By passing through all the phases and uncorking your sadness here, you can come to terms with reality. You will cleanse the pockets of anger deep inside you, lest they fester more. This is the way things are, folks. Now let's begin from here to work the best deal possible.

Be advised you can get locked up in any of the steps, not just the denial. Also, you can recycle through the phases more than once. In fact, you should.

Rob May's mentor, Elaine, happened to know about the grieving process from personal experience; she had undergone counseling when her own marriage fell apart. She was able to explain the process to him and lead him through it. Imagine how surprised he was when his anger, so long suppressed, burst forth, to be vented at last.

For several months Rob worked and reworked his grief, bringing specific incidents to the surface to grieve them through. He grieved his children's anger at him and his ex-wife. He grieved their situation. He grieved his. He trotted out each of his losses and dwelt upon it individually.

It was on the second anniversary of his divorce that he could finally say, "I am ready to move forward. My depression has eased."

Something to Think About

Sign one of the two statements below:

"I understand what the grieving process is and am ready to embark upon it. I promise to work on it. If I don't fully understand, I'll seek out someone who does to help me."
Signed:_____

"I like the way I feel now and refuse to consider the grieving process. My kids are on their own with this."
Signed:_____

—And Now, the Kids—

Rob May couldn't really figure his kids out. Had he known the term "swooping eagle" he would have had to admit he was one. He had never really gotten close to them. He had never really spoken to them much, except to yell when they got too rowdy. He had no relationship with which to help them. He had to start from absolute scratch.

His best plan of approach would not be to dive in instantly in an attempt to help them through their own anger, guilt, and grief. He would have to build a stronger relationship first, earning the right to be heard. From there he could work on the other issues.

The Child's Anger

In a blended family, child A is rebellious, easily enraged, stubborn. Child B tries to get along, cooperating, making the best of things. Question: Which is the angry child?

Answer: Both of them.

As we counsel a wide variety of cases, we have discovered that anger almost always looms bigger than anything else in the life of a child from a broken home (broken by either death or divorce). It can supplant the natural hunger for love and affection. It can displace respect. Dad first and foremost is going to have to deal with his child's anger.

If Dad hasn't adequately dealt with his own feelings, he will probably try to rationalize his child's feelings. "The kid's doing great. Our relationship has never been better. He/she's handling it like a champ. Not to worry."

Worry.

Dad must understand that his child needs that anger, and even more important, that his child is hurting deeply. The child's world has been destroyed. Dad can get so focused on the surface anger that he fails to see the pain underneath. It's the hurt that needs the help. Hurting kids desperately need someone who can embrace them while they're angry. That can be really hard for Dad to do.

An enraged child is damaging to a father's ego, esteem, and feelings of adequacy. After all, a good father would have happy kids, wouldn't he? Dad is tempted to simply back off and chuck the relationship. Bowing out is not only the easiest thing to do, it may well look like the best. It's not.

The stereotypical father wants to shut his child's anger down. To the eagle, no one except the eagle is allowed to be angry. Too, a kid's anger causes a lot of heat and friction. Kids are annoying at times even under the best of circumstances. When they're angry, they can be truly obnoxious.

"A case comes to mind," says Paul Warren, "of a girl about fifteen named Joanne—a child of divorce. Her father told me about the episode.

"She was one angry kid. Rebellious. Defiant. On one of her dad's weekend visitations she began unloading her anger on him. How dare he do so-and-so—I forget just what. It's his fault, and on and on. He was sorely tempted to just get away from her anger. He had cause; it was really hard to take. To his credit, he chose to hang in there. He restrained himself and wouldn't let himself respond with anger. He took it. Pretty soon his daughter was crying and then they both were crying and talking about the pain they both really felt.

"Today they both recognize that moment as the point when they turned around and began the healing process. So, fathers, it's crucially important to understand that when children are angry, there's hurt underneath. Allow them to express anger and love them through the anger to get to the hurt. That anger is part of the process. Don't back away from it."

Dad faces another daunting task: he must help his kids talk through their feelings without being defensive about his role or derogatory toward their mother. To accomplish that task requires constant vigilance. Is this attack on me? How can I best resist responding in kind? Is this attack on their mom? Keep your mouth shut, pal!

The Child's Guilt

"Guilt? But it's not their fault," you say. And then you tell the kids that. It doesn't do any good.

Small children entertain what psychologists call *global guilt*. That is an encompassing feeling that no matter what

happens in the universe, it is somehow the child's fault.
Any anger and arguing is the child's fault. If the dog gets
hit by a truck, it's the child's fault. And when something in
the family structure breaks down, that absolutely, definitely
is all the child's fault. The older child begins to understand—
strictly head knowledge—that things happen outside his or
her influence, but the heart clings to that global guilt for a
surprisingly long time.

Small children will feel guilty about their mother dying.
They will probably feel responsible somehow (they won't
be able to explain why, of course. This is all beyond articulation). This guilt occurs in older children where you would
not logically expect it because it is so illogical. In addition,
older kids feel guilty about not treating their deceased mom
better, or about not obeying perfectly, or whatever. Be
aware that children of widowers feel just as guilty as children
of divorce.

Children are sensitive barometers of what's happening in
their family. The friction and chaos that so often precede
separation will without fail alter children's behavior, and usually not for the better. A bad-behaving child feels even guilt-
ier when the split happens. If only he or she had . . . . **It's
all my fault that Daddy's angry or Mommy left.**

Dad must recognize that those guilt feelings are down in
there, just as he acknowledges the anger. Regardless of the
surface indications, rest assured that at some level of the
child's being, guilt feelings lurk. Dad can help his child work
through guilt in the same ways he himself worked through it.

The Child's Grief

Kids suffer the same grieving processes adults do, but
with this complication: They must regrieve periodically.
When Dad handles (and often finds he must rehandle) his
grief, he's doing it at an adult level, with an adult's depth
of understanding.

A three-year-old has not tasted much of the world yet—
almost none of it outside the sphere of his or her immediate

family. The three-year-old grieves at a three-year-old's shallow level of maturity and understanding. When the child is six, he or she must grieve the losses at this more sophisticated level of understanding. At nine, at twelve, at fourteen, at late-teen, at an adult level . . . the child must process and reprocess losses as the depth of understanding matures.

Whatever the case may be, it is important that Dad accept and understand the prolonged, repetitive grief process his kids are going through. He should be leading them through the same process he experienced, grieving for lost family, for lost happiness.

Things to Think About

Kids express themselves in multitudes of ways, and often, the surface expression is not a mirror of the feelings beneath. What do you see in your child(ren) beneath the surface? Think about each child individually.

This child tends to express anger by:

_____ Blowing up instantly and unexpectedly.
_____ Sulking.
_____ Weird or destructive behavior.
_____ Depression.
_____ Other _____

I am prepared to put up with that.

This child evidences depression by:

_____ A drop in grades.
_____ Increased hostility or moodiness.
_____ Explosive anger.
_____ Withdrawal, apartness.
_____ Ennui; boredom with life, no pep.
_____ Lack of sense of humor, or very bitter humor.
_____ Other _____

I understand that depression is anger inverted, and I will encourage my child to talk the anger out.

My child feels this about his or her mother (whether she is living or dead):

_____ Anger or

_____ Love.

_____ Devotion (or, devotion to her memory) or

_____ Avoidance.

_____ Blind trust or

_____ Distrust.

_____ Respect or

_____ Lack of respect.

I will encourage the child's respect and be vigilant in recognizing my own tendency to put his/her mother down or show his/her mother in a bad light.

—Communication and Visitation—

The widower may believe this section is just for divorced fathers. Not so. Widowers never have as much time as they wish for their kids. When they can, they may try to make up for midweek neglect with a rousing weekend. In that way they're not so much different from the divorced dad. There is never ever enough time, and there is never enough open communication between dad and kid. So widowers should understand that this section is just as much for them as for any other breed of solo dad.

Rob May had to start building a relationship with his kids from the ground up. He had flubbed fathering so far, flubbed it to the max. How could he make up for lost time? Two weekends a month? Was it worth the effort?

"Is it worth the effort? Oh yes. Absolutely." Frank Minirth sits forward in his chair, speaking with the animation of a man talking about his favorite subject—fatherhood. "Dads tend to start paying attention to their kids as the kids enter their midteens. That's when the kids are getting interesting, the dads think. By then, the relationship should be in place, should have been in place since the start.

"But if it's not, it's never too late to begin. No matter

what age you get involved with your children, you can make a positive difference in their lives."

Communication

Let's consider some ways Rob May can get involved with his kids when he is, in essence, an absentee father.

• Buy a Video Camera

"I'm a great one for gadgets," admits Brian Newman, a man who can use the most complex, sophisticated phone system with ease. "I love gadgets, the shinier the better.

"Videotape the place where you work. Videotape your house if the kids don't visit there. Videotape letters. You can be a talking head on the tape, or you can pan around to other stuff while you talk. Anything, so the kids can get to know you.

"And of course, telephone frequently."

Rob May might even find himself having so much fun he'd get creative, telling stories and tall tales, going biking with the camera duct-taped to his helmet . . . .

• Introduce Them to Your Life

Rob could take his kids to work with him, if not during his normal work hours, at least on some other shift. Show them around. Introduce them to people. Show them what he does in the wee hours of the morning. Rob's world doesn't begin and end at the factory. He might take them along to his barber shop, to the garage where he and his buddies talk mechanics, to the library where he catches up on *Sports Illustrated* and *Field and Stream* now and then.

• The Mail Mystique

With the telephone so close at hand, personal letter writing is becoming a dying art. Here's where Rob can revive it. Absolutely nothing carries quite the same impact as a personal letter. Perhaps on the Saturdays when he does not have the kids, he can write each one a short letter. Each one. Individually and personally. The letters can say exactly the same thing to all the different kids, with perhaps some tailoring of each to the child's interest. And yes, he should send letters to kids not yet old enough to read.

What do you say in a letter for crying out loud? Nothing exciting happens, nothing to write home about, literally.

How about:

The weather. Always good for a paragraph. Praise or complain. Snow and hailstorms make especially good topics.

Anything about mutual friends and relatives that you've learned lately. Letters are a wonderful source of family history for kids.

Reminiscences about when you were a kid, things the children have not heard before. Limit one per letter.

Anything about a pet, however innocuous ("The dog is shedding again. Going to start following him around with a shop vac.").

Anything about animals you've seen or heard lately.

Anything that you know is of interest to the child (Johnny likes planes and you watched a 767 come in yesterday; Mary likes roller skating and you saw two kids skating slalom around the fire hydrant and light poles on Sixth Street; the little one is just starting school and you saw the world's biggest school bus go by a couple days ago. It was huge! It needed two zip codes to park in).

Anything about yourself that might be interesting. Limit "I" paragraphs to one per letter (you ran out of gas on the way to work; you made your first tacos based on daughter Mary's recipe; you attended a shop-sponsored safety seminar and learned some interesting things—list some; the factory installed a new phone system. Now everyone finds himself talking to the wrong people).

No preaching, no correction, no discipline, no ranting.

Words of praise and affirmation to the child. Always.

God's blessing on the child (a simple "God bless you, [ ]" written as you pray for blessing is fine).

As Rob thinks of things during the week, he might jot

them down on a scrap of paper or scratch pad he carries just for that purpose.

He can buy a box of crayons and draw pictures to send each kid, especially the little ones. Goofy pictures. Artless pictures. Fun stuff.

He can clip cartoons and articles from the paper to slip in an envelope and mail, relieving himself of the task of writing anything at all.

He can give each child stationery, envelopes, paper, crayons, magic markers, and postage stamps to encourage return mail.

Phone calls do not replace letters; they supplement them.

"Whatever means you use," Paul Warren counsels, "it is so important to keep the relationship up. Try to use age-related means of communication—by that I mean pictures for the very young, tapes for older kids—to express love to that child.

"It's especially hard to do with a distant dad. It takes work, creativity, and a willingness to face fear and inadequacy to keep in touch; to resist the easy way out of losing contact."

Visitation

"Sometimes Dad forgets how kids think. He starts thinking the way an adult thinks, and he can mess up those times when he and his kids are together," advises Brian Newman.

Rob May could use some suggestions for the dad whose visitation rights are limited, whose time with his kids seems much too short (and occasionally, after a hectic weekend, much too long).

Can't Buy Me Love

"It happens so much," says Paul Warren, "the father trying to buy his kids' love. Because of his unresolved guilt issues, he'll overload his kids with gifts, activities, exotic places to go. He tries to hang on to their love by buying it. Bribing.

"This is dangerous for the kid. Destructive. The kid sees that only the material is going to be involved in this relationship. Dad is teaching his child that love is measured in things. The child may learn that whatever he or she wants from Daddy can be had, if you whine enough. Neither Dad nor the kid realizes that material gifts and exciting amusement parks cannot replace relationship. Nothing can replace time spent getting to know his kids. Nothing."

Dad is goal- and gadget-oriented, but his kids are relationship-oriented. The wise dad will put aside toys and gadgets and keep it simple, keep it close, keep it personal. Do something neat (it need not be out of the ordinary). Talk. Have a meal together. Laugh.

Beware the power play, a situation kids quickly and intuitively exploit. If Dad and Mom are at serious odds, they may vie for the purchase of the kids' affection. One parent buys the child a gift. The other, striving to outdo the spouse, buys a bigger, fancier, costlier one. You're up to computers and little red sports cars in no time flat. Like nuclear proliferation, no one wins this war, and the kids, for all their fancy presents, lose most.

Related to gifts are super-weekends. Here's where Dad, out to impress the kids, curries their favor with a trip to the amusement park, and the zoo, and the science center, and the movies, and . . . and . . . and . . . . Dad in his grown-up perspective is impressed by such places, and by the big money he too frequently shells out there. The kids will probably enjoy them, sure.

Such special events are all right now and then; mostly then. But what will serve Dad's purpose far better is a bat and ball and a simple picnic in the city park where he can play catch with the kids.

"We encourage single parents to be very careful with gifts," counsels Frank Minirth. "Rather, give lots of affection. Holding, embracing, listening. Time. Be there for them. That's the most important gift."

Rob May found himself deep in the game, getting costly and often useless stuff for his kids simply because they begged for it. Only when he managed a good grip on his own guilt feelings (with a little insight from his mentor,

Elaine) could he halt the habit. His kids called him cheap. They whined. They contrasted their Mom's generosity with his newfound miserliness. They even dragged him to the community theater production of *A Christmas Carol* to show him what comes of being a tightwad. He treated them to hot chocolate afterwards and engaged them in a lengthy, lighthearted discussion of the relative advantages of skateboarding versus roller-blading.

He noticed, eventually, that although he had reduced the automatic flow of gifts to a trickle, the kids were still waiting eagerly on the stoop when he drove up to the house Saturday mornings.

Don't Bother Being Perfect

When Dad is not custodial, his time with his kids is precious and severely limited. Dad has a pronounced tendency during visitations to want to be on his best behavior, the perfect dad. There are several reasons. One is the time constraint. Another is a desire to show up the custodial parent, to look so good the kids will regret being stuck with her.

If Dad would be perfect, he figures his visits should be positive experiences in every regard. All smiles, all yesses. He may confuse "positive" with "never having to say anything negative." Dad doesn't realize that sometimes a very positive thing is to say "no."

To unconsciously improve that perfect-father image, Rob May let his kids get away with just about anything. He feared disciplining them, lest they hate him.

Just the opposite is true. Kids need discipline, and they know they need discipline intuitively, for that discipline shows them you love them enough to set good boundaries. "Setting good boundaries" is psychology-ese for drawing firm lines as regards behavior and individuality. A firm boundary says, "I am Dad and you are kids. Because I am solid in my Dad-ness, you are free to grow and blossom as kids. The rules are for your benefit, to help you grow well, and I won't relax them just because you may not like them. I love you."

"Dads," cautions Paul Warren, "don't let kids' anger about discipline stop you from doing what's right. Don't allow the kids to manipulate you. Kids in broken families quickly become extremely manipulative. 'Mom lets me do this. If Mom were here, we could . . . .' And you can bet they'll be back with your ex-wife saying "Dad would let us do . . . .' If discipline is for the child's good, hang in with it.

"What kids think is right is very egocentric. Therefore it frequently is not right for them. Unless you the parent are committed to breaking the will but not the spirit of the child, then you'll reinforce the foolishness in the kids' hearts, with negative impact. If kids feel they can get anything they want from their single dad, they don't have the security of that discipline V, and they are damaged."

Although the noncustodial father's visitation time may be severely restricted, he still has the same fatherly duties any other dad has. He is still there to be his children's window on the world and their skills-enabler. He still can teach them the sense of the world and how to cope successfully in it. He can still nurture and protect, to an extent.

"Never underestimate your uniqueness," Frank Minirth advises. "You're Dad, and no one can replace you."

Most of all, the single dad can still build purpose in his kids' lives.

He can dream with them.

—The Impact of Divorce—

"When a couple comes to me with separation on their minds," claims Brian Newman, "they talk about a civilized divorce. They say, 'We want to do this in such a way that it won't have a bad impact on the kids.'

"And I tell them, 'People, forget it. There is no such thing as a divorce with minimal impact on the kids. It will impact them negatively, and it will be profound. No other way.' Then they'll say, "Yes, but . . .' and tell me why it's better for the kids that they separate, and I'll repeat, no way."

"Another myth of divorce," Paul Warren relates, "is that

they're getting away from their problems. The truth is, the divorce won't solve any of their problems. It will multiply them. And it will generate immense bitterness. We challenge divorced parents to put aside their bitterness, because it will invariably work down to the kids."

Brian Newman snorts. "It's good to quench the bitterness. It's necessary. But it's next to impossible because so many complications arise. Dad so frequently checks out because he can't deal with the ex-wife. The ex-wife wants to destroy memories, keep the kids away, stay away herself. They both feel angry and betrayed. The kids lose their dad and they feel angry and betrayed." He shrugs. "Bitterness. It's built-in."

"Bitterness is assuaged by grieving the losses and forgiving your ex-spouse." And then Paul Warren adds, "The best fathers can produce respect for their kids' mom in spite of the divorce."

Respect?

If you are divorced, list three things about your ex-wife that would be worthy of respect in the eyes of a man who did not know her well.

1. _____
2. _____
3. _____

List three things she does as a mother to your kids that you accept and can respect.

1. _____
2. _____
3. _____

List three things your kids say about their mom that would generate respect.

1. _____
2. _____
3. _____

When next you feel anger, resentment, bitterness, and hopelessness well up, remind yourself of these good points in the woman. It's tough. It requires forgiveness on your part. But you can do it if you have to. And for the kids' sake you have to.

You are Dad. For the kids, you can do whatever you have to. They depend upon you.

Things to Think About

Obviously a key to helping children is getting to know them. Perhaps you can use these items to help you get started. Think about each child individually. This means getting to know each one better than you now do. Good. If you're uncertain, ask the child. Use these items not just to better deal with the single-parent situation yourself, but as an avenue toward greater intimacy in your relationships with your children. The benefits of improved closeness and intimacy will multiply as your kids grow up.

This child is best described as (shy, bold, rebellious, cooperative, reserved, outspoken . . .): _____
_____

These traits should be encouraged: _____
_____

These traits should be subtly discouraged: _____
_____

Even as a single father, I can help this particular child grow and develop into a confident, stable adult by:

_____ Encouraging the child's interest in _____
_____

_____ Allowing the child more latitude in (decision-making, likes and dislikes, choices [friends, apparel, foods])
_____
_____

_____ Teaching the child these skills suitable to his or her personality and physical build (crafts, sports, activities, animal husbandry, plant culture, games, practical skills such as woodworking or computer science . . .): _____

_____

Three age-appropriate ways I can express my love to this child would be:

1. _____
2. _____
3. _____

And finally . . . Think of a fourth one.

—Stepping Out—

Single fathers usually become stepfathers, and that opens a whole new horizon of challenges. Daunting challenges. You know men who are; statistically speaking, some of your best friends are stepdads. It behooves you, therefore, to understand some of the mechanics of stepfathering, if only to be able to sympathize with the men who mean a lot to you. We suggest that even if you yourself are not a stepfather, that you not skip this next chapter, Stepfathering. Its information will prove useful in some context, sooner or later.

THIRTEEN

Stepdad

Rob May found love. She was perky, cute, and blonde, and she worked in the personnel office at the plant. Divorced, she had three kids of her own. She was a good, loving woman; Karen was her name.

Determined not to mess this one up, Rob switched over to working days. Rob fondly pictured himself with Karen, settling in as a family, being Dad to her kids, living happily ever after.

Fat chance.

—The Challenges Before a Stepfather—

Of all the twists and circumstances fathers can get into, stepparenting is by far the most challenging. So many personalities are involved that just the mechanics of the new mix can destroy the dreams and the marriage.

Rob is typical in his assumption that he could step in as surrogate father to Karen's brood. He assumed his own brood were happy enough living with their mom, and they weren't a big factor in the new union. He assumed Karen's kids would accept him. He assumed, in fact, that Karen would accept him fully as co-parent and spouse. Rob is also typical in that almost none of those assumptions was valid.

Rivalries, jealousy, control and other power issues, and shattered dreams would invariably come into play. Let's look at them in detail, for they affect all stepfamilies, no matter how well they seem to get along.

The Rivalry

Karen's three kids included a boy of thirteen named Chris, a girl, nine, and a boy, seven. She had been divorced for more than four years, thus when the split happened, Chris was about nine.

For four years, there had been no man in the picture. Chris was used to being "the little man of the house." He had been picking up some of the slack as Karen worked and ran a household single-handedly. He'd been obeying his mom and fighting with his mom, with no interference. Their relationship was stable. Now here came Rob, who, although an improvement over his first dad, was still no great shakes as a father. Rob expected to take over as man of the house where there had been none before—that is none except Chris. And Chris was not going to give way to this new rival easily.

If a boy is among the stepkids as a man and woman blend their families, there will be, one way or another, an element of male competition, even sparring. The longer the household has been without an adult male, the larger will loom this rivalry when a stepdad does enter the picture. Invariably, too, the rivalry issue will be complicated by control issues.

The Power and Control

Control issues are not gender specific. The eldest daughter will be just as loathe to give up her "Little Mommy" role as will any boy his "Little Man."

But Mom, too, may hesitate or subtly refuse to give up any control. She's had it so long, and she knows her kids so well, it just doesn't seem right to let some virtual stranger take over. Moreover, she wants desperately for her kids to accept this man as being Mr. Wonderful. If he disciplines them they won't like him as much. Therefore, she feels he ought not say no to them.

Even as Mom and the kids are resisting the new stepdad's discipline and control, the man is assuming he can jump right in as Dad. Dad's word is law. Dad is the prime discipliner. He expects that right and privilege, and feels angry and frustrated when it is not forthcoming.

Need we say that most of this control struggle goes on below conscious level. No one in the family understands what's really happening, and that in itself is frustrating for everybody.

Karen followed this pattern. She couldn't bring herself to surrender control of her kids to Rob.

"I'm just trying to protect you," she insisted. "Chris and the others will resent you if you come on like gangbusters, and I want them to love you the way I do."

She was indeed trying to protect Rob and make him more appealing to her kids. But she was also instinctively protecting her kids from this virtual outsider (it takes a couple years of marriage to build any real degree of intimacy). And she was protecting her traditional turf, as well.

"There is a sad case I counseled recently," Paul Warren relates. "About like Rob. Mom couldn't bring herself to give the new stepdad any control over her twelve-year-old boy. In this case, however, the child was out of control. Mom was the only one who couldn't see that she couldn't handle him. They ended up shipping him back to his dad, a thousand miles away.

"Now the boy's dad had remarried too. His wife couldn't handle the boy and came to really hate the kid's coming in and disrupting their life. This engendered all sorts of negative feelings toward the mother for sending that disruptive kid to his dad. The father felt so guilty about the divorce that he let the kid walk all over him. Suddenly, they found themselves with a young teenager totally out of control. Outwardly defiant, he was hitting and pushing his father, using drugs, coming and going as he wished. Dad finally had to call the cops to arrest his own son."

The control problems and power struggles, exacerbated by rivalries, are further fouled by a number of interlacing jealousies as the new family tries to blend.

The Jealousies

Every child wants a two-parent-plus-kids home. This goes deeper than wanting, deeper than yearning, deeper even than needing. It is primal. Two parents and the kids.

When Rob was living alone in an apartment, and his kids were living with their mother, that primal image of parents-plus-kids was best served by Mom's place. At least there was one parent plus kids. Rob alone did not drum up the primal picture. But then he took up housekeeping with Karen and her three, and his kids' yearnings kicked in. Instantly they became jealous of Rob's stepkids. Those kids got to live with their dad in a two-parent home, and they did not. Every time the two sets of kids got together, the jealousy caused friction and a lot of noise.

Rob was jealous too. Either he had forgotten how much of Mom's time, attention, and energy kids consume, or being a distant father in his prior marriage, he never realized. Now he coveted all that time and attention Karen's kids were blotting up. This was *his* wife, and they were robbing him of her.

Whether the kids' natural father is alive or dead, he becomes a saint when a stepdad arrives on the scene. Invariably, the stepchildren in a family will compare the stepdad with the natural dad and find the stepdad wanting. Invariably. As the former dad recedes into the mists of time, bad memories are forgotten and the good memories are preserved in crystal. Remember that every child yearns for perfect parents to guide him or her faultlessly through life. Eventually, the natural father emerges as the unattainable perfect parent and the stepfather as a very shabby, nonperfect imitation, no matter how sterling an individual he may actually be. The stepdad may quite naturally feel jealous of this supposedly perfect absent dad, and even more so if the dad is deceased. You can't confront a ghost or change a memory.

As you might expect, how much influence these issues

wield has greatly to do with the age the children are when the new stepfather appears. It's a wild card, something no one can control or determine ahead of time, and it makes a profound difference. How long has the natural father been absent? Did the child have much involvement with the birth father? The stepfather who comes on when his stepchild is very young can grow together with the child. If the child is older, like Chris, when he appears, Stepdad will have a rough time earning acceptance. He may never do it. Rob will have to come to terms with that possibility, as will every stepfather.

"That sad case I was talking about," Paul Warren concludes, "doesn't have an ending yet, but they're getting close. What that boy was saying with his disrespect and physical violence toward his dad was, 'I want you to love me enough to discipline me.' Kids instinctively know that sound discipline comes out of love. In fact, on one occasion, he actually said, "Dad, if you want me to stop, you'll kick me out of the house. You'll make me spend the night on the porch.' He was begging his father to give him the security of discipline. But his dad was afraid.

"The boy has voluntarily entered a drug rehab program. He is finally working out a relationship with his father, as the father comes to realize he has to take a firm hand. The firm hand is doing it."

That boy's dreams about his family had been shattered. Now at last he's starting to put them back together.

Shattered Dreams

When Gerald married Stacy, her sixteen-year-old daughter attended the wedding dressed in black. Her ten-year-old hung tough until the ceremony commenced, and then buried her head in her sister's lap, not to raise it again until it was over. And weddings are happy occasions?

Not to a child of divorce.

Along with the dream of living in a two-parent home, every child of divorce clings to the dream that the natural parents will somehow reunite. When the mom or dad re-marries, that effectively destroys the dream of reunion. "I would say," claims Paul Warren, "that a parent's remarriage is one of the worst moments of a child's life, possibly the absolute worst."

Below conscious level, children, angry about divorce—and all children of divorce are—may want to punish the parent(s) who did them wrong. Again below conscious level, they may actively work to break up the new marriage in order to restore the dream of reunion. Disobedience, rebellion, acting out—in short, any kind of disruptive behavior—might serve the purpose.

Rare is the Machiavellian child who realizes what she is doing. But it happens, all the same.

—Once More, Into the Breach; Stepdad Steps In—

"Being Stepdad takes real guts. And energy," Brian Newman claims. "Talk about your macho job. He's asking himself, 'How can I balance things out, so that I don't play favorite to either hers or mine? How do I balance love and attention? I really do want to make these kids' lives better. How do I keep them from hating me?' And he's not getting any answers, because all too often there aren't any. No matter what he does, both kids will believe he's favoring the other bunch. Kids are so egocentric, he can't win. And there's all those issues of jealousy and everything. The marvel is that he hangs in there and keeps trying."

Says Paul Warren, "I've seen situations where a man marries a woman just to get the kids, and a lot of situations where he refuses to marry because he doesn't want responsibility for the kids. In no way is that a sign of weakness. He's not chickening out. He is realistically judging that he's simply not up to the daunting task."

What is the situation, the daunting task, a stepfather faces, specifically? A blended family goes through six stages.

Stage One—Dream Phase

The new man enters Mom's life. She sees him as a white knight who will bring romance to her beleaguered life. The kids, desperate for a dad, also see him as a hero on a white horse. In fact, the kids are really looking forward to a stepdad; they want the relationship. There are exceptions. At times we see situations where the kids are so enmeshed with Mom that they don't want this guy intruding. In those cases there are almost always serious codependency issues causing other problems as well.

This dream phase has some severe drawbacks. For one, it gives Stepdad the false expectation that he's going to be welcomed. He is, for the moment, but the moment isn't going to last long. Too, kids can't see very far down the road (neither do most adults, for that matter). They can't envision the feelings and tugs-of-war that will mar their happiness shortly.

Stage Two—The Fantasy Phase

Storm clouds begin to gather but nobody will admit they're there. The rivalry, jealousy, and control issues are starting to intrude on the dream phase. Mom and Stepdad are sure it'll pass and shrug it off to temporary adjustment jitters. After all, the new union is only a few months old, and everyone is just now settling in. Give it another few months—a year at most. Everything will be fine.

Fantasy.

The kids are beginning to look beyond the knight on the white horse. Serious questions plague them as they feel increasingly split between conflicting loyalties. "If I like this guy, does it mean I don't like my dad?" If Dad's opinion of the stepfather is not very high, and that is so often the case (the stepfather is usurping Dad's place, remember, in his kids' lives and in their mom's bed, and both he and the kids know it), inadvertently or on purpose, he introduces another source of loyalty conflict into his kids' lives.

The kids begin to resent this guy, especially the older boys, and particularly enmeshed children. His faltering relationship with her kids begins to affect his relationship with Mom. The new stepfather is beginning to feel like he's in a real bind. When does adjustment take place and this unsettled feeling end?

Stage Three—Reality Phase

This man has married not a woman but a whole family. Theoretically included in, he feels like odd man out, and rightly so. The intimacy of years together has laced the kids and Mom into a unit. Stepdad has none of that. He's starting to get messages from the kids saying, "You're not welcome here after all." Overtly or covertly, the kids appeal to Mom to protect them from this guy who's not really their father. It's been less than a year, and already, significant strains on the marriage are beginning.

Stepdad may be feeling a little ambivalent by now, but the kids are really crashing. They must finally come to grips with the fact that their parents are not going to get back together, not ever again. It's the end of the dream. Wipeout.

"That is just so shattering," says Frank Minirth. "About now you're going to see acting out behavior, sadness, playing one parent against the other. The kids were pretty good, but now they're horrid. That's because they're grieving the lost dream and they almost surely don't know it. They don't know what's wrong, but something is terribly, terribly sad.

"If this is a blended family of his and hers, his kids will go to war with her kids. It's part of the bitterness and resentment, the reaction to the loss of the dream. They have to take it out on somebody, and Mom and Dad aren't safe targets."

"A blended family requires ongoing counseling, for every member," Paul Warren says. "Both before and during all this. Besides, for every problem that comes up, there are four you didn't anticipate, and the people here are too close to the problem to see the solution, even when it's perfectly obvious to everyone else.

"Yes, even professional counselors and pastors in this situation need an outside counselor. The point is not whether you have the expertise yourself; the point is, you're too close to the situation to see it clearly. Every person needs a point of view from outside."

Stage Four—Battle Phase

"By now," Paul Warren relates, "the parents are shocked and surprised that it's come to this. They had all these blue-sky expectations. Everyone feels pretty much frustrated by the situation. There's a lot of anger. The stepfather feels in direct competition with the kids for his wife's attention. Frequently, the kids may be positioned by themselves—an 'us against the world' type of thing—or directly between the stepfather and mother. The marriage is beginning to deteriorate in earnest. There's a war going on."

This is normally the stage when other problems become dramatically clear. Logistics, such as kids going back and forth between households, may not be working the way they were intended. The two households may have different sets of rules and expectations. Financial disputes arise. Which father is going to pay for which costs for clothing, medical, incidentals? How will child support, or the lack of it, affect the marriage?

Conflicts, power plays, and rivalries that began tentatively in prior phases burgeon now. They become centered around statements like, "You're not my real father."

Stage Five—Crisis Phase

Here's where something is going to happen. Either the marriage will fall apart or the stepfather and mother will commit to whatever it takes to make their marriage strong. Usually, what it takes is counseling and the special support of people outside the family.

From the outset, stepfathers have to work harder than

natural fathers to keep the new marriage together, because of the adversarial relationship that quickly develops between them and the kids. Where control issues are a major concern (and they almost always are), there is often a we-versus-them clash of mother plus kids against the stepfather. Stage Five only intensifies it.

Stage Six—Resolution

If the marriage reaches this stage—that is, if it survives, say, the first couple years—Mom and Stepdad will be able to achieve accord regarding exactly what roles each will play in the marriage and in their parenting.

- Does Stepdad play the full father's role as skills-enabler, protector, and so on? Or does he fill in where the natural father, still involved with his kids, assumes a large role in their lives?
- Does Stepdad have a full role in discipline and shaping?
- Does Stepdad adopt his stepkids, or do they retain their natural father's name?
- Does Stepdad enjoy the full rights and respect any other husband enjoys? He and his wife must both guard against the creeping assumption that he's a marital fill-in, a substitute, since the original is no longer available.
- Does Stepdad have a realistic expectation of the part he plays in this new family? As we have shown, the stepfather comes into this situation with inappropriate expectations, anticipating having every right and privilege, and the respect, and often even the name, of Dad. He must adjust his expectations to accept that he will play all or nearly all the father roles, and he will be the head of the house, but he will never be the kids' father.

These are all questions without a pat answer. Each must be answered individually according to the case at hand. In every case, Stepdad and Mom should sit down and discuss them together, then answer them as a team. Sometimes Mom and Stepdad will not arrive at a mutually satisfying answer. Not a big problem. The fact that they have examined the issues is the key.

Rob May was immensely harried and frustrated as he watched his new union fall apart. If he had an inadequacy fear before, imagine how big it mushroomed now. It was all his wives' fault, of course, but the failures still reflected on him. He was supposed to be the leader of the household. The kids hated him, and didn't mind if he knew it. His own kids, living with their mom, were becoming strangers; he was neglecting them, trying to make this new thing work, and in the process he was losing everything. Karen was getting second thoughts about the marriage too. She said so. "What did I ever see in you?" is not a reassuring statement. Less than two years after his second wedding, Rob was ready to bag it.

Rob was now sitting smack dab on the turning point. He could admit defeat and cut his losses. Or he could sit down with Karen, discuss the mess, and draw from her (if she was still willing) a commitment to make this work. It would take both of them, fully committed.

Both of them, through counsel or reading, had to first find out about all the undercurrents and undertows working in this stepfamily. Scrub the fantasies and figure out the dynamics, the issues and phases we discussed above. Until they recognized what was really happening, they couldn't do much to really turn it around. Then, Rob was going to have to do something he had never done before. He was going to have to become a real leader in the family.

As leader, he would clarify his own role in his mind. Together with Karen, he would decide on a plan of action. And then he would stick to it. Welcomed or not, the stepdad was about to assume a position of leadership and bring the family together.

There are several distinct steps for him to take.

—Stepdad's Practical Steps—

What Am I?

"There seems to be a lot of confusion about stepfather versus father," Paul Warren says, "and there shouldn't be."

Always, the stepfather must see himself as stepfather and not as the father. Although it's the dream of every man, as he marries into an instant family, to be Dad in every way, he should never try to be the father.

That would be hard for Rob, for he had already flunked fathering once. His ego demanded that he get another shot at it and succeed this time. He must keep in mind that he can still perform all the traditional and modern roles of a true father, but he should not try to take the name.

Stepdad has to remember that, at some level, he will always be in competition with another man, the real father. That other man will be present emotionally, if nothing else, in the hearts of his wife and the kids. If Stepdad is wise, he'll give up trying to compete actively with the other man, or the memory of the other man. He'll never win that competition. His wisest course is simply to be the best dad he can be, and work to avoid getting uptight when the kids (or even Mom) compare him with the other man.

For as kids dream about their original family getting together, so they maintain a sharp distinction between their father (even if he's been dead for years) and this stepdad or adoptive dad. It's one of the truisms kids cling to and the stepfather errs greatly if he tries to destroy it. Besides, biology is on the kids' side. He's not their dad.

Who Am I?

"What do the kids call this guy? Dad? Father? His first name?" Paul Warren says, "I tend to lean to the first name. Rob May would be Rob to his stepkids, Dad to his natural kids. But there are plenty of possible exceptions. We counsel to accept some latitude here. The bottom line is, everyone must discuss it. The whole family—kids, Mom, and

Stepdad—have to come to some sort of common agreement. And the matter should be laid to rest, at least for the time being, by stage two or stage three at the latest.

What Are My Goals?

Rob and Karen would do well to sit down and agree on what they agree upon. We recommend a goals and priorities list something like this:

GOAL ONE AND FIRST PRIORITY: Solidify the Marriage

TO ACHIEVE THAT GOAL:

Schedule time at least weekly to be alone together. Oftener is better. Our time together will be: _____

_____

Schedule at least one time a month to get away from the house and kids completely. During the next three months, we have these possibilities:

1. _____
2. _____
3. _____
4. _____
5. _____

Make no decisions and resolve no issues unless you can honestly say, "We're in this together. What will we do about it?"

All other goals and issues, such as those below, are secondary, though not to be ignored. Stepdad and Mom discuss them together, acting as a team to achieve them.

Discipline: Agree in advance, even thinking up scenarios the kids might get into; must be handled jointly.

Time spent just with the kids of this house and other house.

Decisions regarding finances, education, and miscellany—school, college, (piano, swimming, ballet) lessons, summer camps, orthodontia, pet ownership, jobs, activities.

All the issues we've talked about in this chapter must be resolved in the light of what the stepfather's role is. And because these issues work below the surface, with no one knowing they are there, the family ought to have a counselor to help wrestle with them. That counselor can be a professional trained for the work, a knowledgeable pastor, or a knowing friend.

Understand that the television series *The Brady Bunch* is fiction. Blended families, stepfamilies, do not fuse instantly into a big happy gang war of cooperative kids and adults. It will take any stepfamily a minimum of three years to really settle in.

Many never do. But the kids manage to grow up, all the same.

—What About Adoptive Fathers?—

"The adoptive father," Brian Newman suggests, "is in a somewhat different position from the stepdad. In a step situation, the kids come in a package deal and they know it. The adoptive father is choosing his kid. It's a subtle difference but an important one. It eases a lot of friction before it happens. Too, as kids get older they can understand sufficiently that this was a legal step making the adoptive father, officially, Dad."

"Fathering is fathering," says Paul Warren. "Whether adoptive or natural, Dad is called Dad and he assumes the roles we've discussed. Adoptive issues don't come up, usually, until the Oh-no!-my-parents-aren't-perfect issue comes up. This happens in early adolescence with the onset of real identity fixing and individuation. This is not their real dad. Somewhere out there, a real dad is floating around, the perfect parent every kid has. My adoptive parents aren't it, so it must be him.

"Natural versus adoptive parentage is also important from a medical standpoint. Is this child at risk for a disease or health problem with genetic origins? Cystic fibrosis, for example. Sickle cell. Did the natural dad have an alcohol problem? Children of alcoholics tend to become alcoholics. A lot of surprising things are inherited. It's one of the reasons we suggest that adopted children know the truth about their origins."

—Coda—

Rob May, with a lot of work, managed to turn his life around. He hung on to Karen and he survived her kids. He never did develop a strong, fatherly presence with his own kids. But his ex-wife remarried and, frankly, the guy wasn't all that bad. So his kids weren't totally bereft. And Rob did try to be a dad to them.

But at the back of Rob May's mind, hidden deep where he rarely gave it light, was a persistent, subtle, nagging question: Had he devoted the energy to his first marriage that he poured into this second, would his first union have survived?

Things to Think About

If you are a stepfather, or are contemplating marrying a family, think about this list of items as they apply to each child in the stepfamily, or prospective stepfamily, in turn.

My first impression of this child was:

_____ Positive

_____ Negative.

What either attracted me or turned me off was:

_____ Attitude

_____ Appearance

_____ Actions

_____ Age

_____ What I'd heard about the child

_____ Other _____

I recognize that that first impression could skew my thinking about the child and about the relative position of that child in the family (e.g. most favored, least favored). These factors can offset or balance my first impression:

_____ Promise of the future (what child will grow into)
_____ A firm, fair, loving hand in discipline
_____ Broadening of the discipline
_____ Narrowing of the discipline
_____ Attention equal to what the other kids receive
_____ A little extra effort and attention
_____ Recognition of special needs, advantages, handicaps, gifts

Ten or twenty years down the pike, I envision this child as:

_____ Having blossomed into a really neat adult.
_____ Being under indictment.
_____ Being a good parent in his or her own right.
_____ Having some serious emotional problems.
_____ Remembering me fondly.
_____ Hating me.

—GRANDDAD—

What do you remember about your grandfather? What memories are fond and what do you wish he had been to you that he was not? Let's look at the powerful influence grandfathering can have on kids.

FOURTEEN

Granddad

Cowboy, the big black Labrador, galloped off to fetch the Frisbee yet again. A couple of people in this broad, grassy, city park, perfect strangers, paused to watch the huge dog leap high. He was quite a sight, with his bulky flatiron head and barrel chest. He caught it in midcourse and came galumphing back. He dropped it expectantly at Elgin Mayer's feet.

Elgin took the slobbered-upon Frisbee from his mouth and tossed it under the picnic table. "Enough, Cowboy. Go lie down."

Slurpily, Cowboy licked Elgin's wrist.

Elgin pitched his voice deeper. "Go lie down, I said!"

Cowboy turned away, walked all of six inches, and flopped onto his belly. Casually, he flexed around and began noisily to lick unmentionable parts. His owner, Elgin's son Charles, reached out with a toe and jabbed him. Cowboy shifted to licking his paws instead.

"Grampa? Why does he do that? Lick?" At three years, two months, Sean Michael was asking questions like a Philadelphia lawyer.

Elgin was more than a little proud of his precocious grandson. "Don't know, Sean. Dogs do that, though. Lick you all the time. This mutt especially."

"Grampa? Do you lick?"

"Sure I lick! Ice cream cones. Suckers." He twisted around close to Sean Michael and confided *sotto voce,* "Lick my fingers if I'm eating chicken, too, when Gramma Jean isn't looking."

Sean Michael giggled and glowed.

Elgin Mayer was glowing, too, at least inside. Ever since he cowered in the corner of that delivery room and watched Sean Michael enter the world, he glowed with a special enthusiasm for his grandkids. Sean Michael in particular. Sean Michael had a baby sister now, and a couple of cousins, but he was and ever would be the firstborn grandchild.

Elgin had no inkling that as large as his grandkids loomed in his life, he loomed in theirs just as large. Grandfathers play an important role in the lives of children. And like Dad's role, Granddad's cannot be duplicated by any other person in the world.

—Who Granddad Is—

When Dad becomes Granddad, a quantum change takes place, both within the man and in the relationship between him and his adult children. Reviled as a fuddy-duddy by his adolescent kids, he's been gaining stature as they mature and wise up. He may still be a fuddy-duddy, but now he's one smart fuddy-duddy. Along comes the grandchild, and subtle, unspoken questions come as well.

Inside the son or daughter's head lurks the question "This man bossed me my whole life; is he going to try to rule my child too? How close do I dare let him get; will he steal my child's affection somehow?"

And inside the new granddad is, "My kids have goofed royally now and then; besides, they are still just kids themselves; can I trust them to raise my grandchild wisely? How much do I intrude, and when do I keep my mouth shut? What if I see them making some tragic and lasting error?"

The good and the bad of grandparenthood, the pride and the doubts, all stem from a question of roles and relationships. The specific role of Granddad is a clear one, once you study it.

Granddad the Link

Elgin Mayer was on the road a lot, driving for the moving company. He didn't get to see Sean Michael very often. At

first, when Sean was very, very small, Elgin worried that
he would remain a stranger. Would Sean recognize him as
a family member during his infrequent visits?

Sean did.

Your grandkids know you're Granddad. They will intuitively give you a family place that is neither parent nor
peer. Small grandchildren will accept you as perfect just as
they do their parents. But they need help remembering,
especially when they're small. We therefore encourage
granddads to forge links as strong as possible. Write letters.
Call occasionally between visits. When years stretch between visits, send photos, perhaps even videos.

Links between grandfather and grandchild equal links between the past and the future. Without fully understanding,
grandkids grasp the link, at least to an extent. They have a
passing interest in their history, and only a grandparent can
say, "When your [Mom] [Dad] was your age, [she] [he]
used to spread peanut butter just like that." Or "hated lima
beans." Or "loved to be read to." Links.

"God honors the concept of generations," says Brian
Newman. "The importance of multiple generations turns
up many different ways. Think of all the begats that are in
Bible. 'Children unto the fourth generation.' 'Children unto
the tenth generation.' 'Son of' this person and 'son of' that
person. Not just Jesus Christ's lineage, but so many people
throughout Scripture. The generations and the heritage are
emphasized over and over."

Recorded lineages are not just an artifact of peoples with
a written history. In oral traditions without the written
word, highly trained and respected historians can literally
sit for days, reciting from perfect memory the genealogy,
history, and totems of their clans.

People hunger for their history, and grandparents can
assuage that yearning as no one else can.

"I know so very little about my past," Brian Newman
laments. "So I try particularly hard to give my children a
heritage they can savor when they're older."

Granddad the Mentor

Grandfathers can be the primary support for their sons the fathers. They can offer information as well as support, back-up, encouragement. They can be a wall off which to bounce ideas.

"We do not suggest," Paul Warren assures, "that he should be fathering the father. That needed to end. But Granddad is Dad's best mentor in many situations. He's been there, and he knows his son."

Granddad the Example

Granddad presents by living, breathing example that the values Dad has been providing his kids actually work. Here is a man who has come through a long life okay. Values and lifestyles are not just arbitrary ways to do things. They offer dividends. By observing the grandparents, the child learns that.

Of course, not all grandparents provide a positive example. Some teach by example the folly of pursuing a certain lifestyle or value system. Others demonstrate that despite your lifestyle, disease and misfortune strike. The grandparents thereby illustrate that tragedy can often be a random thing, with no person immune. It is a necessary lesson, all the same.

Granddad the Window

"In my particular branch of government," a federal employee told us recently, "there has been a recent trend to pass over the persons fifty or older when making promotions. They are moving younger people into upper positions, essentially skipping a generation. Early retirements are being encouraged.

"This is fine for the younger people, but the whole branch is losing a vital link with the past. We're losing the continuity—the passing along of skills. And the loss is causing a lot of unnecessary confusion. The younger executives don't have enough experience and knowledge of human nature to handle unusual situations—or even usual ones, at times. The wheel keeps getting reinvented all the time because no one in a particular office can remember what wheels once were."

Grandchildren lack the one thing grandparents have in abundance—experience and understanding of the world. Like the federal workers in our friend's branch, the children need the steadying knowledge about the world that their grandparents can provide.

Does this sound familiar, Granddad? The child's window on the world? That fathering role has not diminished, but now it takes on a new perspective. Granddad can be a skills-enabler, true. And that in no way reduces Dad's role in the same capacity. But Granddad can reinforce skills, show shortcuts, provide plain old, ordinary practice, and offer a different perspective on what Dad has been giving his kids. Granddad's window is set in a different wall from Dad's, a different time; the child will see from it a somewhat different view.

Granddad the Builder of Identity

A grandchild will draw most of his or her identity from the immediate family. What Daddy thinks and what Mommy thinks will shape it. Identity will grow as the child achieves skills, functions, and knowledge. It will develop further depending on what other people think, peers and other adults. Granddad can add to that identity a sense of history and continuity, as we discussed above. But that's not the only way Granddad builds identity for his grandkids.

Paul Warren explains an immediate way Granddad can contribute to children's identity and understanding of themselves. "The grandfather can enrich his grandchild by reminding the child, 'Yes, your father was a little boy.' Most kids can't see their father as ever being young, as being a teen. That's important," he says. "It helps the family feel affiliated. Similar. 'We have similarities, we're together, we've been through the same things.' Granddad, Dad, the kids can all say that. The grandparent by his very presence personifies that. The child identifies with his parents in a new and important way."

Too, by praising good efforts, Ganddad can provide that important recognition and affirmation children need. Granddad is not a parent. He cannot replace Dad's affirmation. But he can multiply it exponentially by approving. And approval greatly fortifies identity.

So does dreaming, and who is better than Granddad at dreaming dreams and imagining purposes in life? Over fast food, down at the mall, in the park, in the car to somewhere, Granddad and his grandchild can talk about dreams. They can imagine the world.

Granddad the Mantle

But more than a sense of history, Granddad provides a mantle, a shawl, a wraparound. The child does not just have a history; learning about history is head knowledge. He or she belongs within it: heart knowledge. That feeling of belonging, of being nested within, is fertilized and enriched below conscious level when grandparents are a part of the family picture.

Imagine a grade-school-aged boy standing alone in a house or apartment. He must depend upon his own resources (the theme and suspense point of the popular film *Home Alone;* can he manage on his own?). Think how isolated he feels. Now add the parents to the picture. He is no longer alone, no longer isolated. Finally, introduce one or more grandparents. The child now has a wealth of resources, both practical and symbolic. He has not just the wisdom of the ages, he is encompassed in it.

A friend confides, "Some of the most vivid recollections of my life were the evenings at my grandfather's. He would invite my brother and me over to his place down the street. Not the parents. Just us. We were maybe eight, ten, twelve; my brother was two years younger.

"Grandpop would dig out dominos or something. Occasionally it was cards, and we'd play three-handed euchre, or gin. I forget what, except that he'd cheat outrageously. We knew it was a game, that he wasn't serious about it and we shouldn't be, either. That was good training, when I think about it. Don't get serious over games.

"Anyway, what we mostly did was be men, as opposed to being domesticated—be 'grown up.' That was what the evening was all about, being grown up. Then he'd say, 'How about a snack?' Does Santa want a reindeer? He'd let us take anything in his refrigerator—half a dozen kinds of pop and fruit juice. I remember we tended to avoid the fruit juices. Hey, we got that at home. He'd open up a can of peanuts and we'd go back to the dominos. We were men, my brother and me and Grandpop. It was so delicious. And so vivid."

Our friend has not played dominos since, though he still loves peanuts.

His excursions into manhood were far more than just game night at Grandpa's. Remember how children try on different roles? His grandfather was allowing the boys to try on the role of manhood where it was safe. Feel tough. Look tough. Drink 7-Up. Grandpop certainly never consciously thought, "My grandsons need to first taste adulthood in a controlled environment, lest they try it out under dangerous circumstances. They need a mentor, an older adult model." He was simply having fun. Incidentally, by enjoying the male night out, he was also thereby reinforcing the boys' confidence in their sexuality.

Grandpop did not just introduce our friend and his brother to the mysterious and secret society of the adult. He included them. He wrapped adulthood around them as a mantle, though they had to leave the mantle behind when they went home. They were history in the making and he was history past. It is one thing to enjoy a sense of history, a linkage with the past. But it is also important to feel a part of it. Granddad, like no one else, can impart that sense of belonging. He can wrap his grandchild in the cloak.

Our friend's reminiscences, above, also bring up the down side of grandparenting.

—Who Granddad Is Not—

Granddads have a definite tendency to go against the parents' wishes and preferences. After all, the grandparent has so much more child-raising experience and wisdom. What does the kids' dad know more than his own dad? The grandparent takes a certain proprietary interest in the grandchild and wants things done right.

Bucking the parents' wishes, though, is not right, and certainly not good for the kids. We do not in any sense recommend it as a way to go. However, we know it happens. In some regards, it does no harm. In others, it does. There are shades of grey, and there is black. And the grandparent more so than the parent must guard against committing the harmful rebellions.

The Harmful Things Grandparents Can Do

Elgin Mayer's schooling never extended beyond high school and his son Charles had a college degree. That sure didn't mean Charles was smarter. The kid could really pull some dumb stuff from time to time. He wasn't as wise or practical as Elgin by a long shot.

Take Little League, for instance. Now everyone knows every boy should have the experience of Little League. But Charles said he didn't want Sean participating. Sean at age three already parroted his dad's line, but baby Sean didn't know any better. He didn't understand what Little League does for you. Charles should have. He was a Little League veteran.

Elgin figured out when Sean would first be old enough to be eligible and began to make plans. He would sign the kid up if his dad wouldn't. He would get a team started through the moving company if there were no suitable slots available for Sean in his neighborhood. That would require at least a year's planning ahead of time. And he would cut back his work load during the season so he could drive Sean to games. Charles could take a running jump; Sean was going to get Little League experience.

Elgin's plans violated the first precept of grandfathering.

• You Don't Make Child-rearing Decisions

Paul Warren explains, "The grandfather has a special opportunity to be grandparent. In fact, he has the special privilege, an enviable position, of spoiling his grandchild a little. He should not ever try to be parent and blur the distinction between parent and grandparent. Besides, it's not his child."

Whether or not to participate in Little League was a child-rearing decision belonging to Charles and Meghan only. Not Elgin, not Grandmom Jean. Not even Sean's, ultimately, although Charles would be wise to give Sean's desires great weight.

Little League is not a critical topic, but some topics are critical. The degree of discipline, for example, will shape the child for better or worse, forever. So will any abuse or neglect. What if Elgin saw signs of abuse? Saw that discipline was not appropriate? Saw Charles and Meghan ignoring Sean's needs? If he wasn't to engage in parenting, how could Elgin stem the damage he saw in the making?

Elgin might begin by choosing—or creating—a nonthreatening place and time to discuss his worries with the parents. Elgin's opinions carry more weight if he is on good terms with his son or daughter, of course, and still more weight if his relationships with his children are both comfortable and close. But he is voicing an opinion. Nothing more.

He will be wise to have more than just opinion on his side. Is his opinion buttressed by the informed opinions of others? Are there facts and figures behind his position?

He will do well to offer solutions and alternatives along

with opinions and worries. Is there a better way? An easier way? Include that in the discussion.

Should there be no positive change, Elgin must remember that the grandkids are not his children. Just as Dad has to raise his daughters as he raises his sons, by letting them be free to err, so Elgin must release his children. They may be erring. But it is their responsibility, their choice now.

Even if Elgin sees trouble brewing because of his children's decisions, he should be very careful to avoid breaking off his relationship.

"That's easy to do," says Frank Minirth. "I see it so much. A's father disagrees strongly with something A is doing. It may have to do with child-rearing or something else. A's father says, in effect, 'Until you shape up, you're not welcome here'—using his relationship with his child as a club, you see. It's so sad, for the grandchildren as well as the father-child relationship. They lost their granddaddy. He just drove a wedge between A and himself, and he's lost any chance to work some kind of improvement, to have his side be heard. I've seen feuds go on for years that way."

Elgin, then, regardless of his opinion of Charles's parenting decisions, needs to maintain a warm, close relationship with his grandchildren and, as best he can, with his children.

Now there is one line to draw—illegality. The grandparent who sees actual illegal conduct should never condone it. Child abuse in particular requires immediate intervention. What sort of intervention? That decision must be made on a case-by-case basis, for no two situations are alike.

Grandparents must set their minds to seeking counsel themselves if a problem involving possible illegality comes up. Who knows the current law? Who knows how to best help the child in today's legal and social climate? Go there for advice. Handle the issue, as much as possible, to the grandchild's advantage.

As regards Elgin's problem, the Little League question did, in fact, come up in conversation. Elgin didn't initiate it, but since the subject was on the table . . .

"Why are you so dead set against it, Charles?"

Charles thought a moment, weighing words. "I don't want to hurt your feelings or anything, Pop." He hesitated. "I hated it. I hated every minute of it."

"Whaddaya mean? You were in Little League five years!"

"Worst experience of my life. It was just plain painful. Ruined my summers. The coaches stuck me where I'd do the least damage, and . . ."

"They never gave you a chance to blossom. I'd talk to them about that."

"I know you would. And that would get them on my case worse. They didn't like you telling them how to run their team, so they'd take it out on me. Pop, I couldn't hit or catch or field worth anything. I wasn't coordinated enough, or fast enough, and I didn't want to learn. I just wanted out."

"I don't believe that! Why didn't you ever say something?"

"I did. You wouldn't believe it then, either." Charles leaned forward. "Sean's a lot like me. I don't think Little League would do any better for him than it did for me." He straightened. "But I'll give you this promise: If Sean decides he wants to, because all the other kids are doing it, for instance, I'll help him as much as I can, short of second-guessing the coaches. But it has to come from him. And if he says he wants to quit, he can."

• You Don't Undermine the Parents' Authority

"No grandparent," says Paul Warren, "has the right to interfere with or undermine the parents' authority. You don't raise kids by committee. The parents have the final word, regardless of what you think."

Unfortunately, grandparents have a way of undermining parents both indirectly and directly.

Indirectly, they use the children as unwitting messengers to deliver a word contrary to the parents'. "For instance," Paul Warren says offering an illustration, "the parents decide to raise only one child. And the grandparents want a whole gang of grandchildren. The children might get a frequent, subtle string of messages such as, 'Wouldn't you like a little brother or sister?' 'Tell Mom and Dad you want a baby brother or sister.' 'Your house has that extra bedroom; wouldn't a brother be nice?'

"Those kinds of messages say, 'Your parents don't know what's best. Your parents are making a wrong decision.' It casts the shadow of doubt in a child who should not have to think about that sort of thing. Parenting is tough. The grandparents shouldn't be making it tougher by trying to control through innuendo."

Grandparents can also attack the parents' authority in direct, not-so-subtle ways.

"In counsel," says Paul Warren, "we find ourselves constantly telling kids, 'Be careful how you pick your friends. Pick good friends.' The kids ask us what makes a good friend, and we give them a couple rules of thumb, criteria. One criterion of good peer friendship is that the child's friends should never try to undermine parental authority. You know, something like, "Don't listen to those old fogies. They don't know best.'

"It's the same with grandparents. More so, in fact. Grandparents sit even higher in respect than peers do. When they say 'Your dad's all wrong; we'll do this instead,' there's a lot of power and influence behind that."

The grandfather who invited his grandsons to men's night out never disturbed the parents' authority. Never did he say, "We're going to get away with something here." Never did he suggest the parents were too strict or too narrow or in error. He was supplementing what the father primarily provided—a look at manhood and the company of adults.

• You Don't Practice to Deceive

Brian Newman smiles at the memory despite himself. "My grandfather was a man you used to call kind of ornery. Not mean ornery, at all. Lovable ornery. Crusty, I guess, is the better word. Every now and then, he'd let loose with some cuss word when I was with him. Then he'd say, 'Oops! Don't let your Gramma know I said that.' It was a sort of man-to-man secret, and I really liked the way he included me in it, and how he treated me as a grown-up. You know, those days, men swore and women didn't and kids didn't dare.

"I was an adult before I realized that Gramma knew perfectly well what kind of language he used."

That sort of thing—keeping secrets—is not the way to go with kids. Neither is any behavior you don't want them to emulate, either as children or as adults.

• You Are Not the Primary Caregiver

"Well," the concerned grandfather complains, "if I didn't do it, it wouldn't get done." And with that rationalization he proceeds to buy his grandchild the bunk beds, or a garment he thinks the child should have. He takes the child into his home because the parents can't find a baby-sitter that suits him. He hovers over his grandchildren as a mother hen protects her brood, watching for some shortfall on his kids' part that he might step in and fill.

"If it doesn't get done, it doesn't get done," Brian Newman advises. "That's between the parents and their kids. The parents may well have reasons you don't see for handling matters in ways you don't like. Limit your role to what it should be. Enricher. Link. Friend."

• You Are Not a Financial Institution

We strongly recommend against grandparents supporting either kids or grandkids financially.

We recognize, though, that there are situations when this set of should-bes or oughta-bes are simply not possible. Today's economic climate is exceedingly unstable. Parents' financial difficulties may force the grandparents to become their grandchildren's primary caregivers or financial support. It happens all the time. We are not talking here about grandparents who must out of necessity step into the role of parents again. We are discussing the grandparents in families with one or both functional parents.

What should Granddad do when his empty nest suddenly fills up? "Boomerang Babies," they're called—the kids who left the nest, built families, and for one reason or another are suddenly back in the fold. Children made single by divorce may show up alone. Frequently, though, the whole family moves in.

A moment ago, Granddad felt comfortable with the adult-to-adult relationship he had with his kids. Now he's finding himself back in a parent-to-child relationship, simply because his kids are under his roof. It's automatic, a throwback to times gone by. That parent-child relationship is the first thing he must resist, and resist strenuously.

Dad/Granddad must sit down with his adult child before the move takes place and set the ground rules. Here are some suggestions for that groundwork.

Dad/Granddad (let's call him the host dad) will not set curfews or impose rules that would be appropriate for a child not yet fledged. We're dealing with adults here. There are a few exceptions we might make. If the child's lifestyle conflicts with the parents' moral or ethical standards, the child bows to the parents' preference. An obvious example: John is dating again after his divorce and wants to bring his date home overnight. Dad and/or Mom (it needn't be both; the feelings of one is enough) hold to moral standards that won't allow that. Even though John is an adult, making his own moral decisions, he follows his parents' wishes, at least while he's under their roof. And if John is really smart, he won't stay out overnight, either.

John should not even consider any illegal or suspect activity, of course.

The host dad need not countenance behavior that irritates or causes significant friction, either. John may have to keep his music down; he may not be able to slam doors or stomp around in heavy boots the way he did when he was on his own. Avoiding such irritations is common courtesy, and both the host dad and the kids should be sensitive to common courtesies. Other than those exceptions, the host dad should think of his adult child as a tenant. A roomer.

A temporary roomer. With the arrangement for an adult child to move in, with or without the family, should come a tentative arrangement for the child to move back out. Set up a time frame. Why did the child move in? Economic reasons? "As soon as you get a job . . ." is pretty nebulous. Rather, "You should be able to find work in the next six months. I'll expect you to be on your own by (six months from now)." A definite date. Call it a deadline.

Are the reasons personal? "As soon as you feel better . . ." is an open invitation for the kid to live with the host dad the rest of his or her natural life: "Let's give it (three months) (six months) (a year). Then it will be to your best interests to be out on your own again." Again, a definite end in sight.

Who pays for what? That should be arranged ahead of time, and it should be equitable for all concerned—at least, as much as possible. The adult children are still responsible for their family. The grandparents are not. On the other hand, the grandparents may have more resources if the adult kids are strapped by job loss, divorce, or other financial blows. Work things out not according to fixed rules, but according to common sense.

Who does what? The adult kids moving in should never make more work for Grandma or Grandpa. They would have to be handling chores, laundry, and such were they living apart. They can do it here, too. The host dad should keep a watchful eye that this guideline is not abused. It is ever so easy to say, "Well, John/Jane is working long hours, and I'm washing today anyway . . . ." "Well, the kids are tired and upset. I'll clean up the kitchen just this once." Keep chores distributed according to the agreement.

Holding to the terms of the original agreement is not cruelty. The fact that they have to move back in with the parents raises a lot of self-doubt in the adult kids. By hewing to the agreement faithfully, they are keeping a promise, and keeping promises is an excellent builder-upper. They need the boost. The host dad can help them regain their esteem by treating them firmly, fairly, and consistently, as adults.

In those households, grandparents are bound occasionally to cause friction. You can't mix any combination of individuals of any age without getting friction now and then. Grandfathers should be on the lookout for common sources of friction and smooth them out if possible. But there are some sources few people realize exist until those sources have done their dirty work.

—Granddad Causes Friction—

The retiree is not time-driven. It's one of the greatest things about retirement. In fact, older people, retirees and pre-retirees both, can deliberately slow their pace a lot easier than they could when they were thirty. They can kick back and do whatever their grandchild wants to do.

When their own kids were growing up, today's grandparents didn't have time. Their resources were more limited. They were under more stress. In their era, parents didn't interact with their children and play with them the way parents are invited to do today. At last, with so many constraints such as time relaxed, they can enjoy a relationship with the grandchild that they could never achieve with their children, the parents.

And that can be hard on the parents. They see their children getting along much better with these people than they themselves ever did. "I never got to play catch with Dad. He does it with my son every time he comes over." "Dad never had time to read to me. Look at him with my daughter in his lap, for an hour at a time, book after book."

In a way, that sounds like jealousy. It is loss. Something precious, something yearned for, something needed—a parent's full attention—has forever slipped away, never to be reclaimed. It is a poignant loss, and the parent very rightly mourns.

"We have a friend right now," Brian Newman relates, "who's experiencing just that source of friction very strongly. She has a nine-year-old daughter who thinks her granddaddy hung the moon. But she has never gotten along well with her father. They've been at odds most of her life. They still treat each other horribly.

"She can't understand what her daughter sees in that autocratic, bossy old man, and it really hurts her, how her daughter dotes on him. In her eyes, he doesn't deserve it. And then her daughter gets mad at her for her hostility and sides with the granddaddy. And that causes more upset.

"None of them can see that the grandparent-grandchild relationship is completely different from the parent-child relationship. The parents are adults. The grandparents' situation is much different—more time, more patience, all that. And the little kids still have that naivete that all adults are perfect. The parents outgrew that one long ago. So you see how the dynamics have changed."

"Now and then," says Paul Warren, "I see a sick situation that stems from this lack of relationship during the parents' childhood. In this situation, the parents force the grandkids onto the grandparents—they deliberately turn their kids away from themselves and toward the grandparents—in order to receive vicariously the love they never got. Granddad loves his grandchild and the parent taps into that. In a sense, the parent is offering his kids as a sacrifice in a certain dark way."

Brian Newman continues, "That wasn't the situation in the particular case I just cited. But both the grandfather and the mother are frustrated and sad at missing out on that relationship that never happened."

And therein lies the secret for grandparents to ease this point of friction. Empathy. Sympathy. For instance, the granddad above might simply share his own frustration and sadness with his daughter.

- You know, I always wanted to do this with you and never had the time while you were growing up. By the time I went to a forty-hour week, you were in high school."
- "I wish I could have been a more involved father, like I am with my granddaughter."
- "There's no way I can make it up to you, [daughter], but I'm grateful for this relationship with my grandchild."

After expressing your feeling, be prepared to listen—really listen—to the response.

Whether or not it eases the friction (and it usually does), it heals the parent-child bond to some extent. Sharing of feelings almost always does.

Asking forgiveness is also an essential healer. If you have any misgivings or regrets at all about how you raised your kids, now is the time to unabashedly ask forgiveness. No fair citing the mitigating circumstances: "Yes, but we were only making ten thousand a year." "Yes, but . . ." Relationships lost are relationships lost, regardless of the reasons or justification. Seek forgiveness.

Forgiveness works in the other direction also, from parent to grandparent. And it functions in the same ways.

But what if the grandparents are unavailable?

Not all grandparents can have enough contact with their kids to generate warmth, let alone friction. Some may have died. You must get a little creative, if that is so.

—Grandparent Lost—

Let us assume for the moment that one or more of the grandparents is deceased. Beyond forgiving face to face. Beyond enjoying. How would you the father, or you the surviving grandfather, help make up, at least in part, for the loss of that important grandparent?

We suggest stories.

Kids respond innately and eagerly to stories. Tell them war stories of the past, casting the missing grandparent in

the role of hero or trickster or victim or orchestrator—it
matters not what role.

The purposes of your stories are twofold. You want the
children to get to know their lost grandparents, at least
secondhand. And you want to convey to the children the
values their grandparents would convey in person, were
they able to do so. Both purposes are served well by stories.

Just plain talking about the absent persons is a good way
to help children feel comfortable and familiar with them.
Talk naturally, talk in an upbeat way.

Show the kids all the pictures you can. There are many
of us who know our grandparents only through fading photos
in a plush-upholstered album. Have you any news clippings?
Even the obit from the paper is all right. Read it with the
child. Since no obituary is ever correct in all its facts, talk
to the child about the errors as well as the highlights.

If you can, take the children to places where Granddad
lived, where he went to school, where he raised his children. Did he enjoy major league baseball? Take the kids to
games when his favorite teams are playing. Sports are a
fine way to link the generations.

"Oh, sure," grumbled a friend of ours. "My old man
played the horses."

Okay, so skip that and find something else. You're conveying values as well as memories and history, remember.
In fact, the methods above for helping a child become familiar with a deceased grandparent work well for keeping alive
connections with a distant grandparent who can visit rarely
or not at all. And yet, frustrated grandfolk need not go
without the pleasure of being Granddad.

—Grandfathering Beyond the Family—

"Many cities have substitute grandparent programs in
place," Paul Warren relates. "I cannot understate the difference that groups of volunteer grandparents can make.
Health facilities such as hospitals and hospices, orphanages,

schools, libraries, volunteer service organizations—many, many people need grandparent types. In some programs, the older people actually act as surrogate grandparents.

"There's often more women then men, and they need male role models. They love to get the grandfathers in there."

Granddads can do something as simple as read books to small kids at the library on Storyteller Morning. They can help the high school vocational ed class hang windows and doors. They can visit ill children and help chaperon field trips. There are a million potential grandparenting situations out there. The first step is to seek out the organizations and sign up.

Granddads can listen. They can nod. They can offer a shoulder to cry upon. They can show you how to bait a hook without running it through your finger. They can unsnarl the backlash on your reel and help you wash the car. They will tie you to the past and encourage you into your future.

They can love you.

Judd Swihart says all persons need someone who has an irrational love for them.

That's Grandpa.

Things To Think About

Whether or not you are a grandfather now, build yourself a family compendium. This is an assembly of family information, filed in ring binders or boxes. Use the suggestions below as memory-joggers, and expand them to fit your family's circumstance.

If possible, enlist the help of your children. You will be amazed at how valuable this information will become, for several reasons. One, your children, and most likely also you yourself, will someday want to know about the family's heritage. Now is the time to gather information, while the sources who know the most are still around to be interviewed. Two, biologists are linking some unusual diseases to a hereditary base or tendency. Some diseases they are investigating at the moment, for example, are Parkinson's and multiple sclerosis. Knowledge of your family's genetic heritage may one day prove extremely valuable.

You want to know:

Your parents' full names and birthplaces:

_____

_____

Your wife's parents' full names and birthplaces:

_____

_____

Your grandparents' full names and birthplaces:

_____

_____

Her grandparents' full names and birthplaces:

_____

_____

Now build a tree with all the aunts and uncles, great aunts and uncles and their spouses and offspring. If you can, mention intimate friends of these people who could offer information about them. Whom can you reach? Whom can you interview, in order to gain information to fill the holes you'll discover in your tree?

If you are a grandfather (even if you are not, just yet), a valuable gift you can give each grandchild is a personalized family tree of what you've found, a link between him or her and the past.

Another gift you alone can present to them is a memoir of experiences from your youth and their parents' youth. Prepare it by simply narrating stories into a recorder. Don't worry about sounding "professional." They want to hear *you*. Or you can write it on paper. Whatever, however, your gift will grow in value as your children and grandchildren mature.

As memory joggers, write a few words here, describing various stories you want to tell. Use this list as the talk

outline, or skeleton, of what you would talk about on record.
How about . . . ?

Funny anecdotes:
_____
_____

Poignant stories of pets, neighbors, relatives:
_____
_____

Heartwarming tales, the kind you'd tell around the fire at
Christmas:
_____
_____

Tragic stories of accidents, misfortunes to family members and close friends (as sad as such stories are, family
members want to know about them):
_____
_____

Who-married-whom and whatever-happened-to-so-and-
so stories:
_____
_____

Places you found information, possible places where
others may go to seek information in the future:
_____
_____

Interesting background stories about particular pieces of
furniture, collectibles, and other memorabilia in the family (the stories go with that old teapot, the rocking chair,
the faded picture of a St. Bernard protecting a hypother-
mic little Victorian girl in the snow, the gizmo in the
kitchen cupboard that no one can identify but everyone's
afraid to discard):
_____
_____

A precious trove the grandkids will want to know about someday is the art works in the family. Inventory them all, detailing the maker/artist and approximate date where known. And include not just fine art—paintings, sketches, and such—but also include:

- Crocheted pieces: doilies, bedspreads, afghans, table-cloths, lace trims
- Knitted pieces: handmade garments, afghans, table-cloths, bedspreads, lace trims
- Wall hangings and pictures in crewel, cross-stitch, and other embroidery, weaving, hardanger, needlepoint, other
- Quilts and coverlets, even raggedy ones (certain old bat-tered quilts can be quite valuable)
- Handsewn garments and small items
- Dolls and toys with a history
- Hand leatherwork
- Wooden items, carved items, marquetry pieces, hand-made furniture, ship models and such
- Sculptures, figurines with a story, hand-detailed ceramics

Catalog all collections in the family, especially collections you made as a youth. (One of our friends, now a grandfather, received salt-and-pepper sets as a child, from several rela-tives who traveled a lot; he has over two hundred, no two alike, and hasn't the slightest idea what he's going to do with them. Another friend, a farmer, collects pig figurines. Many collect stamps.)

Make sure all the photos and clippings your family is storing in albums and shoeboxes are labeled with names, dates, and places.

Make several copies of your family compendium. Scatter them among interested relatives and put yours in a safe place.

FIFTEEN

The Bottom Line

He had just turned sixty, this man named Gil. His eyebrows were greying, but they still beetled into a thick, solid line across his face. Nature graced him with broad, ham-sized shoulders and slim hips even now in his later years. His pals at the gravel pit where he worked called him "Duck," because he tended to waddle with a rolling gait. After he separated from his second wife, they called him "Lonesome Duck," but not often, nor to his face. He was the manager.

Duck came into the world the youngest of five kids, three of them stepsisters from his father's side. When he was barely two, his Dad left—said good-bye to the kids and not a word to Mom and walked out. Within twenty years Duck had lost contact with his brother and three stepsisters. For fifty-eight years, he felt abandoned, rejected by his father, cheated of any chance to know his father or even to know about him. He left his native Moline when he was twenty, settling in the Dallas area, and returned only when his mom died, and only for the funeral.

There at the funeral, he ran into some relatives that he did not even know about. They in turn led him to other stepbrothers and stepsisters he had never heard of. He made contact immediately.

Within days, one family called saying they were in town, visiting from Minnesota. Duck and his newfound relatives got together. He took his two granddaughters along. He met May, a stepsister in her seventies. She commented over and over how much like his father Duck was. Mannerisms, the beetling brows and beefy shoulders, the tone of voice. "Uncanny!" she said. She noted how he responded to his grandchildren in the same way their father had responded to children.

Duck never knew his dad, but in many ways he could see his dad by looking in the mirror. He heard about his dad's three marriages (that May knew about) and he thought about his own two. His father's marriages had all ended bitterly. So had both of his.

And he wept.

—The Yearning to Know Dad—

Duck illustrates in microcosm the sheer impact that fathers have, whether they are present in a child's life or not. He also illustrates what so many of today's men, young and old, are discovering. Far beyond what you would expect, far beyond what logic would dictate, men seek to know their fathers. Duck found it satisfying—even soothing—to learn that the things he fancied about his dad, the fantasies both good and bad, weren't accurate. The truth felt better than any fond imagining, even if it wasn't pretty.

Seeking Security

We speculate that a part of this seeking to know Dad has to do with security. The world has gone haywire in so many ways, with rampant change, inconsistency, lies, and unpredictability. And if it's spinning out of control now, what will tomorrow bring? Selective memory makes the past seem much more stable and reliable. Men therefore look backward for security, not into the frightening future. This is probably at least part of the reason people are returning to nostalgia, from Andy Griffith to wood stoves and quilts. The past is now set in cement. No more unsettling changes.

But in the very deepest recesses of men's hearts, a small voice sees the frightening future and calls to the traditional window on the world, the protector. "Daddy . . . ?"

"In October of '91," says Brian Newman, "fathering was

the issue at an international conference on the men's movement. The age mix was very interesting—the average age of the men there was fifty plus. It was surprising, because these were the men who were our fathers." He can say that; he's under thirty-five.

"They were never really fathered, you see? They were searching for a sense of fatherhood for their past, while men today, the men my age, are wanting to father their children in the present, for the future. So many of the men at that conference were done with their own kids, but still seeking the meaning of fatherhood."

We mentioned previously that Brian Newman, because he gained hardly any sense of family history from his father, is trying to build one in his children. He grins. "Okay, I admit it. I'm building it for myself, too." He pauses. "Mostly for me."

A sense of security and safety, then, could explain the interest in part. But not the hunger, not the intensity of the yearning as a man grows older. Neither is it just a yearning to be fathered, exactly.

We will always be our child's father, no matter what the age. "That doesn't mean we always operate as the father," Paul Warren reminds us. "We must say good-bye to the child. Release our children. But we will always be the father."

And in a sense, we will also always be the child.

Seeking Self

Frank Minirth frequently quotes in counsel the old adage "The acorn falls not far from the tree." The kids owe the parents much more than chromosomes full of genes. Kids' cultural, moral, spiritual, and emotional profiles all will depend upon the parents.

Charles Mayer's wife, Meghan, recited Charles's strengths and weaknesses (well, all right, she called them "faults"). "He can't go to bed at night and he can't get up in the morning. If he stays up past eleven, he gets his second wind and he's good for the night. But even if he goes to bed at eight, the next morning you can't pry him out of bed with a crowbar. A couple times, I've planted my feet in his backside and just plain shoved him out of the bed. He's not a happy camper when I do that."

Jean Mayer, Meghan's mother-in-law, nodded sagely. "Obviously inherited. Elgin can't wake up either."

"And he putters." Meghan continued her litany of woe. "I mean, he is so pedestrian. He just slogs along, doing one thing at a time, piddling. Like, he'll be late headed out for work, but he'll still take his breakfast toast plate and empty coffee cup out to the kitchen, rinse them under the faucet, turn them upside down—"

"All at the same rate of speed," Jean chimed in. "Can't just depart from the routine and get on to work. My, yes, that's his father! He has to go through all the motions, as if he had all the time in the world—"

"Oh, gravy!" Meghan moaned. "It must be in the Y chromosome. Sean Michael is doomed!"

The women were being partly, though not entirely, facetious, but the principle remains. To see yourself, look at your father. Conversely, when your father is missing from your life, a part of you has not quite fallen into place.

What is the heritage you want to give your children?

Keeping Contact

If your children are small and still in your home, pledge now to maintain contact regardless of future circumstances. A big fight, some catastrophic wedge might separate you from your children as they grow up. Don't let it become permanent. No matter how much they disappoint you or enrage you, hang in with them, for your own sake as well as theirs.

If you are a divorced father, be reminded once again that most men lose contact with their children within two years of the final separation. You will have to take special measures to ensure that that won't happen.

Your children who are teens and older are ready to fly the nest, and may have done so already. The teen years are also the time when parent-child relationships reach a nadir, what with Dad's imperfections becoming glaringly obvious, and the kids' separation and individuation in full swing. It's surprisingly easy to lose contact here.

If friction or bad blood has separated you from your kids and you cannot see reconciliation in the offing, we recommend that you at least establish minimal contact. Give your kids your address and phone number and notify them when you move (a postal card form provided by the post office will suffice). Request, formally, if formality is appropriate, that they provide you with a current address for emergency and legal use if nothing else, should something happen to either of you.

"When my grandfather died at ninety-some," Jack Brubaker recalled, "we had a terrible time finding his stepdaughter, my Aunt Minnie. She had married a couple times and changed her name, and spelled it a different way, and was a general all-around flake. The estate couldn't be divided until she was found. We thought she was in southern California someplace.

"I have a friend whose cousin works for the Los Angeles County Sheriff's office. He told her about our problem and she did a computer check in records and found my Aunt Minnie from her description. She had been slow about paying up on a couple of speeding tickets. If she'd paid the tickets promptly we might not have ever found her. Did I mention she's cheap too?"

Had family contact been maintained, Minerva would have learned of her inheritance promptly. As it was, she learned of the money nearly a year after the grandfather's death and almost never received it at all.

"There's a friend down the street from us," says Paul Warren, "who grew up in Topeka. Her dad is still there, but she and her six brothers and sisters have scattered, literally, all over the world. (She has a brother in Thailand.)

Her father is in his sixties, and he's been sending out family newsletters her whole life to all the grown children out across the country and now to some of the grandchildren who are away from home at school. He serves as a clearing-house for family information. He offers bits of wisdom, seasonal tidbits—even an occasional recipe. He's keeping a very far-flung, close-knit family together."

You may not resort to a newsletter (in fact, statistically, you don't have seven kids plus grandkids, either), but use some means to maintain contact. "That's my wife's duty," many fathers claim. So long as she assumes the responsibility voluntarily, fine. But if she does not, the privilege falls to you.

Drop back to seasonal greeting cards with a dry-copied newsletter, if all else fails.

There are reasons beyond those considered so far that Dad's shadowy presence extends so far. "Head of the household" is the least of his roles.

—The Importance of Being Dad—

Says Brian Newman, "When I counsel adults, eighty percent or more of the issues we have to work through are kids-and-parents issues."

Paul Warren echoes that: "At least eighty percent," and adds, "By far, most of the kids I see don't need a therapist as much as they need a dad."

Claims Frank Minirth, "The men with the healthiest attitudes were loved and nurtured by a father."

Consider the statistics offered in the *Journal of the American Academy of Child Psychiatry* (23:681, 1984). An article by H. S. Goldstein compared parental presence and supervision with behavior problems in kids twelve to seventeen. Among boys, whose fathers were present at home, 8.8 percent got in trouble with the police, one way or another. Almost twice as many—16.6 percent—boys who were fatherless found themselves in hot water with the police. Girls showed the same tendency, though less dramatically:

1.2 percent got in trouble with police when Dad was home, compared with 1.8 percent of fatherless girls.

Trouble at school showed up just as clearly. Over twice as many fatherless boys (9.9 percent) as fathered boys (4.4 percent) got called on the carpet for discipline and behavior problems at school. Girls showed an even stronger contrast: 1.2 percent of girls with fathers got in trouble, compared with 3.8 percent of girls without Dad at home.

Leading Sensibly

Paul Warren thinks about the cases he serves. "Most of the families I see who are going through difficult times, the father is not in his place leading the family in dealing with the problem. Again, here's that stereotype, swooping in to straighten it out after it's been boiling for some time, then getting back to whatever he was busy with. Back to his more 'important' interests.

"That's not leading. Leading is being involved in the family, in the problem and in the solutions. Leading, again, is relationships. As the leader, Dad has the responsibility to make a plan, a way to resolve the problem. A resolution."

Dr. Minirth added this. "If I would preach anything at all to fathers, it would be 'common sense.' Be flexible. Be open. Many, many kids I see in the hospital come out of homes where either rules are too rigid or there are no rules at all. No common sense.

"Some Christian parents in particular have trouble being flexible. They can't bend when you have to. I'm not talking about relaxing standards. There are standards set by God that you can't compromise. But some perfectly sincere parents somehow don't grasp . . ." He searches for words a moment and starts over. "They don't recognize that grace and mercy do not negate justice. And that kids are kids. You can't be absolutely rigid with kids because they're not absolutely in control of themselves."

Grace. More favor than you deserve.

Mercy. Less punishment than you deserve.

Kids, of all people, stand most in need of grace and mercy.

Things to Think About

From you, your children are going to receive their psychological development, emotional health, self-image and confidence, socialization and morality, understanding, self-expression, self-control, love, and affection. Primarily you will teach them not with lessons and lectures, but by being you and being with them.

1. Let your imagination soar. What are some things you wish your father had done with you? for you? to you? that he didn't (it may be something like playing games, that he never did, or something like reading to you that you wish he had done more of)?

a. _____
b. _____
c. _____

2. In what ways are you parenting like your father?

a. _____
b. _____
c. _____

Is that good? _____

Or bad? _____

3. In what ways are you parenting the opposite of your father (i.e. in reaction against his methods)?

_____
_____

Are your kids better off because of it? _____

Or worse off? _____

And the big question: Do you like the way you're doing it, all right?

_____
_____

—The Final Word—

Brian Newman points to the final two verses of the Hebrew scriptures. "Malachi 4, verses 5 and 6. The very last words before Jesus arrived years later. The last thought God left the Hebrew people.

"God says He's sending Elijah to 'turn the hearts of the fathers to the children, and the hearts of the children to their fathers, lest I come and strike the earth with a curse.'

"Four hundred years later, Luke repeats these words among the first in the New Testament, the message to be sent at John the Baptist's announcement of Christ. When the Old Testament ends with it and the New Testament starts out with it, God's making a point.

"You see, too, from the way it's stated that the dads have to initiate it. The fathers turn first. As a natural response, then, the kids' hearts are turned."

He watches his daughter, Rachel, a few moments, as she colors quietly at her desk. Benjamin is squirreling around on the floor amid his bright baby toys, exploring the heady prospects of crawling in excess of two miles an hour. Kids.

"But you start with the fathers."

— APPENDIX A —

Resources
for Fathers

We believe the materials listed here contain useful information. We do not thereby endorse everything found in them. We recommend you evaluate them according to your own needs and convictions.

—Books—

Bly, Stephen. *How to Be a Good Dad*. Chicago: Moody, 1986.

Campolo, Tony and Bart Campolo. *Things We Wish We Had Said*. Dallas: Word, 1989.

Carlson, Randy. *Father Memories*. Chicago: Moody, 1992.

Cole, Edwin Lewis. *Real Man*. Nashville: Thomas Nelson, 1992.

Conn, Charles Paul. *FatherCare*. Dallas: Word, 1983.

——. *Dad, Mom, and the Church*. Cleveland, TN: Pathway, 1989.

Dalby, Gordon. *Father and Son—The Wound, The Healing, The Call to Manhood*. Nashville: Thomas Nelson, 1992.

——. *Healing the Masculine Soul*. Dallas: Word, 1991.

Dargatz, Jan. *52 Simple Ways to Build Your Child's Self-esteem and Confidence*. Atlanta: Oliver-Nelson, 1991.

Davis, Phil. *The Father I Never Knew*. Colorado Springs, CO: NavPress, 1991.

Dreizler, Carl. *52 Simple Ways to Have Fun with Your Child*. Atlanta: Oliver-Nelson, 1991.

Farrar, Steve. *Point Man*. Portland, OR: Multnomah Press, 1990.

Gaither, Gloria, ed. *What My Parents Did Right*. Mountain View, CA: Starsong, 1991.

Hansel, Tim. *What Kids Need Most in a Dad*. Tarrytown, NY: Fleming H. Revell, 1984.

Heidebrecht, Paul. *Time to Go Home: Turning the Hearts of Fathers to Their Children*. Norcross, GA: Great Commission Publications, 1990.

Jones, Brian and Linda Jones. *Men Have Feelings, Too*. Wheaton, IL: Victor Books, 1988.

LaPlaca, David and Annette LaPlaca, eds. *I Thought of It While Shaving: Ideas for Devoted Dads*. Wheaton, IL: Harold Shaw Publishers, 1992.

Lewis, Paul. *Famous Fathers*. Elgin, IL: David C. Cook, 1984.

Lockerbie, D. Bruce. *Fatherlove*. New York: Doubleday/Galilee, 1985.

MacDonald, Gordon. *The Effective Father*. Wheaton, IL: Tyndale House, 1989.

McCartney, Bill. *What Makes a Man?* Colorado Springs: NavPress, 1922.

McDowell, Josh and Dick Day. *How To Be a Hero to Your Kids*. Dallas: Word, 1991.

McDowell, Josh and Norm Wakefield. *The Dad Difference*. San Bernardino, CA: Here's Life, 1989.

Miller, John. *Biblical Faith and Fathering*. Mahwah, NJ: Paulist Press, 1989.

Neal, C. W. *30-Day Journey to Being a World-Class Father*. Nashville: Thomas Nelson, 1992.

Oliver, Gary and H. Norman Wright. *When Anger Hits Home*. Wheaton, IL: Moody, 1992.

Osherson, Samuel. *Finding our Fathers*. New York: Free Press, 1986.

Pruett, Kyle. *The Nurturing Father*. New York: Warner Books, 1987.

Rand, Ron. *For Fathers Who Aren't in Heaven*. Ventura, CA: Regal Books, 1986.

Simmons, Dave. *Dad the Family Coach*. Wheaton, IL: Victor Books, 1991.

_____. *Dad the Family Counselor*. Wheaton, IL: Victor Books, 1991.

_____. *Dad the Family Mentor*. Wheaton, IL: Victor Books, 1992.

Smalley, Gary and John Trent. *The Blessing*. Nashville: Thomas Nelson, 1986.

Stanley, Charles. *How to Keep Your Kids on Your Team*. Nashville: Thomas Nelson, 1992.

Swindoll, Charles. *You and Your Child*. Nashville: Thomas Nelson, 1981.

Taylor, Daniel. *Letters to My Children*. Downer's Grove, IL: InterVarsity Press, 1989.

Temple, Todd. *52 Simple Ways to Teach Your Child about God*. Atlanta: Oliver-Nelson, 1991.

Wilder, James. *Just Between Father and Son*. Downer's Grove, IL: InterVarsity Press, 1990.

Williams, Charles. *Forever a Father (Always a Son)*. Wheaton, IL: Victor Books, 1991.

Wright, Norman. *Always Daddy's Girl*. Ventura, CA: Regal Books, 1989.

—Other Resources—

Christian Service Brigade
Box 150
Wheaton, IL 60187
(708) 665-0630
    Newsletters: *On the Father Front* and *Man to Man*

Dad the Family Shepherd
PO Box 21445
Little Rock, AR 72221
(501) 221-1102, 1-800-234-3237
    Seminars (live, video, and audio), men's ministries, small group materials, books, newsletter

Focus on the Family
Colorado Springs, CO 80995
(719) 63FOCUS (719-633-6287)
1-800-A FAMILY (1-800-232-6459)
   Videos/films: *A Father Looks Back* and *Christian Fathering*
   Newsletter: *Parental Guidance* (for parents of teens)

Upbuilding Ministries
Ron Rand
4222 Hamilton Ave.
Cincinnati, OH 45223
(513) 681-5669
   Fathers' Ministry Team Curriculum
   The curriculum has positively influenced men and their
   families by revealing practical insights and methods that
   turn fathers' good intentions into specific plans of action.

National Center for Fathering
217 Southwind Place
Manhattan, KS 66502
(913) 776-4114
   Personal Fathering Profile, research

Promise Keepers
PO Box 18376
Boulder, CO 80308
(303) 421-2800
   Leadership and men's conferences

On the Daddy Track
P.O. Box 13D
Boyertown, PA 19512
(215) 367-4252
   Produces drive-time audio cassettes practical fathering
   issues.

Handy Pocket Guide to Exasperating Your Kids

Here's a summary of how not to father. We base this on the cases we encounter daily in our professional practices. The man who has not stepped beyond the traditional roles of fatherhood may see himself in more than one of these situations. Let us hope he does not see himself in many of them and that he is willing to move beyond them.

Abuse them. Check out various books on codependency issues and pay closer attention to the daily newspaper. Learn what's "in" with abuse—sexual, physical, emotional, passive abuse, active abuse. Researchers are learning that over 60 percent of teen mothers were sexually abused in their childhood. There is no faster road to really messing up your kids.

Refuse to spend time with them. Kids sit in Paul Warren's office literally angry to tears because Dad always has something more important he has to do than to be with them. If you really want to warp them, replace time and affection with purchased things. Works every time.

Compete with them. Kids are into competition anyway, so get the jump on them. You're bigger and stronger; you should have no trouble winning.

Compete for Mom's attention. After all, you knew her first.

Says Paul Warren, "I see a lot of older boys and girls who got the subtle message throughout childhood, 'Don't you ever try to be better than me.'"

Brian Newman adds, "Kids, including adult kids, so often get the message that you'd better back off of any areas of competition with your dad. When Dad feels inadequate, he passes the feeling along with 'You'll never amount to anything.'"

To really be effective, start in on them early.

Keep an iron fist on those reins. Control everything completely.

"I learned the folly of trying to control too much," Brian Newman admits sheepishly. "The rule when Rachel is going to bed is that she gets to choose the bedtime story. Well, she always picks these long, long ones. This one night I was tired. I wanted to be the one to choose the story because I'd pick a short one. Rachel started crying, 'I want Mommy to come read me a story, because she'll read the long one.' Ask me how *that* made me feel."

If the kids resist your absolute control, clamp down harder.

Complete that task. Get it done! Having fun doing it is strictly for sissies.

"This is a big problem with me," Paul Warren claims. "My focus is always on finishing the task, not enjoying it. Vicky and Matthew were working on one of those vast jigsaw puzzles. They were picking around at it in their spare moments for weeks.

"Finally, I couldn't stand it anymore. I sat down at it and worked until three-thirty in the morning finishing it. Great sense of achievement.

"You guessed it. Vicky and Matthew were disappointed. That's putting it mildly. They told me, 'You took all the fun, Dad.'" He smirks self-consciously. "'It's framed and on the wall in the den now. A constant reminder. I wanted it done, they wanted to do it. I've never forgotten the lesson."

Make sure your expectations are "way up there." Expect your kid to act like a sixth grader when he's in first grade. Hey, he's up to it. He's a sharpy. Exceptional. Don't let him whine. That's childish. Or cry. He can be a little adult if you just twist the thumbscrews right.

"Females tend to be more in touch with kids," says Paul Warren. "They usually have more realistic expectations because they're with the children more, thus understand them better. Besides, women generally have more of a moment-to-moment kind of love that doesn't require that certain preconceived expectations be met."

Says Brian Newman, "One of my clients considered his kids grown up for years before they actually were. Then he let loose prematurely, causing some serious problems, because he had such trouble relating to his kids as kids."

Don't bother loving your wife. Don't even bother showing affection. This will exasperate your kid about as quickly as anything you can try.

"The most important, the number one thing in a child's life," says Frank Minirth, "is for you to love your wife and raise the kids as a team. Kids are incredibly sensitive to that. I'm romantically in love with Mary Alice, and there's security in that for my kids."

Keep your lip shut about sex. Remember, people with sexual disorders can almost always trace the problem back to Dad. You hold the key to your kid's sexuality. Mom doesn't. So use that power!

Don't ever let the guys catch you changing a baby. But then, that goes without saying.